IN HIS
IMAGE

IN HIS IMAGE

VOLUME I

A Devotional on Spiritual Transformation

KENDALL DAVIS

Davis Publishing
Devotion and Vision Increase Security

Davis Publishing

Unless otherwise noted, all scripture quotations are taken from the World English Bible (WEB) 2020. All texts of the WEB are dedicated to the public domain. The World English Bible is an updated revision of the American Standard Version of 1901.

Scripture quotations marked KJV are taken from the King James Version. Public domain.

Printed in the United States of America

ISBN: 978-1-965441-02-2
eISBN: 978-1-965441-03-9

CONTENTS

Acknowledgment xi

Preface xiii

Serving with my whole heart 1

A Bondservant of the Most High 3

Waiting silently before Him 5

Adjusting my Course 7

Calling on the name above all names 9

Yes, I'm His Child 11

Expelling the World's Love from my Heart 13

Considering My Ways 15

Provoking God's Favor 17

Praying for Somebody 19

Reaping and Repenting 21

Called Goodie Two Shoes 23

Not Disregarded 25

With Dove Eyes for God 27

Taking Heed 29

Not Complaining 31

Drawn by Him 33

Not fighting Alone 35

Motivated by Love 37

Not taking the Donut off the Buddha plate 39

Seeking to Give Him Great Joy 41

Orchestrated to and Through the Heavens 43

Inherit Your Blessing 45

Growing and Growing Up 47

The Road to Recovery.. 49

House On Fire 51

Nobody Greater 53

Cleaning Up Your Act.. 55

The War We Forget About... 57

Public Successes and Private Failures................................... 59

Turn the Knob Up 61

Sprinkled By The Blood 63

Overcoming Manipulation.. 65

Let It Sink In 67

Super-Size Your Love... 69

Stay In Your Own Seat... 71

Love Conquers Me 73

Don't Be a Disappointment to God..................................... 75

Dealing with Difficult Believers... 77

It's God's Fault 79

Love on a New Level 81

The Standing Spot 83

The Fruit of the Tree of Life... 85

Please Visit My Fran's.. 87

Breaking the Siege.. 89

Not A Place For Us 91

Made By Christ.. 93

Don't Let Your Fall Become Your Failure.............................. 95

Oil Laid Upon Me 97

Grace Givers and Forgetters 99

Blame Shift..101

Contempt in the Divine Court..103

Let God Have His Way...105

Don't Slip... 107

Sheep Invasion 109

Rewritten and Redeemed 111

Get Fed..113

Set Your Mind For The Kingdom 115

Wait on the Rock 117

A Good Answer 119

Tune Into God 121

A Heart for His People.. 123

Man's Curse/God's Blessing 125

Pressed Into Service For Christ....................................... 127

Don't Cut Your Blessings 129

Empowered By Christ 131

Depart From Me 133

Press on to Know the Lord 135

Cultivate It Into To A Blessing 137

Delighting In Mercy 139

Do You See Them...141

Let There Be Light.. 143

Prophetic Plagiarism..145

An Active Word For An Active Life 147

A God Perspective 149

Salvation is Yours 151

Lord Send Me 153

Love Like Never Before...155

Give Me My Vision 157

God Is In Control 159

Covered, Blessed, and Increased 161

Moving Forward 163

The Blame Game 165

Pentecost for the Soul..167

Instruction for Construction 169

Break Me Off Something..171

Fight Until We All Win 173

Victory Verses 175

Putting it in God's Hands.. 177

Running Into Things 179

Harvest Time...181

Keep Me In The Right Position 183

Enabled to Serve 185

A Time for Prayer... 187

Getting Our Lives in Order to Receive the Blessing 189

Finding Yourself...191

Grateful to Share..193

Blessing Folk 195

A Righteous Return on Sin 197

One Day You'll Understand 199

Walking the Gray Line.. 201

In the Face of Christ 203

Maintaining control of your spirit 205

Clever Little Devils 207

It's Only For A Season...209

Great Things In Small Packages...211

Headed Toward Death 213

The Power to Become 215

Last Words...217

Most Blessed Forever..219

What God Seeks 221

Give Yourself Away 223

Total Submission... 225

Financial Stability 227

Man's Second Image 229

The Marriage Triangle 231

For This Reason 233

Better to Be Blessed... 235

It Won't Work 237

Thrive or Survive 239

Sleeping In 241

Destined For Greatness 243

Led by His Love 245

The Mark of a True Believer 247

Seven Calls of the Believer 249

The Welcomed/Unwelcomed Spirit 251

Victory Commanded 253

An Opportunity to Obey 255

Superpowered Faith.. 257

Possessing with Honor 259

The Image of Your Faith 261

One and Done 263

Self-Guided or Shepherded.................................... 265

Close, But No Cigar... 267

Too Legit for God to Quit...................................... 269

Servant Authority... 271

Working with the Right Things................................ 273

Too Many People In Your Life 275

Not Falling Away 277

Piercing, Tattoos, and the Lord 279

Don't Look Inside 281

A Thriving Vision 283

Evangelizing the Found... 285

Taking Power Over Your Storms............................... 287

Praying the Vision of God 289

An Appointment with the Sword...............................291

Don't Fear But Fight 293

Declaration of the Doorkeeper 295

Knowing God 297

100 Fold.. 299

No Fear in Their Hearts 301

Preparing For A Sacrifice.. 303

Much Forgiveness, Much Love.. 305

Ouch, That Hurt 307

Lock Them Out 309

Waiting For A Word 311

Kingdom Fit 313

A Good Heart 315

Get the Want by Fulfilling Needs 317

I Need to Reschedule an Appointment..............................319

Purpose of Financial Woes 321

Have You Found What You're Looking For........................ 323

What Kind of Harvest 325

Simon Says.. 327

The Breakfast of Conquerors.. 329

Come and Get It 331

Women of Power... 333

Who is He..335

Watch Your Step 337

Getting Back on Track 339

You Control the Flow.. 341

Voice of A Stranger 343

A Good Reason to Give Him Praise.................................. 345

The Resting Place 347

Expect to Win... 349

Reset Your Attitude...351

A Dramatic Victory...353

Grace Instruction 355

For the Sake of His Name 357

Cleaned Up 359

Strangers not Welcome..361

From Manna to Maturity.. 363

Starting Over 365

ACKNOWLEDGMENT

This book is the second in a series of devotional guides I pray will be used to awaken a daily routine of devoting ourselves to the word and prayer. I want to continue acknowledging my outstanding debt to those who supported me in writing. I thank my wife, Makisha, and my children for always believing in me. My church family and ministry partners far and wide gave feedback as I began writing this devotional guide, and I am grateful.

Most importantly, I acknowledge the savior of our souls, Jesus Christ. We are to give thanks in all things, and I realize that during restless nights, as I struggled, the Lord was with me, drawing me closer. Thank you for waking me up, showing me things that needed prayer, and giving me the insight to write a devotional guide to manifest your presence. We are your co-laborers, and I acknowledge your leading this work. I also appreciate everyone using this devotional to draw themselves into a more intimate relationship with God. You are fantastic, and I am glad to be your brother in the Lord. Thank you all very much. We are on this journey together to conform to Christ's image.

Acts 6:3-4 Therefore select from among you, brothers, seven men of good report, full of the Holy Spirit and of wisdom, whom we may appoint over this business. But we will continue steadfastly in prayer and in the ministry of the word."

PREFACE

*Acts 2:42 They continued steadfastly in
the apostles' teaching and fellowship, in
the breaking of bread, and prayer.*

In His Image Volume I is an instructional devotional for continuing the example of the apostles and the early church. We do this through introspective reflections from the word of God that cast light on the dark areas of our souls. Using short daily scripture readings that you can meditate on throughout the day, In His Image will teach scriptures and speak to the heart of the soul in small daily increments, strengthening the believer's faith. Use this guide as a catalyst for personal growth and a tool to encourage others with scriptures and simple explanations. The devotional is excellent for family devotions or small group fellowships. We encourage you to share your insights daily with others over a cup of coffee or a meal and use the prayers to voice your needs and to pray those prayers for the needs of your loved ones.

*Romans 8:28-29 We know that all things work
together for good for those who love God, for
those who are called according to his purpose.
For whom he foreknew, he also predestined to
be conformed to the image of his Son, that he
might be the firstborn among many brothers.*

The title, "In His Image," brings light to God's work in a believer's life to restore His likeness marred by sin. God calls those who love Him according to His purpose. God also foreknew all who love Him and predestined them to be conformed to the image of His son Jesus so that Christ will have preeminence over us all. The goal of God's love for us and our love for Him isn't just to make it to heaven but to recreate the Lord of heaven within us. We hope this devotional is used in the lives of those who love the Lord, making them more like Christ. For this reason, we pray that the Lord will bless those receiving this guide richly.

Genesis 1:27 God created man in his own image. In God's image he created him; male and female he created them.

As we walk through life, we find ourselves surrounded by many images that do not reflect who God is and how He sees Himself through us. In His Image is designed to assist you in seeing God in your everyday life, as you spend devoted time with Him. In His image will lead you to have a stronger spiritual relationship, as it motivates you to read the Bible. It is essential, before each devotional day, to pray and ask the Holy Spirit to guide you on this journey. Also, after reading the daily devotional, it is also paramount that you read the entire biblical account and take time to reflect, meditate, and record to achieve the total fulfillment of your devoted life in God.

Serving with my whole heart

---✦---

2 Chronicles 25:2 He did that which was right in Yahweh's eyes, but not with a perfect heart.

To win, you must get off to a good start, prepare and pace yourself properly and be confident. King Amaziah began doing what was right in God's sight but fell away. When he avenged himself on those who had murdered his father, he was careful not to kill any of their children.[1] When he made an unwise choice, he listened to the prophet and took a loss,[2] but something happened. Pride began to sink in. He started doing things on his own.

How often have we run into half-hearted service? When things go our way, we serve God. However, if things go against us, self-will creeps in.[3] A half-hearted Christian will eventually fall out of fellowship with God, and they believe in God's word but no longer apply it to their lives. Eventually, God sent a prophet to warn him, but Amaziah didn't want to listen.[4] How many half-hearted believers leave the fellowship of the saints, not listening to the watchman of their souls? We may still follow the Lord, but not with all our hearts.

---

[1] 2 Chronicles 25:3-4 compare with Deuteronomy 24:16
[2] 2 Chronicles 25:6-10
[3] Genesis 49:6
[4] 2 Chronicle 25:16

It is possible to love God half-heartedly. Here's the test. Do you fellowship, serve, and accept correction? What about an excuse for inaction, blame for failure, and failure to appear in God's house? The rejection of any of the principles of His word is our roadmap that shows where our heart lies. When Amaziah turned away from following the Lord, people conspired against him.[5] Half-hearted service opens the door to the enemy. We must ensure that we serve Him with our whole hearts so it can be said we did right in the sight of the Lord with all of our hearts.

Prayer: Lord, I ask you for your strength and help not to do anything halfheartedly. Keep my fire burning so that I will stay my course and finish well. Please remove the distractions and delays that hinder my progress. Help me develop the skills needed to succeed. Let my testimony be that I served you with my whole heart, mind, soul, and strength, in Jesus' name. Amen.

---

[5] 2 Chronicles 25:27

A Bondservant of the Most High

---⯘---

2 Peter 2:19 promising them liberty, while they themselves are bondservants of corruption; for a man is brought into bondage by whoever overcomes him.

Bondage is horrible. It arrests the body, deprives the heart and mind of the hope of freedom, and restricts the soul. Peter warns about submitting to people who feign holiness but are in bondage to corruption.[6] They can't deliver on their promises. The purpose of a promise is to bring hope. But undeliverable promises only bring despair. Whether you're forced or submit willingly, what overcomes you enslaves you. You are overcome by whatever you submit to. If you submit to sin, then you become sins puppet. You will remain in bondage to depravity unless you know the way to freedom.

2 Peter begins by saying, "Simon Peter, a bondservant and apostle of Jesus Christ.[7] Bondservants are those who choose to serve. Peter chose to be overcome by nothing except Jesus Christ and Him alone. Bond service to what is good is not slavery but liberty to fulfill our purpose. By continuing in Christ's word, we become disciples who know the truth and are set free.[8] Peter knew that only through Christ he could obtain victory. The

---

[6] 2 Peter 2:1-2
[7] 2 Peter 1:1
[8] John 8:31-32

bondage of sin and death could not overcome his submission to Christ, who overcame sin and death.

There were problems even among the 12 where the other apostles did not know Judas was a false brother.[9] Peter learned that the problems he encounters while serving are the issues he would have to deal with when called to lead. Whatever problem you may have, Jesus Christ has already overcome it. Every yoke and bondage are under Christ's feet.[10] Will you come to Christ's feet so you can have victory? It is better to sit at His feet than to be placed under His feet. Let Christ and His Holy Spirit overcome you so that you can become a slave to righteousness.

Prayer: Father, I come surrendering myself as a bondservant of Jesus Christ. I pray my life reflects your kingdom's come; your will be done on earth, as in heaven. I ask that you grant me greater discernment so I will not take the counsel, advice, or suggestions of falsehood. Surround me with people who love you so we can encourage each other on this walk together. I asked you to guard my house and my family and place every problem under the feet of Christ in Jesus' name, Amen.

---

[9] Galatians 2:4
[10] Ephesians 1:20-22

Waiting silently before Him

Lamentations 3:25-26 Yahweh is good to those who wait for him, to the soul who seeks him. It is good that a man should hope and quietly wait for the salvation of Yahweh.

Waiting through hardships can be challenging. Our tendency to fight or flight tells us to instinctively attack or run and hide. Waiting calls us to stand amid our problems and let God attack them.[11] Lamentations is a prophetic expression of grief to the heartache caused by sin. Some deserved the punishment that came upon the nation. However, the faithful remnant suffered for the actions of others. Many believers suffer due to their sin or a lack of preparation. Others may suffer because those around them have done wrong, and they are feeling the repercussions. Either way, The Lord is good to those who wait on Him.[12]

Our scripture translates two different Hebrew words as "wait." The first word is Qavha, which means "Eagerly looking for." We should be eager but not anxious. God is good to those who know the Lord will keep His appointed time and those who keep looking for Him to arrive.[13] The second word for wait is the Hebrew word Yachil, which means "Expect with hope." It describes the mindset of the person. He eagerly awaits God's

---

[11] Psalms 46:10

[12] Isaiah 30:18

[13] Genesis 18:14

arrival because He trusts that God will handle the issue. Many don't trust the Lord and lose their expectations, confidence, and reward.[14]

Waiting is difficult, but it is the way you wait that brings God's goodness. To wait quietly means praying without griping, murmuring, or complaining.[15] How many of us charge God with wrongdoing and blame God and everyone else instead of looking inside to see where we are at fault? Being patient and having the proper attitude brings support from our Lord. We activate God's favor by waiting with calm assurance and hope that He will provide for all our needs.[16] If you are in need, wait for the Lord, who will show you His goodness.

Prayer: Lord, thank you for all the times you waited for me when I was messing up; now, help me to wait on you without being fearful, anxious, or complaining. I trust you and wait for you to renew my strength. Your word says that my confidence gains me a reward, so I ask that you bless me now because I expect you to come through with Hope. Thank you for your grace and love in Jesus' name, Amen.

---

[14] Hebrews 10:35-36
[15] Psalm 62:5
[16] Philippians 4:19

Adjusting my Course

---✦---

Ezekiel 3:17 "Son of man, I have made you a watchman to the house of Israel. Therefore hear the word from my mouth, and warn them from me.

God called Ezekiel to minister to stiff-necked people who refused to listen.[17] The Lord would send prophet after prophet, but they would not turn. They were stubborn and set in their ways. Nevertheless, God has set watchman over the house so that they would hear the words of the Lord and give warning to the people. It is good to know that God appoints watchmen to speak words of warning to us. Like a ship steering through the sea, sometimes unforeseen dangers enter our lives.

The watchman is God's signal that you're going in the wrong direction. An old anecdote tells of how a ship's Captain saw what appeared to be the lights of another ship heading toward him. He sent a message, "Change your course ten degrees to the north." The reply came, "Change your course ten degrees south!" The captain responded, 'I am a Navy captain; change your course. The response came, 'I am a seaman first class; you change your course.' The captain was furious. He said, 'I am a battleship! you change your course.' The seaman replied: 'I am a lighthouse! So, you better change your course.

The watchman is to the believer what a lighthouse is to a ship. When we Captain our own ship, we may miss things happening or refuse to get

---

[17] Ezekiel 2:3-8

out of the way. When we start depending on our position and power to get what we want but ignore the watchman's call, we shipwreck our faith.[18] We are to submit to those God has placed over us.[19] Just as Ezekiel was accountable to God to warn the people,[20] our pastors, and leaders are responsible for speaking and living the truth of God's word. Everyone needs their watchman. Pray for your watchman and hear what God says through them. They are your lighthouse sent to tell you to get on course.

> **Prayer:** Lord, give me an ear to heed your warnings and a mind that does not lean to my own understanding. I'm sorry for all the times I have been hardheaded and have stalled my progress by not listening to your voice. I asked you to restore the blessings I have laid away but not received. Help me to live in your truth and walk in your favor as you show your love and devotion to me in Jesus' name. Amen.

---

[18] 1 Timothy 1:19
[19] Hebrews 13:17
[20] Ezekiel 33:1-7

Calling on the name above all names

Jude 1:9 But Michael, the archangel, when contending with the devil and arguing about the body of Moses, dared not bring against him an abusive condemnation, but said, "May the Lord rebuke you!"

Michael is one of God's most powerful angels. He is called one of the chief princes, the prince of Israel[21], and the great prince who stands as a watchman over the nation of Israel.[22] Scripture tells us that the angels are more powerful than us but will not bring a slanderous accusation against the devil.[23] The lesson learned from the angels is that we need God to fight on our side when we battle.

Some may wonder why Jude wrote about a fight in the heavenly realm that is not found in the Old Testament. We don't know why satan tried to steal Moses's body, and it could have been that he would try to reanimate Moses's body and possess it to cause people to worship him. He will do this with the antichrist, who will resurrect fully possessed by the devil after suffering a fatal head blow.[24] Whatever the reason why Satan wanted the

---

[21] Daniel 10:13 & 10:21

[22] Daniel 12:1

[23] 2 Peter 2:11

[24] Revelation 13:3-4

body, while Michael was fighting with Satan, God intervened and buried Moses somewhere nobody knows.[25]

God wants to use you as the instrument of victory, and he will fight the battle as you submit to His will and call upon His name. Demonic forces are too strong for us to handle alone, but they submit in the name of Jesus.[26] Like the archangel Michael, we don't have to curse Satan. No, instead, we call on God. Speaking Curses and accusations brings more darkness to a dark situation, and calling upon Jesus brings the light to dispel the darkness. If you get in a struggle, don't blame others or make accusations. Just call on Jesus, and He will work it out.

> Prayer: Father, I pray that you will be with me in every battle I am facing. I called upon your name and asked you to move. I shall not use the tools of darkness but will bring the light of Christ's power to the forefront. I asked you to rebuke the devourer and cause my light to shine. Grant me favor, peace, and love in Jesus' name. Amen.

---

[25] Deuteronomy 34:6

[26] Luke 10:17-20

Yes, I'm His Child

Hosea 1:2 When Yahweh spoke at first by Hosea, Yahweh said to Hosea, "Go, take for yourself a wife of prostitution and children of unfaithfulness; for the land commits great adultery, forsaking Yahweh.

Hosea lived what he preached. For him to understand the pain of reaching an unfaithful people, God led Hosea to marry a prostitute named Gomer. Their oldest son was named Jezreel, meaning "the Lord will sow."[27] He was a sign that God would judge the bloodshed committed at Jezreel. His second child, a daughter named Lo-ruhamah, meaning "not pitied."[28] Reflecting the fact that God would give no compassion to sinning Israel. Their last child was named Lo-ammi, meaning "not my son."[29] Yes, Gomer had a baby with another man while married to Hosea, and she left him and went back into prostitution.

God does not break His covenant, but we often do. God did not allow Hosea to divorce Gomer; he had to redeem her.[30] The Lord is compassionate and merciful but is also a fair judge. Just as Hosea spent all he had and even gave away his food supply to get Gomer back, The Lord gave His most prized possession to redeem us. Yet many of us remain unfaithful.

---

[27] Hosea 1:4

[28] Hosea 1:6

[29] Hosea 1:9

[30] Hosea 3:1-3

Hosea's call to repentance was in his children's names, which, when given in order, state, "For the actions you have sown, I will not pity for you are not my child."

Why was Israel, not His child? Because they had sold themselves off to serve their own desires. They did not heed God's warnings or listen to His prophets. God does not consider the unfaithful His. Some of us have no fear of the Lord. James says that even demons believe but shudder at God's presence.[31] Only those who receive Him as the true light become the children of God.[32] Those who walk in darkness are not His. If you are a child of God, He will redeem you from every situation and bring you back to His presence.

> **Prayer:** Lord, thank you for redeeming me from all my troubles. I receive your covenant blessings and submit to remain faithful. Help me to turn towards your word, whether written, spoken, or placed upon my heart. I ask you to move by your power and keep me free. Watch over my home and life in Jesus' name, Amen.

---

[31] James 2:19
[32] John 1:9-12

Expelling the World's Love from my Heart

--- ⚓ ---

*2 Timothy 4:10 for Demas left me, having loved
this present world, and went to Thessalonica;
Crescens to Galatia; and Titus to Dalmatia.*

Three men and fellow laborers in the gospel left Paul in Rome. Two of them had his blessing, but the other did not. Whatever we may say about Demas, he served God, working with one of the most excellent teachers in the New Testament, Paul.[33] He experienced genuine love and cared for the saints as they collected money to send to the poor.[34] He also saw what it was like to be in a ministry that did not compromise the gospel. He had all the things that made a healthy, well-balanced church. Nevertheless, he still loved the world.

Many people who were once active in ministry are no longer involved. However, all reasons focus on the self rather than on God. Believers who have Christ-centered lives heal in a faith community. The Greek Agapaó translated love deals with preference and self-choice. Demachose the world over the gospel. They focus on their acts rather than others and sustain their walk with Christ. Those who walk in God's light should do so with other believers who walk in the same light, having fellowship with God and a cleansing relationship.[35] Still, others never crucified their flesh, so

---

[33] Philemon 1:24
[34] 1 Corinthians 16:1-4
[35] 1 John 1:6-7

they still loved what the world offered them. These fall into sin and end up in bondage.

When we love the world, our lust drives us and reveals that the love of the Father is not in us.[36] Believers who play with sin, desiring their previous life, have evicted the love of God from their hearts. We must ask ourselves, "Is the love of the Father still in us"?[37] Have we become self-deluded like Demas was when he served God but still clung to possessions, position, and pride? Have we let the love of God drive us into the will of God? Love not the world, and let the love of the Father Abide in you.

> **Prayer:** Heavenly Father, I come to you, asking you for strength is separate from all affection for the things of this world. Set my mind on things above so that I may please you and walk in your ways. Keep me planted in your house and faithful to your word so that my home may prosper and your spirit will heal all around me; in Jesus' name, Amen.

---

[36] 1 John 2:15-16
[37] 2 Corinthians 13:5-6

Considering My Ways

Haggai 1:5-6 5 Now therefore this is what Yahweh of Armies says: Consider your ways. You have sown much, and bring in little. You eat, but you don't have enough. You drink, but you aren't filled with drink. You clothe yourselves, but no one is warm, and he who earns wages earns wages to put them into a bag with holes in it."

Haggai was a post-exile prophet sent to speak to those who returned from Babylonian captivity. Though God had blessed the Israelites by keeping them in the hard times, they continued to put God second. God planned to prosper them[38], but they gave God little (Hebrew: Meat meaning what is few or less than enough) to bless. They harvested little, so they had to ration their food. They could not afford luxuries like wine and wore extra clothes because they couldn't afford burning oil. Lastly, the money was already spent on bills whenever they got paid. All of this is because they lost focus on God.[39]

Like many of us today, the Israelites had not considered their ways. They thought they would have time for God's work later[40] but didn't realize their hindrances came because they left God behind. God brought

---

[38] Jeremiah 29:10-11

[39] Haggai 1:9-11

[40] Haggai 1:2

them into the land, and they thought they could prosper by giving God half-hearted devotion. Sometimes, people live paycheck to paycheck and fear trusting the one who can do exceedingly abundantly more than we could ask or think.[41] Whatever job, business, home, family, or ministry God has given you, you need the Lord to prosper.[42]

Everyone you meet is fighting a battle you don't know about. However, those who have made God a priority have the upper hand. Consider where you have placed God in your life. Consider your household and finances if you have not given Him the first portion so that He will make the rest holy.[43] Where there is no peace, keep your mind on Him and consider your ways.

Prayer: Heavenly Father, I commit to walking in faithfulness, living right, and building the kingdom. I ask that you pour out the latter rain, causing the increase. Increase my faith. Provide for every need and the abundance that you desire me to receive. I ask for your hand in relieving and paying off all debt. In Jesus' name. Amen

---

[41] Ephesians 3:20

[42] Deuteronomy 8:18

[43] Romans 11:16

Provoking God's Favor

---◆---

Zechariah 8:14-15 For Yahweh of Armies says:
"As I thought to do evil to you when your
fathers provoked me to wrath," says Yahweh
of Armies, "and I didn't repent, so again I have
thought in these days to do good to Jerusalem
and to the house of Judah. Don't be afraid.

God is sovereign, and no one can force His hand. However, we can provoke His favor. The Israelites provoked wrath through their unrighteous deeds. They had not dispensed justice, practiced kindness, or shown compassion to their brothers.[44] When they began to backslide, God did not immediately judge them but showed love and patience. He sent prophets to encourage them to get back on track.[45] Nevertheless, they refused His mercy and would not listen, so God refused to relent from pouring out His wrath.

John Piper said, "God is most glorified in me when I am satisfied in Him." Understanding what provokes God to move is the key to living a fruitful and blessed life. God is a jealous God.[46] Most of us think that jealousy is a negative thing. We witnessed jealous people who did not control their emotions and actions, and God is not that way. Jealous means that

---

[44] Zechariah 7:9-11
[45] Jeremiah 3:22
[46] Zechariah 8:2

God can show a righteous preference for or against you. The rejection of God's mercy removed favor from the Israelites, but faithfulness brought it back.

Our faith, faithfulness, and zeal are what provoke God's favor. God has an unstoppable devotion to those who are committed to Him. Through faithfulness, the people would see God restore what was lost, heal brokenness, and open up the windows of heaven.[47] Favor promotes God's agenda and is a setup to heal every setback. We must ask ourselves, "Do we have the right attitude, service, and deeds to provoke blessings in our lives"? Favor requires maintaining covenant relationships and doing the right things for the kingdom and our future. Are you committed to being like that? If so, get zealous for God and provoke your favor.

Prayer: Gracious God, thank you for choosing my life to reflect your son's love, character, and compassion. Lead me by your Holy Spirit and keep me from straying away from your grace. Ignite the fire of my faith and zeal for you so I will walk in your favor. I need your touch, so keep your hands on me and your graces near me. So, I might serve you with an excellent spirit in Jesus' name. Amen.

---

[47] Zechariah 8:11-13

Praying for Somebody

---✦---

Daniel 9:13 As it is written in the law of Moses, all this evil has come on us. Yet we have not entreated the favor of Yahweh our God, that we should turn from our iniquities and have discernment in your truth.

Some think that when their loved ones reach the end of their rope, they will come running to God. The truth is all hell could be breaking out, and some still do not seek the favor of the Lord. Daniel recognized that broken homes, death, and injustice did not turn many back to God. When the time came for the Israelites to be set free, most stayed in Babylon.[48] So what did he do? He prayed.

There are hints that Daniel may be a priest who, in his old age, returned from captivity[49] and that the mention of him being of the sons of Judah did not mean he was from the tribe of Judah but from the Southern Kingdom of Judah.[50] Daniel was a powerful intercessor, and he prayed three times a day and ministered on God's behalf before kings.[51] The Hebrew "Chalal" described soothing God's face through prayer. Daniel knew that to turn the people back, someone had to pray and seek the face of God.

---

[48] Ezra 1:5-6
[49] Nehemiah 8:10
[50] Daniel 1:6
[51] Daniel 6:10

Turning from iniquity and giving heed to the truth is repentance. With only one thing required to receive the Lord's favor, many chose to continue in their calamity. God required repentance to restore homes, families, and everything our calamities tried to destroy.[52] Our mothers and grandparents' prayers saved many of us today. But are we praying like Daniel for the people? Will they return or stay in their own Babylon? Let's pray to soothe God's face and seek our generation's favor.

Prayer: Lord, I come before you, seeking your face and turning from my iniquities, asking you to show favor again and restore blessing to my family, church, and community. I pray your hand of peace be upon this nation and our economy. Provide real solutions for the poor, the sick, and the elderly. Use me and stir others up as your change vessels to bring revival and restoration to our communities and do good works in Jesus' name. Amen.

---

[52] 2 Chronicles 7:14

Reaping and Repenting

---◆---

1 John 1:9 If we confess our sins, he is faithful and righteous to forgive us the sins, and to cleanse us from all unrighteousness

Remember when you first became a believer? You probably confessed your sins every day, if not more. However, as we grow in Christ and begin to have victory over sin, we may find ourselves confessing less and less. Are we still taking an honest look at ourselves?[53] Since our knowledge of the word has increased, shouldn't our awareness of sin grow? God judicially forgave us at the cross, but what about relational forgiveness, where we address offenses and disappointments, keeping our slate clean?

1 John mentions fellowship with God or one another four times in five verses, speaking of our confession as cleansing our walk.[54] The sins the Lord mentions are not willful but self-denied sins that we often overlook or don't admit.[55] Denial of sin causes a break in fellowship, not loss of salvation. But if we look inside ourselves and confess, He is faithful and right to forgive and cleanse our walk with Him. Cleanse Greek Katharizó means to purge or purify. To be faithful and just means that God is consistent in the relationship and shares His light with us, overcoming our darkest places.

---

[53] 2 Corinthians 13:5

[54] 1 John 1:3-7

[55] 1 John 1:8

Confession doesn't admit to God something He doesn't already know. It means to come into agreement with God regarding sin. Without confession, a believer will feel prideful or unclean before God. Light cannot walk with darkness.[56] Wearing a silk outfit doesn't mean you have clean undergarments. We need to bathe regularly by confession and put on righteousness.[57] If you want to be clean before God, look at what you have overlooked, agree with Him, and you will be clean again.

Prayer: Father, I come before you confessing my sins that affect my walk with you. The times I haven't helped, given, served, or prayed when I should have. I confess that attitudes, judgments, and bad habits I have overlooked. My thorns and secret sins are all laid bare at your feet. I submit my will and ask you to heal my thoughts and cleanse my acts so I can walk in sweet fellowship with you. Help me where I am weak and keep me from all harm. In Jesus' name. Amen

---

[56] 2 Corinthians 6:14-16
[57] Isaiah 59:17

Called Goodie Two Shoes

---

1 Peter 4:3-4 For we have spent enough of our past time doing the desire of the Gentiles, and having walked in lewdness, lusts, drunken binges, orgies, carousings, and abominable idolatries. They think it is strange that you don't run with them into the same excess of riot, speaking evil of you.

Peter reminds us that we have already committed enough sin to last us a lifetime. It's time to leave old things behind and put our PET (Pride, Ego, Temptations) on a leash. We have carried out the desires of others long enough, and we must eliminate all competing desires to have God's love live in our hearts.[58] The Spirit of the Lord will conquer the desires inside us. Following the desires of old acquaintances can hinder your renewal in Christ Jesus.

It's hard for those who once knew you to accept who Christ has made you. You must understand that people who fit your past may not fit into your future. When you have no vision, motivation, or goals, the partying and excesses fit your life. However, now we have hope for better things, and the bitter things no longer fit.[59] The bitter things occur when you take a new you into an old life. Some will respect your change, and others will slander you for not going along with their program. Their slander reveals

---

[58] Romans 5:5
[59] Hebrews 6:9-11

that they are either jealous of us for bettering our lives or never really cared for us.[60]

Let's ask ourselves, have we left behind the desires of the Gentiles? Has the Spirit of God renewed us? Separation is the precursor that breeds both spiritual growth and transformation. We only renew ourselves to the extent that we can detach from sin and unite with the mind of Christ.[61] God's love shapes our hearts, so we learn to trust Him enough to surrender. If believers desire to reach their potential, we must come out and be holy as He is.[62] The time is already sufficient for all the wrongs we have done. Let us walk in faith and Christ's forgiveness.

> **Prayer:** Heavenly Father, I come putting away stubbornness, stagnation, and stress. Please help me to form good habits that work. Progress me towards my goals. Remove the people who no longer serve a purpose in my life. Surround me with those who can match my purpose and vision. I declare you have made me above and not beneath. I will be the lender, not the borrower, and will rest in your favor in Jesus' name. Amen.

---

[60] John 15:18-19
[61] Philippians 2:5
[62] Leviticus 11:44-45

Not Disregarded

Titus 2:15 Say these things and exhort and reprove with all authority. Let no one despise you.

Every believer needs to know authority and submission.[63] Whatever positions you may find yourself in, you are there because either you have placed yourself there or God has installed you. Titus found himself in a dilemma. He was to encourage and appoint the faithful to accomplish God's work. However, at the same time, Titus would have to rebuke those who desired spiritual authority but did not have the character it demanded.[64] For Titus to accomplish his charge, he would first have to recognize who God had appointed him to be. He was not to be disregarded by any.

Many do not recognize who God has called them to be and submit to wrong things by not operating in His power and authority. We carry the banner of Christ and operate as His soldiers and ambassadors in this world. We must submit to God first and then to those he has set in authority second.[65] However, if those in authority resist God, we heed God's voice rather than man's.[66] When you operate in the authority of God, no one can disregard you.

---

[63] Matthew 8:8-10

[64] Titus 1:7-9

[65] 2 Corinthians 8:5-6

[66] Acts 5:29

We are to speak, exhort, and reprove with authority. We are to talk respectfully but with confidence that God is with us. We are to speak according to the word with faith that God will move. We must also reprove some and live by God's standards of a faithful and holy life. When you speak with God's authority, people take notice of you. You become too significant to be ignored and too substantial to discount. Encourage others with the conviction that God will bring them through. Firmly reprove believers who do wrong as if you have a biblical mandate.[67] Don't let anyone disregard you.

> **Prayer:** Father, prepare me to walk into the authority that you have given. Please help me speak what is in my spirit while I am still calm. Forgive me for all the time I internalized rather than speaking against wrongs done and allowing stress and pressure to build in my life. I ask that others forgive me for blowing up when the issue was more about me than it was about them. Help me to recognize the authority you have placed me in and under so I may do what is pleasing to you in Jesus' name, Amen.

---

[67] 1 Timothy 5:20

With Dove Eyes for God

Songs of Solomon 4:1 Behold, you are beautiful, my love. Behold, you are beautiful. Your eyes are like doves behind your veil. Your hair is as a flock of goats, that descend from Mount Gilead.

King Solomon was the wisest man ever and had more women than you could shake a stick at.[68] He was a master at romance and described his love in seven ways. She had bird eyes, and her hair looked like a bunch of wild goats, her teeth resembled a herd of sheep, her lips were like a red piece of thread, her temples like fruit, her neck looked like a building, and her breast was like a building two deer.[69] Saying this nowadays would have you either sleeping on the couch for a month or divorced.

Let's revisit what Solomon said. Doves wink seductively to each other to reinforce their relationship and continual court and mate for life. Her hair was beautiful, like a flock of goats cascading down a mountain. Her teeth were as white as washed ewes, her lips anointed, and only loving words came out of her mouth. When he complimented her, she would turn blush red like the inside of a pomegranate. Her neck was desirable, like a tower where warriors hung their shields during peace. He said her breasts were evenly sized and placed like two fawns. How beautiful she was.

---

[68] 1 Kings 11:2-3
[69] Songs of Solomon 4:1-5

Like Solomon, our words should let those we love know how beautiful they are to us.[70] Songs of Solomon is about reciprocations. Every time Solomon did something nice, she didn't just accept and expect it; instead, she responded kindly. We can never outlove God, but we can try. Even God wants your appreciation.[71] If we each showed more love, there would be more love for people to love us back. Please don't wait until someone dies before you bring them their flowers. If you love someone, build them up, make good memories, and show appreciation. Love now, laugh often, and show them you care.

Prayer: Lord, I appreciate you for everything you have done. Help me reciprocate through praise and faithfulness. Stir me to give as I receive and give voice to my attitude of gratitude. Increase my consideration for my loved ones so they know my heart for them and are encouraged. I will be a builder and fisher of men by your grace. In Jesus' name. Amen

---

[70] Proverbs 16:24
[71] Psalm 9:1

Taking Heed

---※---

Mark 4:24-25 He said to them, "Take heed what you hear. With whatever measure you measure, it will be measured to you; and more will be given to you who hear. For whoever has, to him more will be given; and he who doesn't have, even that which he has will be taken away from him."

Nothing will help you on your walk with God as much as having an ear sensitive to His word. Jesus gathered his disciples to explain parables of how to have a fruitful walk with God, letting them know that they need to be receptive hearts.[72] Next, he instructed them to be transparent before God and not hide what he already knew.[73] Before he ends, He introduces a warning about watching what you hear.

Things we should avoid listening to, like unbelief, gossip, rumors, malicious speech, and lies, are apparent. Other things like speculations and manmade teachings are more covert. These are under the umbrella of profane speech and can lead people astray.[74] Profane means to make unfit or unclean for use and speaks of anything that defiles or degrades, whether from a conversation, music, or multimedia. Listening to wrong

---

[72] Mark 4:14-20

[73] Mark 4:21-22

[74] Ephesians 4:29-30

things makes you unfit because you may reflect on it rather than using the measure of faith God gives.[75]

What you heed will either grow your faith or take you out of touch with Jesus.[76] The same measure we apply what we hear to our lives is that measure we grow or shrink back. Those who heed the instructions of God will increase, But for the one who does not listen, what he has will be taken away. The question is, "Do we want more of Jesus or less." The family of Christ hears and does the word of God.[77] When you read the bible, hear a sermon, or pray, do you respond with faith and obedience? If so, expect to receive more and be blessed.

Prayer: Lord, thank you for desiring to speak to my heart and guide me by your Holy Spirit to heed your word and increase. I covenant to shut my ears to every profane thing that does not build kingdom living. You have desired to give me an abundant life where I will fulfill my purpose and receive your peace. I ask you to guide me through every challenge and help my life to reflect your image. Protect my family and home and draw us to a closer walk with thee, in Jesus' name. Amen.

---

[75] Romans 12:3
[76] Romans 10:17
[77] Luke 8:21

Not Complaining

Numbers 17:10 Yahweh said to Moses, "Put back the rod of Aaron before the covenant, to be kept for a token against the children of rebellion; that you may make an end of their complaining against me, that they not die."

It is a pity that the people complained even when God revealed His presence. God directed Moses to write each tribe leader's name on their staff and leave them in front of the ark of the covenant. During the night, Aaron's staff budded, producing ripe almonds, which solidified that Moses and Aaron were God's chosen representatives and those coming against them were in rebellion.[78] The staff Moses retrieved would be a sign that the people need to stop murmuring and complaining.

Biblically, complaints are against enemies, not kingdom comrades.[79] When God places someone in authority, they become His ambassador on the earth. An attack on the ambassador is a rejection of the one who sent the ambassador.[80] Moses wanted to serve the Lord, but the more he tried, the harder people made it for him. However, they weren't just coming against Moses by complaining; they were attacking God. The punishment

---

[78] Numbers 17:1-8
[79] Philippians 2:14
[80] Luke 10:16

for such acts was fire from heaven, a plague, and the earth swallowing up the rebellious.[81]

Sometimes, people disagree with leaders because it isn't their way of doing things. Abraham Lincoln said, "You can complain about rose bushes having thorns or rejoice that thorn bushes have roses." Without the proper perspective, we may do things that fight against God.[82] Disagreements should be prayed over and addressed practically. Go to someone in love rather than others in gossip. Get help when needed; if it doesn't work, take it to the congregation for reconciliation.[83] Without these, you may be a rebel against God.

> **Prayer:** Heavenly Father, as I take my complaints to you, I ask you to give me the proper perspective on the things in my life. Please help me support those doing good and shield against evil from rising. Knowing your sacrifice on the cross gives me no reason to complain about suffering. Strengthen me when I am weak and weary. I can do all things through Christ, who strengthens me to be bold in faith and continuous in love. In Jesus' name, Amen

---

[81] Numbers 16:28-51
[82] Acts 5:38-39
[83] Matthew 18:15-17

Drawn by Him

Jeremiah 31:3 Yahweh appeared of old to me, saying,
"Yes, I have loved you with an everlasting love.
Therefore I have drawn you with loving kindness.

Some wrongly imply that God in the Old Testament shows judgment, and in the New Testament shows love, and nothing could be further from the truth. God does not change, and His love for His people has never changed. The New Testament shows His ultimate love in Christ's sacrifice[84] and His ultimate judgment on sin.[85] The Lord has an everlasting love for those who are His and draws them with His loving kindness.

In the Old Testament, God gave standards through laws to live by, but people kept doing things their way. In the New Testament, God reveals His standard in the person of Jesus Christ, who is the way.[86] Our sinful propensity has always been to set our standard and live in God's world our way.[87] Living according to God's standards would release us from bad habits, hurtful thoughts, and negative attitudes. So, God reaches out by lovingkindness to draw and show us something better.

---

[84] John 15:13
[85] Revelation 20:11-15
[86] John 14:6
[87] Proverbs 3:5-6

It is God's goodness that causes us to change.[88] The Lord takes and transforms us. By the world's standards, most of us are expendable and replaceable. However, to the Lord, we are precious in His sight. People forget that difficult roads often take you to the best places, and storms make trees grow deeper roots. God's love doesn't quit but waits for us to discover our need for Him.[89] God draws us into a relationship of peace, protection, and prosperity through goodness. Grab hold of His tender hand by faith and surrender to His lovingkindness.

Prayer: Heavenly Father, I ask you to draw me near in your lovingkindness. When my thoughts seem distant, and I struggle to live by your standard, hold me close in your everlasting love. Please show me how to renew my mind, refresh my soul, and yield my spirit to your goodness. I ask you to heal the hidden sorrow buried in my heart and reawaken my devotion to follow the leading of your Holy Spirit. Continually cover my home and family and draw each one towards you in love. In the name of Jesus. Amen.

---

[88] Romans 2:4
[89] 2 Peter 3:9

Not fighting Alone

---⫝⋆⫝---

Deuteronomy 20:2-4 It shall be, when you draw near to the battle, that the priest shall approach and speak to the people, and shall tell them, "Hear, Israel, you draw near today to battle against your enemies. Don't let your heart faint! Don't be afraid, nor tremble, neither be scared of them; for Yahweh your God is he who goes with you, to fight for you against your enemies, to save you."

Have you ever been on the verge of a battle that seemed like something you couldn't win? God would have small men face giants, few men face armies, and women destroy generals, so we will learn to trust Him rather than fear our foes. Moses instructed the Israelites to call the priest forward to speak to our faith and fear whenever they had to fight an impossible battle.[90] Our first battle is within ourselves, whether we trust God or fear men. Without faith, you won't see yourself for who you are.[91] When the deck stacks against you, come out fighting through faith.

God doesn't just jump in; we must invite Him into our difficulties. We proclaim His name, and He shows up. The priest would allay the people's fears and proclaim God's presence. The Lord waits for us to gather the priest and sound the trumpet declaring His name. We fight the same

---

[90] Deuteronomy 20:1
[91] Numbers 13:31-33

enemy, but the battle is different when God is there. He gives strength where we are weak, confounds the enemy, and gives us victory.[92]

Some of us are on the verge of battle and have gone in alone. We have not called on the priest to proclaim God's presence in our struggle. We face the enemy at his full strength and have not increased our strength against him. We fight against enemies we can't see, but God sees them.[93] When we conquer our fears, God conquers our foes. One may put a thousand to flight, but you may face much more. Have you called upon the servants of God to assist you in putting the demonic forces to flight? Sound the alarm, call upon the priest, and proclaim your victory in Christ.

Prayer: Lord, I ask that you be with me in every trial. I will not be bullied or intimidated. I come against those times when I am mentally strong but emotionally weak. I meet every challenge, obstacle, and problem with faith, not fear, because I trust you. I call on your name, and you are with me in every storm and attack. Give me skills for the battle and make your presence so I will conquer every giant in the name of Jesus. Amen

---

[92] Isaiah 41:10
[93] Ephesians 6:12

Motivated by Love

---⚜---

Philippians 1:16-17 The former insincerely preach Christ from selfish ambition, thinking that they add affliction to my chains; but the latter out of love, knowing that I am appointed for the defense of the Good News.

When Paul penned the Philippians, he was chained and in prison in Rome.[94] Instead of having a quieting effect on the church, people began to proclaim the gospel with renewed boldness. Getting the gospel out is indeed more important than our motivations.[95] However, we should ensure we do the right things for the right reasons. Some preached, looking to fill the void in leadership. Others preached to promote the legalistic doctrine of the Judaizers. Still, others preached simply out of love for Christ.

There are two primary motivators for serving God. The first is selfish ambition, which is serving God for the benefit of our own. Getting recognition or a position bolsters our pride. People like this serve in visible ministry and resist the behind-the-scenes stuff. The second motivator is love. Many people do nothing for the Lord, showing a lack of appreciation for

---

[94] Philippians 1:12-14
[95] Philippians 1:18

the one who saved their souls.[96] Our love for God and His people should motivate us to serve because we are nothing without love.[97]

The difference between religious ceremonies and service is love. Without love, we do everything out of a sense of duty. That kind of Christian life is about the ceremony, and it looks good but has no life to it. Prayer, fasting, giving, and helping others become a burden instead of a joy when no love exists. If you aren't serving, check your life; if you have no love, check your heart. The world knows we are Christian by the love we show the brethren.[98] Make sure you give the gospel, do good, and love.

> **Prayer:** Lord, help me keep the right thing the right thing. When I am wrong, help me see the flaws and know what to do to make it right. Open up opportunities for me to encourage others and share your gospel. I pray you give me the boldness to speak your word and walk in your victory. Renew my mind to faithfulness and focus on the cross of Christ in the name of Jesus. Amen.

---

[96] Luke 7:47
[97] 1 Corinthians 13:2
[98] John 13:35

Not taking the Donut off the Buddha plate

---*---

1 Corinthians 8:1-2 Now concerning things sacrificed to idols: We know that we all have knowledge. Knowledge puffs up, but love builds up. But if anyone thinks that he knows anything, he doesn't yet know as he ought to know.

In Corinth, temple servants of the various false gods would sell the leftover meat dedicated to their gods. The meat was sold cheaper and provided them with extra money. Normally, you would buy the meat belonging to the god you served and eat it as a form of worship. Some churches at Corinth ate the meat previously sacrificed to idols. They knew that the idols were nothing and, therefore, the things sacrificed to them were nothing. Doing so offended the sensitivities of believers who recently emerged from idolatry and wanted to separate from that life.[99] Knowledge without love causes some to stumble in their faith.

Knowledge without love is reckless and moves forward without constraints.[100] New believers saw seasoned saints in the pagan temple market.[101] Since buying the meat of the God you served was considered a form of worshipping that idol, it offended those coming out of pagan worship.[102]

---

[99] 1 Corinthians 8:7-9

[100] 1 Corinthians 13:2

[101] 1 Corinthians 8:10-12

[102] 1 Thessalonians 5:22

Without love, knowledge will cause us to be insensitive to our brothers and sisters in Christ. We may begin to look down on those God has saved because they don't know what we know. But if we think like that, we don't know what we should.

Many believers have head knowledge without heart knowledge.[103] Knowledge puffs up because it is simply an accumulation of information. But love builds up because it is an impartation of divine affection.[104] Knowledge without love has a mind for God instead of having the mind of God. Without humility, knowledge becomes arrogant. Knowledge does not mean understanding. Only when the mind of God meets with the heart of God within us do we understand. If you want to seek the things above, then seek to have the heart of God. Don't seek to be puffed up, but be built up in the faith.

Prayer: Father, never let my head knowledge outshine my heart knowledge. Help me to consider my ways and do what is right for all around me. I will not be an offense in the church but a defender of the weak. Help my life reflect both faith and faithfulness to your word and your love in the name of Jesus. Amen.

---

[103] Proverbs 4:23
[104] Romans 5:5

Seeking to Give Him Great Joy

⬥

***3 John 1:4 I have no greater joy than this: to
hear about my children walking in truth.***

Whether you are their spiritual or biological offspring, a parent's greatest desire is knowing their child is following their instructions. The apostle John felt this when he heard that Gaius, one of his sons in the faith, walked in the truth.[105] Gaius became known for helping others. He had a ministry of help, and word of the love he showed others, reached John, who was about to be exiled to the island of Patmos.[106] John's ministry is at a close, and it did his heart well to know that his children would continue to push forward.

When we think of the things that please our heavenly Father walking in the truth of His word would be at the top of our Lord's list. To walk in the truth is to heed God's voice and call in your life. It is to live with the integrity of the word. Jesus is the way, the truth, and the life.[107] Walking in truth conforms us to the image of the one who is the truth. The apostle's goal was not to replicate himself in his spiritual children; instead, he would see Jesus replicated in the believer's lives.[108] God's joy is to see Christ take hold of the life of God's children.

---

[105] 3 John 1:1-3
[106] 3 John 1:5-8
[107] John 14:6
[108] Galatians 4:19

When we don't walk in the truth, we portray the illusion of a Christian life, lying to ourselves about how much we love God.[109] Knowing the truth is not enough; we must also walk in it. Are you willing to walk in the truth of Christ's life, love, and word and bring God great joy? God has no greater joy than seeing His creation function according to the truth. When we walk in truth, we return to God's original blueprint for our lives. God created us to bring Him glory and great joy.[110] So make God smile and walk in the truth.

> **Prayer:** Father, you greatly desire to see me walking and the truth. I ask for your help to reflect the reality of your grace rather than the illusion of my works. Please help me to live by the blueprint you have for my life. I ask that the Holy Spirit construction company remove all defects and restore the image of Christ to me. Lord, I ask you to do the same for my family and loved ones by your grace and through your love in the name of Jesus Christ. Amen.

---

[109] Mark 12:30
[110] Isaiah 43:7

Orchestrated to and Through the Heavens

Psalms 32:8 I will instruct you and teach you in the way which you shall go. I will counsel you with my eye on you.

Life is a divine orchestration that God uses to benefit those who love Him.[111] Like in an orchestra, each move of the conductor's hand tells us how to operate in whatever circumstance we find ourselves. Life is better when we cooperate with the conductor of our orchestra. God's judgments are moves of His hand, making decisions and plans for our future.[112] We can resist and meet a bitter end or ask God what our next move is.

You may not have control over your life, but God does. A divine orchestration is when we allow God to guide us through actions from above.[113] God guides us all the time, but many ignore His moves. Scripture tells us what notes to play, the Holy Spirit helps us make the right sound, and the Lord above calls the heavens and earth to move on our behalf.[114] His guidance is always moment by moment, step by step, day by day. We have to move with each movement of God.

When the Lord calls down to earth, His voice goes through the heavens and activates them on our behalf. He speaks to the heavens and

---

[111] Romans 8:28

[112] Jeremiah 29:11

[113] Proverbs 16:9

[114] Isaiah 66:1

watches over His word to perform it.[115] He judges His people to see if we order our lives by His divine orchestration. Our faithfulness and obedience on earth pull down the favor, blessing, and protection spoken into the heavens from above. Imagine how many blessings we may miss because we have not followed His orchestration. By faith, we have access to His grace.[116] Let us call down every grace spoken from above and receive the abundantly blessed, divinely orchestrated life.

> **Prayer:** Father, I appreciate how you anticipate my needs and help me in every circumstance. Please assist me in hearing your voice and acting in accordance with the wisdom of your word. I stand against disturbances and disruptions that want to distract me from my purpose and peace. Create harmony in my life, family, and house. In the name of Jesus, teach me your ways and uphold me with your holy hand. Amen

---

[115] Jeremiah 1:12
[116] Romans 5:2

Inherit Your Blessing

---✦---

1 Peter 3:9 Not rendering evil for evil, or insult for insult; but instead blessing, knowing that you were called to this, that you may inherit a blessing

Guilty as charged. That is what most of us would say if asked if we have returned evil for evil or insult for insult. When someone pushes us, we push back. It's a natural reaction; we are good at hurling insults or talking about others when offended. However, we must respond with God's supernatural character and power in Christ. I am talking about a spiritual reaction that blesses others when they curse and forgive those who have insulted you.[117] For this, you were called and set up to inherit a blessing.

How many times have we had the opportunity to inherit a blessing and messed it up by returning evil for evil? The truth is this: there are some blessings we can't receive until our character changes.[118] When we respond to natural situations unnaturally, supernatural favor comes upon us. To inherit anything, someone has to die. When they die, it releases the inheritance of blessings they have been holding up from us. When we die to ourselves, we inherit the blessing for which Christ died.[119] When you repay evil with blessing, you have killed your pride and selfishness.

---

[117] Luke 6:27-28

[118] Psalms 1:2-3

[119] Matthew 16:24-25

Godly character produces a godly inheritance, and evil character is like sowing to the wind and reaping the whirlwind.[120] Are you letting natural reactions block your blessings? Think about how much you may have lost by reacting naturally instead of walking in the spiritual. The cliche "when praises go up, blessings come down" has been misunderstood and misapplied. God is praised by our spiritual reactions to natural situations, bringing blessings down from heaven.[121] God calls us to have supernatural spiritual reactions that bring blessings from heaven. Make sure you inherit every blessing.

Prayer: Lord, just as we expect the child of a great person to reflect the greatness of their character, help me reflect your character. Forgive me for all the times I didn't act like a child of the most blessed king. When others mistreat me, I won't worry about what they say; instead, I'll keep you in the forefront of my life. I will inherit the blessing and ask that you pour out your favor as I crucify my desires daily in the name of Jesus Christ. Amen.

---

[120] Hosea 8:6-7
[121] Malachi 3:10-18

Growing and Growing Up

---◆---

Ephesians 4:16 from whom all the body, being
fitted and knit together through that which
every joint supplies, according to the working in
measure of each individual part, makes the body
increase to the building up of itself in love.

It is from Christ that the whole body we call the church is put together
and caused to grow.[122] However, placing parts together does not cause
them to stay together or work in tandem. Unity and growth happen with
the proper working of each part. As we commit to Christ, we also commit
to His multifaceted body.[123] For the church to be healthy, each component
must work together and receive what it needs.

Christ has supplied all we need for the church to grow. When each person in the body functions, then Christ is working to build up His body.[124]
Each of us is to cause growth through what we supply. Understand that
only through our proper working within the church is the church built
up in love. God cares for each person in the body, and those rarely seen
are important and have great honor.[125] Ephesians shows us that church

---

[122] Ephesians 1:22-23
[123] 1 Corinthians 12:12
[124] Colossians 2:6-7
[125] 1 Corinthians 12:22-26

growth stems from spreading God's love in our service, unity, speech, and actions.[126] When we show this, then the church is built up by Christ.

The Church at Ephesus didn't advertise; they evangelized. Growth doesn't come by putting up signs or websites; it comes from what every part supplies. It came from building itself up in love at the direction of Christ. Advertisement draws a crowd but only lead to transfer growth when believers leave one church to go to another. It's good to reach out to nonfunctioning members of Christ's body, but that is congregational growth, not growth of the body of Christ. What are you supplying to the body to cause growth? The Christian life is involved in Christ's body. Get involved and make a difference.

> **Prayer:** Lord, I pray for everyone sidelined needing to heal and commit so they will again participate in the work of your body, the church. I know you have strategically placed me and given me your Holy Spirit to empower me as a faithful witness. Please show me the chances to serve. Put a hedge of security around my home and family, stirring us up in love and good works. I thank you for your continued comfort, healing, and blessing in the name of Jesus. Amen.

---

[126] Ephesians 4:13-16

The Road to Recovery

---✦---

Mark 10:50-52 He, casting away his cloak, sprang up, and came to Jesus. Jesus asked him, "What do you want me to do for you?" The blind man said to him, "Rabboni, that I may see again. Jesus said to him, "Go your way. Your faith has made you well." Immediately he received his sight, and followed Jesus on the way.

What are you doing today to get closer to where you want to be tomorrow? Bartimaeus's name meant son of Timaeus, and no one bothered to call him anything else. Everyone tried to discourage him from seeking the Lord, telling him to remain quiet and let the Lord pass him by. He was blind but still could see that the difference between success and failure was giving up. Overlooked and in need, Bartimaeus kept calling until Jesus heard him call.[127]

No matter how busy Christ is, He will help whoever calls Him. It doesn't matter what your station in life is or if no one knows your name. God listens to the one who seeks Him.[128] Bartimaeus started his road of recovery by calling out to God to help him when no one else would. Yet before he could come, he had to cast aside his beggar's garment and never

---

[127] Mark 10:46-49
[128] Psalm 4:3

pick it up again.[129] When Christ saw that he did not approach him as a beggar but as a believer, He said his faith made him well.

By removing his garment, he approached Christ in a way that made Him say, "What do you want me to do." It's not till we leave behind those things that kept us bound, labeled, and tied to the past that we are ready for Christ to do something new in our lives.[130] No one knows your path until they walk it, but too many follow Christ were never made whole. Why? Because they drag their past into their road of recovery. Inability, failure, unforgiveness, and the like are garments that weigh down our faith and slow our walk with God.[131] Let's travel this road to recovery, free of everything that holds us back, and call on Christ until healed.

> **Prayer:** Thank you, Lord, that my past no longer determines my future. As I get closer to you, its control over me is broken and left behind. Please give me strength as I follow you. I look forward to the glorious future I have in you. I ask you to reveal to my family and loved ones how to live a life of freedom in the name of Jesus Christ. Amen.

---

[129] Ephesians 4:21-24
[130] Zechariah 3:1-4
[131] Hebrews 12:1

House On Fire

---◆---

1 Samuel 30:2-3 and had taken captive the women and all who were in it, both small and great. They didn't kill any, but carried them off and went their way. When David and his men came to the city, behold, it was burned with fire; and their wives, their sons, and their daughters were taken captive.

Ziklag was home for David and His men. From there, they would regularly raid the enemies of God who still inhabited the land of Israel.[132] However, they were allied with King Achish, who called for help he did not need.[133] While they were away fighting someone else's battle, an enemy brought the battle to their doorstep. They left their homes unprotected in their haste to help someone else. No one died, but the women and children were distressed because no men had stayed behind to protect the city.

People will ask you for help without trying to deal with their problems first. We return only to find our Ziklag burning. While away, the enemy has been throwing fiery darts at our families.[134] Unless we take measures to secure Ziklag, we will come home to the burning issue of life. Men feel dishonored, women feel uncovered, and our children feel neglected. Why?

---

[132] 1 Samuel 27:5-12

[133] 1 Samuel 29:6-9

[134] Ephesians 6:16

Because we didn't protect our Ziklag. We return home only to find that the enemy has attacked, and fires of contention, strife, and anger are burning.

Trying to fix someone else's problems while your home is burning is unwise. Part of providing for our homes is making sure they are protected.[135] Preparation is prevention, and prevention is nine-tenths of the cure. You may find it burning if you don't spiritually, mentally, and physically protect your home.[136] Yet, people deplete their strength by answering the cries of others while ignoring the cries of their own homes. No matter who calls, your issues come first. Deal with your problems, or they will deal with your happiness.

> **Prayer:** Lord, please keep my house safe. Please give me the wisdom to handle emerging problems and the foresight to identify every attack before it reaches my door. Please help me avoid being sidetracked or spending more time on others than in my house. I need to establish boundaries and balance to serve you and my family. Help me be more considerate and resourceful in dealing with my family. In Jesus' name, Amen.

---

[135] 1 Timothy 5:8
[136] Matthew 24:43

Nobody Greater

Luke 7:19 And John calling to him two of his disciples sent them to Jesus, saying, Are you he that should come? or should we look for another?

Have you ever said, "This is not how things are supposed to be"? You're serving God but not where you want to be, and things aren't going your way. It's supposed to be different for us. Well, that's probably how John the Baptist felt, and he sacrificed all the comforts of home in the family to serve the Lord, only to find himself stuck somewhere he couldn't get out of.[137] Is this all life has for me? Where is my Messiah? Should I be looking elsewhere?

Sometimes, we have to decrease so Christ can increase. Even the strongest believers can be shaken in their faith and wonder if they have missed God's words.[138] Have I been on the right path, or should I be looking for something different? Questions arise as we look at our lives to see if we are fulfilling our purpose. Reflecting on his ministry, John wanted assurance that he had done the right thing and completed his work.

Jesus has come and fulfilled all that scripture said he would do, yet we still look for others to validate us. I'm sure John received his answer with joy. The sick are healed, the blind sees, and the gospel is preached.[139] Jesus

---

[137] Luke 3:18-20

[138] Mark 9:23-25

[139] Luke 7:22

did all the things John had expected Christ to do. Instead of looking for another, we must examine what Christ has done for us.[140] He is worth the service and sacrifices we make daily. He is what we are to long for, search for, and live for. There is nobody greater.

Prayer: Father in heaven, I've come to do your bidding and carry out your mission. I pleaded with you to accompany me as I move on with what I must accomplish and to respectfully accept the things I cannot change. Please provide me with good people with whom I can work to finish the work you assign me. Help me lower my pride and gain control over my desires. One day, I want to hear you say well done and call me a friend, so continue walking with me in Jesus Christ's name. Amen.

---

[140] Hebrews 12:2

Cleaning Up Your Act

---✦---

Isaiah 1:16 Wash yourselves. Make yourself clean. Put away the evil of your doings from before my eyes. Cease to do evil.

How can it be put more plainly? We are responsible for our spiritual condition before God. However, people often blame others for their condition. The truth is that no matter what others are doing around us, our habits determine our spiritual condition.[141] We have slandered, lied, stolen, and resisted God's Spirit, and we haven't washed the blood off of our hands.[142] We can blame no one else.

The precursor to all spiritual cleansing is our physical contact and actions. Our environment does not defile our spiritual nature; it rests inside the inner man.[143] The inner man only meets our outer man or flesh, not the world. Defilement happens through acts of the heart acting on the temptations of the outer man. Our surroundings can only touch our flesh, but our actions touch our hearts. Every temptation or test is external and will only defile us through the actions of our flesh.[144]Therefore, only when we cooperate with the temptations of the flesh are our spirits defiled.

---

[141] Romans 12:1-2
[142] Isaiah 1:15
[143] 2 Corinthians 4:16
[144] Mark 7:15

Confession cleanses our consciousness, but what about our actions? Before we can learn to do well, we must first cease from evil.[145] We must leave that fatal condition called sin alone and get right before God's eyes. Let us wash and make ourselves clean before the Lord. Stop touching what should not be touched and lift the same defiled hands to the Lord in prayer. Cleanse yourself before you pray and come clean into the presence of the Lord.

> **Prayer:** Forgive me for when I asked you to wash me through confession but didn't wash my deeds. I come for your aid in purging myself of pride, pretense, and performance. Help me develop the spiritual habits necessary to withstand temptations by relying on my faith, your word, and restraint. May your Holy Spirit burn away my shortcomings and anxieties like dross in the furnace of refinement. Free me of all shame, so I do not hide sin from your presence in the name of Jesus. Amen.

---

[145] Isaiah 1:17

The War We Forget About

---✦---

Proverbs 18:12 Before destruction the heart of man is proud, but before honor is humility

Wars have already been fought and forgotten. The War of 1812 is one such conflict. Referred to as America's second war of independence, in 1812, America declared war on the British Empire, including Canada, for acts that insulted American sovereignty. This war was called the Humiliation of America and led to the capture, occupation, and burning of Washington, DC. It also led to the destruction of the Tecumseh's Indian Confederacy and ended Britain's Atlantic Coast blockade, yet only the most ardent history buffs even know these things happened.

Psalm 18:12 describes the overlooked war that wages inside of our hearts. A war of pride insults God's sovereignty over our lives. When we walk in pride, our every action is an effrontery to God.[146] Our arrogance offends God's love through its smug attitude, and our conceit attacks the dignity of God through its self-importance. Pride clashes with grace and resists the Holy Spirit's work.[147] Pride thanks itself rather than giving thanks for God's goodness, love, and grace.

It was pride that changed angels into devils. Pride is short-lived because it brings us down.[148] However, if our heart is lowly before Him, He will

---

[146] Psalms 138:6

[147] James 4:5-7

[148] Isaiah 2:11

lift us. Where we position our hearts will determine where the Lord will position us. If you're waiting for God to honor you, then humble yourself. Pride is concerned with its rights; humility concerns itself with doing right. God guides and teaches those who are humble.[149] Keep fighting against all pride and work with a servant's attitude. Then, the Lord will bring you honor and great reward.[150]

Prayer: Lord, I ask you to break the root of pride in every aspect of my existence. I hold captive to every idea that seeks to elevate itself above what is right and devalues the contributions of others to my achievement. I humble myself under your hand and ask you to lift me. Lead me by your Spirit and instruct me on what is right in the name of Jesus. Amen.

---

[149] Psalm 25:9
[150] Proverbs 15:33

Public Successes and Private Failures

Proverbs 22:4 The result of humility and the fear of Yahweh is wealth, honor, and life.

Who are the elite in this world? Many look up to those with privilege and influence, never knowing that many so-called elites are spiritually poor, dishonored by their own families, and whose lives are in shambles.[151] They are public successes and private failures and are disasters waiting to happen. They have money, power, and respect publicly, but privately, they do not possess the true riches, honor, and life reserved for those who walk in humility and the fear of the Lord.[152]

What does it take to be both publicly and privately successful? Does it come from a positive outlook and determination, or is it our confidence in specific skills? To become a private and public success, we must have the winning combination of humility and the fear of the Lord.[153] First, we must maintain a humble attitude that submits to God's authority over our lives. Secondly, we must approach every situation by making our choices in fear of the Lord. These are to be our attitude and our approach.[154]

Rosalind Russel said, "Success is a public affair, and failure is a private funeral." Neglect of home, family, and mental and spiritual health bury the

---

[151] Revelation 3:16-17
[152] Amos 6:1-3
[153] Job 28:28
[154] Psalms 111:10

joy of success. The right choices with the right attitude will bring rewards from God and make us successful in all areas of life.[155] Too many have sacrificed their well-being and family to attempt to become public successes, only to find failure in their private lives. Let those who want success seek humility and fear the Lord God fixes broken things. God will do the rest when you have done everything possible.

> **Prayer:** Lord, I pray that focusing on my public success won't lead to failure in my private life. Set my feet on solid ground so I will maintain a life of devotion, consideration, and balance. I will not sacrifice peace of mind for profit nor stray from integrity for gain. Help me stay humble and walk in fear of the Lord, and then I can find the wealth, honor, and life I long for. Grant that your Spirit will guide me to open doors and give me the wisdom and boldness to make the most of every opportunity in the name of Jesus. Amen.

---

[155] Isaiah 33:6

Turn the Knob Up

---✦---

Psalms 51:2 Wash me thoroughly from mine iniquity, and cleanse me from my sin.

It's nice to ask God to gently and caringly wash us, pouring water on our heads; however, sometimes, we need a thorough cleansing. King David asked God to be his fuller, an ancient launderer who would wash and repair torn and soiled garments. He uses the Hebrew word "Kabas," which means to wash by stamping with the feet. Kabas describes their work of repeatedly submerging and walking on a garment to remove heavy stains.[156] When cleansed, the fuller would repair any damage by restoring the garment to a better condition before returning it to the owner.

This washing consecrates the believer to return to God's presence after broken fellowship. Like dirt on clothes, our sin tries to stick hard and stain us. David wrote Psalm 51 after God sent the prophet Nathan to challenge him face-to-face.[157] If the Lord sent someone to rebuke you for your actions, would you respond as a fragile article or say, Lord, wash me till I am clean?[158] Admitting your part is sometimes the most challenging part of the restoration.

We love the gentle cycle, but it does not remove heavy stains. A good friend cannot bear to see stains that will ruin your otherwise good

---

[156] Isaiah 1:18-19

[157] 2 Samuel 12:1-10

[158] Jeremiah 4:14

testimony. God can cleanse us, but we must prepare for the heavy cycle. Hard choices demand a clear break from what is trying to put us in bondage.[159] We can't avoid admitting what's wrong and getting back right with God. When sin has pulled us from God, the heavy-duty washing will pull us back into His presence with the white garments of righteousness.[160]

> **Prayer:** Father, I come to you with my life's torn and stained garments, seeking your restoration. I'm grateful you love me and don't want me marred by sin or past pain. I ask that you wash me thoroughly and cleanse me from all sin so I can stand in your presence. No condemnation exists for those in you, so help lift every prideful, fearful, and damaging thought. I ask that what you do in me, you do in my family also. Amen.

---

[159] Acts 8:22-23
[160] Isaiah 61:10

Sprinkled By The Blood

---⊹---

Psalms 51:7 Purify me with hyssop, and I will be clean. Wash me, and I will be whiter than snow.

What is hyssop? Reading the text, many assumed it was a type of soap, but it's not. Hyssop was a plant bundled together and used as a paintbrush to apply sacrificial blood and mark someone as belonging to God.[161] The priest also used it to sprinkle water and pronounce someone ceremonially clean after a time of consecration.[162] Sometimes, hyssop was used to apply both blood and water simultaneously.[163] We see the spiritual significance in the water and blood pouring out of Christ when pierced with the spear.

The water and blood represented the certainty of Christ's death. To be purged with hyssop is to be proclaimed clean by the blood of Christ. It is to be a holy vessel belonging to Christ and set apart for His purposes. David had recently killed his servant Uriah and taken Bathsheba for his wife.[164] He needed to be purged and free of all contamination by changing his ways and coming to God for forgiveness. Though David still had to deal with the consequences of his acts, he wanted to be valuable to God and didn't want his wrongdoing to destroy his purpose.

---

[161] Exodus 12:22
[162] Numbers 19:18-19
[163] Leviticus 14:51
[164] 2 Samuel 11:14-26

The nation needs revival, but first, God's people need renewal. To be cleansed, strengthened, and motivated to move forward in Christ. We need cleansing with hyssop by sprinkling the blood of Christ on our conscious minds so we can focus on God and His will for our lives.[165] When was the last time you felt clean before God? Do you bow your head in worship or fear in His presence? Are there concerns about how he feels about things you have recently done? Maybe you must be purged with hyssop and sprinkled by the blood.

Prayer: Lord, I come to the tree covered in blood where the waters of salvation flow, pleading for your purification and pardon. Purify my heart, mind, and soul so that my deeds are untainted by my flaws, faults, and failures. Bless me to accomplish my purpose for my generation and leave a moral legacy. I ask that you have mercy on my loved ones and renew our minds, hearts, and faith. By the precious blood of Jesus. Amen.

[165] 1 John 1:7

Overcoming Manipulation

---⚓---

Colossians 2:18 Let no one rob you of your prize by self-abasement and worshiping of the angels, dwelling in the things which he has not seen, vainly puffed up by his fleshly mind.

One of the things people hate the most is manipulation. Manipulation is craftiness and deceit disguised as righteousness. It lures those who have lowered our discernment because we have wrongly trusted a manipulator who mixes a little truth with a big lie.[166] They want you to empathize with them but remain untouched by your situation. Their machinations draw people away from their reward in Christ because they depend upon man's plans instead of being derived from Christ, the head of the church.

The difference between manipulation and motivation is who benefits. People who motivate move you toward mutually advantageous things. Manipulators only make it appear that going along with them means you are finally getting on the right track.[167] Their façade of false humility draws you emotionally into their scheme. They appear very dedicated to what they are speaking about and have all the details covered, so your mind will be at ease. They often speak of great things and vision, yet their grand plans are figments of their minds.[168]

---

[166] Matthew 7:15

[167] 2 Corinthians 11:13-14

[168] 2 Timothy 3:2-5

I'm sorry to say some believers will act under the satanic principle of manipulation.[169] They cross boundaries to get what they want. Deceit was Satan's method in the Garden of Eden and remains his primary tactic today. In overcoming manipulation, we must focus on God's will for our lives and not stray from it. People will try to have us fulfill a vision or plan we have no connection to. Some may mean well, and others are not so good-minded.[170] People can only manipulate those who have let them in. Stay your course with God, follow His lead, and keep the manipulators out.

Prayer: Father, cleanse me of any trace of manipulation that may still be present in me, and grant me the wisdom to spot deceivers. Let me collaborate with other motivators to get a better result. I'm asking for your help in a spirit of faith. Safeguard me and lead me to the right relationships. Keep me in peace and good health, in Jesus' name. Amen.

---

[169] Ephesians 4:17-20
[170] Jeremiah 17:5

Let It Sink In

Colossians 3:12 Put on therefore, as God's chosen ones, holy and beloved, a heart of compassion, kindness, lowliness, humility, and perseverance;

We behave according to the greatest desire in our hearts.[171] Our heart's thoughts become our life's actions. If the thoughts of our hearts tell us to live as one chosen by God, we live holy in the love of God. Our behavior reflects our thoughts, and that is why having the mind of Christ is so important. Christ-like thinking causes our hearts to believe that as the holy and beloved of God, we can clothe ourselves with the character of God.[172]

The Greek word "Enduo," translated as "Put on," literally means to sink down into a garment. Figuratively, it pictures us clothed from above as we lift our hands in surrender. Since we are already holy and beloved in God's eyes, we must surrender our hearts to be more sensitive, kind, humble, and enduring. God desires for us to let these things sink into our hearts so they can saturate our character.[173] When we add the patient endurance of longsuffering, the good qualities that sink into our character become a garment we will never take off.

---

[171] Proverbs 23:7

[172] 1 Corinthian 2:15-16

[173] 2 Peter 1:5-6

We become like whatever we pour into our hearts. If the fact that you are holy and beloved hasn't sunken down into your heart, then it won't sink into your character. Being righteous is more important than being right. It's good that the blood of Christ makes us positionally righteous, but unless that sinks in, we won't practice righteousness.[174] Our holiness in God's thoughts for us will become our holy conduct when it sinks so deep into our hearts that we live it. Let what you are in God's heart sink into your heart, and you will be truly holy and beloved by Him.

Prayer: Father, I appreciate your support in helping me endure everything. I now pray that your love, goodness, and patience find a deep place in my soul since you are my pillar of strength and heart. When I reflect on your work, I give you thanks. Help me maintain a good character so that I might demonstrate your ways to others. Teach me righteousness and true holiness until we are all united in the faith, in the name of Jesus, Amen.

---

[174] 2 Corinthians 5:21

Super-Size Your Love

---✦---

Luke 10:27-29 He answered, "You shall love the Lord your God with all your heart, with all your soul, with all your strength, and with all your mind; and your neighbor as yourself." He said to him, "You have answered correctly. Do this, and you will live." But he, desiring to justify himself, asked Jesus, "Who is my neighbor?

The answer rang out from the mouth of an expert of the law who questioned Jesus about eternal life. When Christ asked about his understanding of it, he resounded with the words from the Jewish Shema, which every pious Jew would pronounce twice daily.[175] Coupled with his reply was a plea for neighborly love. Christ Himself had previously taught others these very words, and here, this man comes up with it through his study.[176] However, it was not enough for him because his love was too small.

Sometimes, the answer is so plain it seems too simple, and yet it can be the hardest thing for some of us to do. God desires us to super-size our love. It's not a lot to ask of us, especially considering the price He paid to show His love on the cross of Calvary. Yet, there is a desire to limit the love we show. To many Israelites, the scripture equated their neighbor

---

[175] Deuteronomy 6:4-5
[176] Mark 12:29-31

only with other sons of Israel.[177] The scribe's problem wasn't whether it was right or not to love God. No, instead, his issue was with loving the gentiles around him.

Christ calls us to live as brothers. He knew our neighbors would look, think, and act differently from us and said to them love anyway. Are there people that seem hard to love? Maybe they're from a foreign land like the Samaritan in the parable that Jesus would tell this man.[178] Loving your neighbor doesn't mean you need to remove your fence, but it does mean you help those on the other side of the road. Think about how hard it was for Christ to love us while we were still in sin, yet He still died for us.[179] The one that bothers you the most may be the one you must love the best. Super-size your love and inherit eternal life.

> **Prayer:** Father, make my heart receptive to love always and everywhere. I stand with my neighbor in the face of illness, anxiety, and anguish. If I can make a difference, I won't walk on the other side of the road. Fill my heart with your love and grace. I ask you to draw my neighbors to the open doors of your church, where they will find welcome and healing in the name of Jesus. Amen.

---

[177] Leviticus 19:18
[178] Luke 10:30-37
[179] Romans 5:8

Stay In Your Own Seat

---

1 Thessalonians 4:11 and that you make it your ambition to lead a quiet life, and to do your own business, and to work with your own hands, even as we instructed you

We should all aspire to lead a quiet life. Life can become very complicated with all the complexities of work, relationships, and hardships. The quiet life is not a life free of disturbance but a life of focus. It is a life where we sit down and work on our business.[180] Refining and improving our lives is a decisive move that will keep us from criticism and competition. How is this done? By setting your mind to your affairs and getting out of the affairs of others. We have to learn to take a chair, sit back and relax.[181]

The Greek term Hesuchazo, translated as "quiet life," means to refrain from laboring, meddling, or talking. Picture yourself busy at your desk tending to your work. Your hands are not idle because you are working on things pertaining to your own life and not focused on the lives of others.[182] That's the quiet life, where the Lord can speak freely and minister to your heart because you have the proper focus to steady the foundations of your life.

---

[180] 2 Thessalonians 3:10-12

[181] Psalms 37:3

[182] Proverbs 11:5-6

It's one thing to have a nose for business and another to have your nose in other people's business. Busy people are never busybodies. Busy bodies interfere and exert false control in the lives of others. They are idle and negative and cause conflicts while robbing themselves of a peaceful life.[183] Keep your mind in its chair and aspire to lead a quiet life. Don't worry about what others say or think. Don't try to fix anyone else; stay in your chair, work with your hands, and let God work on you.[184]

Prayer: Father, help me sweep before my door before I peak into the door of others. I need your strength and the power of focus to accomplish my task. Instead of being busy, I want productivity and perspective to operate in vision. Please guide me in completing my tasks and projects rather than squandering time. I pray that you remove ungodly interference, resolve family conflict, and restructure my life to stay blessed on purpose in the name of Jesus. Amen.

---

[183] Proverbs 17:14
[184] Ephesians 2:10

Love Conquers Me

---✦---

John 14:15 If you love me, keep my commandments.

How do we quantify our love? Is it through the words someone says or through their actions? Love is an inward affection found in our hearts and is known through its expression to be known. It's easy to express love from our mouths, but the tongue is deceitful and leaves doubt.[185] Our deeds, not our words, show others our love. How often does the Lord hear us say we love Him, yet we fall flat when it comes to obedience? We readily tell God we will obey, but when His word clashes with our desires, we ponder whose voice we should listen to.[186] How can we say we love God and at the same time we fight to obey Him?

The most accurate measure of our love is obedience. Obedience derives from love, which naturally gives us respect and a willingness to sacrifice. We see obedience in the small, inconvenient things done daily and the big things we occasionally do. If you have not decided to follow God, you will struggle to obey regardless of what happens. Obedience becomes a battle of will when our love for ourselves or our desires outshine our love for God. Your love for God, or lack of it, will determine who will be victorious. Those who love Christ will obey Him and draw in His love and presence.[187]

---

[185] Psalm 120:2-3
[186] Matthew 21:28-31
[187] John 14:23-24

The command to love God more than anything else isn't because God needs love.[188] On the contrary, He knows that the only way we can walk in obedience is to love Him greater than any other. The question is, "Do you love God enough to conquer yourself"? Love gives us the strength of character to triumph over our will.[189] We obey what we love the most, so it takes our love for God to conquer our love of self and desires. If you genuinely want to follow God, you can conquer yourself and keep His commandments.

> **Prayer:** Lord, grow my love until I can firmly declare that it is not my will but yours to be done. I commit to returning to your commandments because you said the person who loves you would do so. Please give me strength so I may abide in you. Father, I know you see every work of sacrifice and ask you to pour your favor and love on me abundantly. I give you control over my home, family, and life in the name of Jesus. Amen.

---

[188] Deuteronomy 6:5-7
[189] Psalms 73:26

Don't Be a Disappointment to God

John 15:9-10 Even as the Father has loved me,
I also have loved you. Remain in my love. If
you keep my commandments, you will remain
in my love, even as I have kept my Father's
commandments and remain in his love.

Have you ever felt that you let God down or haven't lived up to other's expectations? When we fall, we disappoint those we care about. That's what happens when we haven't lived in the love of God. When we have disobeyed, his commandments and conviction come upon us. We go through feelings of embarrassment, guilt, and shame because we think we have disappointed everyone and fear they may judge us cruelly. Falling doesn't mean you are a failure; when we don't get back up, we genuinely fail.[190]

Keeping the commandments will cause us to stay in Christ's love.[191] Through abiding in love, God transforms our hearts and minds. However, those of us who have fallen and disappointed God's heart can get back to abiding in God's love. We regain our proper standing with Him by asking forgiveness and seeking to obey Him.[192] Our forgiveness affords us the re-

---

[190] Proverbs 24:16
[191] John 14:21
[192] 1 John 1:9

ward of knowing that we are not disappointments to God or our brothers and sisters in Christ because we now abide in His love again.

If we haven't kept the commandments, we can return to and abide in Christ's love. Christ's love is not a judgmental love but a love of understanding. He walked this earth and experienced the same temptations we do so that He could relate to our trials.[193] He makes no excuses for our sins but waits with loving arms for us to repent and abide again in His love. Even if others judge you, what does it matter as long as you are now abiding by Christ's love? They may not see Christ's love in your life, but you do. You have received a host of second chances through His forgiveness and a chance to abide in His love.

Prayer: Lord, I hear you tapping on the door of my heart. I invite you in so that your love might abide within me. I will hold your word dear to my heart and obey your commandments to stay in your affection. Forgive every time that I have stepped away from you. I ask you to change my life, heart, and mind so that I might become righteous and in control. Shelter me in your love and grace and cause me to stand in triumph, in the name of Jesus, Amen.

---

[193] Hebrews 4:15-16

Dealing with Difficult Believers

---⚓---

Ephesians 4:1-3 I therefore, the prisoner in the Lord,
beg you to walk worthily of the calling with which you
were called, with all lowliness and humility, with
patience, bearing with one another in love, being eager
to keep the unity of the Spirit in the bond of peace.

On April 29th, 1992, riots broke out in Los Angeles. Anger at the acquittal of four officers in a videotaped beating of Rodney King sparked six days of assaults, looting, and vandalism. King's plea for peace two days later had little effect on the outcome, ending with 53 deaths, 2300 injuries, and a billion dollars in damage. However, the question King asked, "Can't we all just get along," was addressed to a more receptive crowd who understood the damage of mob mentality, where some believers sided against others.

We must learn to put up with difficult believers to walk worthy of your call. Sometimes, we wonder why some believers can be riotous and have senseless drama and spiteful criticisms. It seems that it would be so easy for us to avoid conflict. We all serve the same God, don't we?[194] Yet because of contentions, it takes a lot of humility, gentleness, and longsuffering to bear up with each other in love. Difficult people drain you of joy and strength,

---

[194] James 4:1-4

so you don't want to spend a lot of time on them, but you do want to invest a lot of peace into them; this will take work on our behalf.[195]

The primary thing is that we can't outwardly agree with difficult people to avoid conflict when we know they are wrong.[196] Unity doesn't happen naturally, even for the saved. It must be endeavored for and sought after. It must be preached, taught, and lived out before people. It takes longsuffering, which is patience under fire. We must use love to lift those who mess up and quickly resolve our differences.[197] Endeavor to walk worthy of your calling and be unified in the Spirit, keeping the bond of peace

> **Prayer:** Lord, we encounter disputes in our homes, places of employment, and places of worship. I ask you to make me a unifier in a divided world. Give me peace so I can patiently await your Spirit's reconciliation work while I strive for oneness. If I have offended someone, please forgive me and guide me to make amends. I ask for your help in living up to my call to grace, faith, and holiness in the name of Jesus Christ. Amen.

---

[195] Hebrews 12:14
[196] Proverbs 17:1
[197] Ephesians 4:32

It's God's Fault

---⟡---

Jeremiah 44:16-17 As for the word that you have spoken to us in Yahweh's name, we will not listen to you. But we will certainly perform every word that has gone out of our mouth, to burn incense to the queen of the sky and to pour out drink offerings to her, as we have done, we and our fathers, our kings and our princes, in the cities of Judah and in the streets of Jerusalem; for then we had plenty of food, and were well, and saw no evil.

It must have crushed the heart of Jeremiah to hear these words. These people differed from those who doubted that Jeremiah spoke from the Lord. No, these Jews fled to Egypt after Nebuchadnezzar had conquered the southern kingdom of Judah. They saw the things Jeremiah had prophesied come to pass, and they knew what he said came directly from the mouth of God.[198] They didn't care. Instead, they blamed God for their problems and listened to what people said instead of doing what God was saying.[199]

Maybe you wonder why they didn't realize that the sins they were committing were the cause of their problems. Well, it's easier to justify ourselves and serve our desires than to deal with our issues. Many professing

---

[198] Jeremiah 44:1-5
[199] Jeremiah 44:18-19

believers treat God as the problem instead of the solution.[200] While calling ourselves believers, many do what comes from our mouths. We don't heed God because the god of this world has blinded our minds.[201]

The difference between a faithful follower and the crowd comes down to who gets blamed for problems. People spend years blaming God for their choices instead of giving the Lord thanks for everything.[202] People blame God for not healing when it was sin that brought sickness and death to the world. Bad stewardship and choices lead to financial troubles, but when it happens, people figure God is not blessing them. The next time adverse events occur, check who you blame and who gets the thank you.

> **Prayer:** Lord, help me not to be a problem to myself. Renew my mind so I heed your voice instead of my choice. Please resolve every conflict, contrast, and contention that arose from following my own lead. Guide me by your Spirit into the principles of your word that will direct my path and show me the right choices for my life and family so we can walk in your blessing and favor, in Jesus' name. Amen.

---

[200] Proverbs 27:23

[201] 2 Corinthians 4:4

[202] 1 Thessalonians 5:18

Love on a New Level

---✦---

John 13:34-35 A new commandment I give to you, that you love one another. Just as I have loved you, you also love one another. By this everyone will know that you are my disciples if you have love for one another.

Christ was preparing for the cross. He had just eaten His last supper and washed the disciple's feet.[203] Judas, already having departed to betray Him, Jesus sits at the table and gives a new commandment. That commandment was to take their love up to a new level. In the old dispensation, Christ had said it was enough to love your neighbor in the same way you love yourself.[204] However, in this new time, Christ commands us to take it further and love our brethren as He has loved them.

The Greek word "Agape" describes and translates into our word for love. It has many variations; however, at its essence, it is a love of your own choice that does what is best for another. Agape love is a decision to love; it is love on a new level that denotes a willingness to sacrifice one's desires to help another. The Holy Spirit working in our hearts receives the God type of love.[205] This selfless love would be the mark of recognition of true discipleship.

---

[203] John 13:3-30
[204] Mark 12:30-31
[205] Romans 5:5

Where is the love? It's with Christ's faithful disciples. Before the disciples could be united in power, they had to join, together showing love. Love is the perfect bond of unity.[206] Agape tells us we are not alone and brings purpose to our lives. Love brings families who have drifted apart back together. It restores and redeems. Love compels us to change and live as the beloved of God. Let's show the world that we are His by loving one another. That's love on a new level.

> **Prayer:** Lord, help me to love on a new level and be a unifier of the church. I pray that everyone will know I am your disciple by the love I show others. Please give me your grace to be a healing force in my home, family, and community. I ask for your help in all things. May your light shine upon and through me. In the name of Jesus. Amen.

---

[206] Colossians 3:14

The Standing Spot

---✦---

Psalm 91:1 He who dwells in the secret place of the Most High will rest in the shadow of the Almighty.

Did you know there is only one place of promised protection? A place where we stand and angels take charge to guard, deliver and promote us.[207] Where is it, you may ask, and how do we get there? Well, it's a place of surrender, where you are standing in the secret place of God and covered under His almighty hand. If we look at all the protection in this Psalm, we find God's desire to deliver us from traps, sickness, and death.[208] While we pray, "Lord, do it for me," God says, "Position yourself so I can."

A position of protection is based on fear of God, faith in God, and favor with God. Godly fear is a level of honor and respect that causes us to want to do what pleases the Father. Faith is the fence that keeps us from straying into sin and places a hedge of protection around us.[209] Faith removes anxiety in our hearts and sets us up for deliverance. It keeps us steady in the storm and safe from outside influence.[210] When we have faith, we renew our strength and hope in the timing of God and His blessing.

---

[207] Psalm 91:11-12
[208] Psalm 91:3-8
[209] Psalm 34:7
[210] Proverbs 29:25

It is our loving devotion and faithfulness to God that gives us favor.[211] It is living with life empowerment to succeed, and favor plugs us into God's heart and presence where we cannot fail. The secret place is where the fire of our trials shines a light on the hidden things so no darkness remains around us. It is where we worship in spirit and truth while God deals with our issues. Many want God's promises and protection but struggle to stand in the godly fear, faith, and devotion that brings favor. If you are standing in the wrong space, move to the secret place and watch God do everything He has spoken.

Prayer: Abba Father, Help me stand in your secret place, trusting and believing in you. You are my strength and haven. I'll put my trust in your protective hedge rather than my fear of what I see. Wrap your loving grace around me and soothe my spirit during the storm. Protect me from sickness, disease, and the work of the enemy. I receive your authority to win every victory and ask you to cover my family and home with the same grace you give me by faith in Jesus Christ, Amen.

---

[211] Proverbs 3:3-4

The Fruit of the Tree of Life

---✦---

Proverbs 11:30 The fruit of the righteous is
a tree of life. He who is wise wins souls.

In the middle of the Garden of Eden, there were two trees.[212] The most recognized is the tree of the knowledge of good and evil, to which Adam and Eve partook, bringing sin and death into the world. The second less known tree was the tree of life; if one ate of it, they would live forever.[213] This tree is proverbially compared to the life of faithfulness that wins souls so others will live with God forever. Those who partake of the fruit of their labors will taste the tree and live forever.

A life filled with the goodness and love of God becomes more intentionally missionary. Charles Spurgeon said that soul-winning should be the primary pursuit of every true believer. The unrighteous only partake of the knowledge of good and evil. They often know what's right but decide to do what they want, and their fruit has only brought sin and death. We must live our lives righteously to persuade others to partake of the healing of the tree of life.[214]

Often, we try to push others into the kingdom of God because we see the problems they face without the Lord. However, if we don't enter into a life of righteousness ourselves, what good are we? We are won by

---

[212] Genesis 2:9

[213] Genesis 3:22

[214] Revelation 22:1-2

righteousness before we win souls. We can't expect others to change if the gospel does not transform us into soul winners.[215] If your life is not about the cross of Christ, then how can others partake of any fruit? Make sure you produce fruit of righteousness and win souls to the tree of life.

Prayer: Lord, I pray you to anoint me with the wisdom and power to win souls. Allow me to have joy in good times, peace in hard times, and trust in the face of adversity. I pray that my fruit will abide and that others will recognize your good hand. Make a difference in my life and enable me to spread the good news of Christ to others. I ask you to save family, friends, and foe alike. Thank you for your Holy Spirit's work in refreshing, renewing, and restoring me so I will bear the fruit of righteousness in Jesus' name. Amen.

---

[215] Revelation 2:7

Please Visit My Fran's

---

1 Peter 2:12 Having good behavior among the nations, so in that of which they speak against you as evildoers, they may see your good works and glorify God in the day of visitation.

F.R.A.N is an acronym for remembering those we should be reaching for the Lord (**F**riends, **R**elatives, **A**ssociates, and **N**eighbors). How we behave in front of our F.R.A.N makes all the difference. Godly conduct is the forerunner to Godly contact. The Lord sends a messenger to prepare His way before the day of visitation.[216] Regardless of what the devil may speak to our F.R.A.N., our actions will always speak louder than his words. If we behave in a manner that pleases God, especially in times of adversity, then our Fran's will glorify the Lord on the day of their visitation.

What is this day of visitation? It is the day when instruction, trials, or discontentment brings the unbeliever to the place where their heart is open to God. The believer is to pray that God gives them the understanding needed to tell the gospel,[217] then pray that the Spirit does work to open the unbeliever's heart to receive the gospel at the time of visitation. [218] If we conduct ourselves as the light, we will become conduits for God's light

---

[216] Mark 1:2-3
[217] Luke 24:44-47
[218] Acts 16:14

before our F.R.A.N.'s. Through our light, the light of God will shine in their hearts bringing all the glory to our God.

Leonard Ravenhill said, "Any method of evangelism will work if God is in it." Evangelism is an overflow of our worship and is not the job of a gifted few but the responsibility of all believers. Don't be concerned about what people say against you because they treated all the forerunners of old this way. It's how you behave that makes the difference.[219] All their evil speaking and acts against you will turn to the glory of God on the day of visitation. Pray that all your F.R.A.N.'s will have their day of visitation and glorify God by your honorable conduct.

Prayer: Father, I ask you to open my mind with new, straightforward ways to share the gospel. I pray for the heart of all my FRANs to open to heed and receive your word. Call forth a mighty force of the faithful to pray and share your message of hope so our nation experiences a revival of righteousness. As our light shines, teach the new converts love, responsibility, and faith in the name of Jesus Christ our Lord, Amen.

---

[219] Philippians 1:27-28

Breaking the Siege

Lamentations 3:22-23 It is because of Yahweh's loving kindnesses that we are not consumed, because his mercies don't fail. They are new every morning. Great is your faithfulness.

Sometimes it amazes us how situations go from bad to worse as if problems were to come multiplied in pairs. We often find ourselves dealing with multiple issues at one time. It is called siege warfare. We are fighting on the home front for our families, the work front for our livelihood, the school front for our children, and the church front to see people set free.[220] The enemy compounds problems on all sides and tries to lay siege to our lives, but the through the Lord's mercies, we are not consumed. His compassions fail not. They are new every morning; great is His faithfulness.

A siege aim is to conquer by consuming you. The enemy waits and attacks to lock us in and deprive us until we become too weak to fight. Yet it is darkest just before dawn. We should gain strength because you become a fighter when you're constantly under siege. God's mercies will rescue you in your greatest need like an army coming over the hilltops at dawn's first light.[221] His compassion will not fail to be by our side amid our

---

[220] Nehemiah 4:14
[221] Isaiah 59:19

troubles. Problems may surround you, but God's faithfulness to provide what you need is great.[222]

The enemy sees how close you are to receiving favor and tries to attack you from all sides. It's time to break through the gates with a counterattack of our own.[223] The remnant remains with you to fight with God's new mercies and compassion, tearing down the devil's fortifications and battle lines. He will find himself caught between the faith and prayer of the saints and the new mercies of God.[224] The siege he sets will be the trap that makes him fall. Great is the faithfulness of our God.

Prayer: Father, I ask you for assistance when I feel like I can't even catch my breath before a new problem occurs. I know you will provide if I only keep your promise and try to do what you say. I am not alone when because you are here with me. A breakthrough is imminent, and your new mercies will include me. I thank you for bringing me through. Great is your faithfulness in the name of Jesus, Amen.

---

[222] Philippians 4:19
[223] Micah 2:13
[224] Revelation 8:3-4

Not A Place For Us

---✦---

Revelations 20:14-15 Death and Hades were thrown into the lake of fire. This is the second death, the lake of fire. If anyone was not found written in the book of life, he was cast into the lake of fire.

Hell is real; its purpose was to torment disembodied spirit entities rather than torment men.[225] Scripture describes three places commonly referred to as hell. The first place consists of Abraham's Bosom/ paradise, where the righteous dwelt, and Hades, the abode of the wicked in torment.[226] The second place we call hell is the Abyss or bottomless pit where some of the most powerful demons remain chained.[227] Lastly is the lake of fire, the ultimate destiny of the men in Hades and the spirits who dwell in the Abyss.

In the first death, the body still exists, but there is no longer any life in it. Likewise, in the second death, the spirit exists without the renewed life that comes from God and without purpose. Hell isn't for us, but many are headed there, not by God's choice but because of our own choices.[228] We must be born again and have our names written in the book of life. After their physical death, those who refused the new birth will continue in the

---

[225] Matthew 25:41

[226] Luke 16:22-26

[227] 2 Peter 2:4

[228] 2 Peter 3:9

spiritual death they were born into. This is the second death to have your place in the lake of fire.

Is your name written in the book of life? The second death is not a place for us. Tertullian said, "After the present age is over, God will judge his worshipers for a reward of eternal life and the godless for a fire equally perpetual and unending." We know salvation is not something we achieve but what we receive by the grace of God. Let's take that grace and reach out to pull others from the fires of hell. But let's make sure we are escaping the fires first.[229] Hell is not for us.

Prayer: Lord, please grant me a long and satisfying life. Also, thank you for including my name in the book of life. I profess my faith in the gospel of Your Son and reaffirm my commitment to obey Your Word. Hell has no hold on me, neither living in hell on earth nor dying and going there. So now I ask you to work overtime to save my loved ones and those struggling in bondage, in the precious name of Jesus Christ, Amen.

---

[229] 1 Timothy 4:16

Made By Christ

---※---

Matthew 4:18-19 Walking by the sea of Galilee, he saw two brothers: Simon, who is called Peter, and Andrew, his brother, casting a net into the sea; for they were fishermen. He said to them, "Come after me, and I will make you fishers for men.

Go after Christ, and He will make you into something new. Your destiny is determined by what you pursue, for good or bad. Everyone is pursuing something, but not everyone is pursuing the right things. Hope and ambition direct our minds, but they remain a dream unless we chase after them. If you follow your desires, they will create what you become.[230] As long as Peter and Andrew chased after fish, they would only be fishermen. But if they followed Christ, He would make them much more.

We will either resist God's truth or become made new by it. All that is required is to let go of our nets and follow Christ. This they did, realizing that if God were going to do His work, they would have to release what was holding them back.[231] Some want to follow Christ from afar. Still clinging to their nets, they drag along the life they made for themselves. We call them secret saints because no one knew that they were believers.

---

[230] Psalm 81:10-16
[231] Philippians 3:13-16

Some are close enough for God to heed certain things but too distant to walk openly with God.[232]

What about you? Does Christ make you, or are you making yourself? We can be a useful vessel or stubborn clay. It doesn't matter what Christ will make you as long as Christ does the making.[233] He knows your call; if you answer, He will make you something incredible. Sandwiched somewhere between your purpose and your destiny is your response to follow.[234] How available are you to make yourself to Christ? The closer we connect to Him, the more consistent the change He will make in us. Stand close and be made By God.

> **Prayer:** Lord, sometimes I am unsure what to do. I ask you to mold and shape me till your thoughts are what I think. Please guide me in dark times, strengthen me in hard times, and use all things to conform me to your image. I submit to your plan for my life and ask you to do great things. Help me also be a fisher of men so my loved ones will come into your saving grace in Jesus' precious name. Amen.

---

[232] John 19:38-39
[233] Ephesians 2:10
[234] John 8:12

Don't Let Your Fall Become Your Failure

---◆---

John 21:7 That disciple therefore whom Jesus loved said to Peter, "It's the Lord!" So when Simon Peter heard that it was the Lord, he wrapped his coat around himself (for he was naked), and threw himself into the sea.

After denying Christ three times, Peter eventually returned to his old life.[235] When faith fails, we often fall back into our old habits. For Peter, it was back to fishing. For you and me, it would be something different. Christ had changed Peter's life. He was no longer to be a fisherman but a fisher of men, but here he was, standing half naked and exposed on a boat fishing.[236] Falling short doesn't mean you will become a failure. Christ can handle any personal breakdown we have, but what He has a problem with is when we fail to follow.

Most believers live with the sense of how easy it is to fall back into old habits. That's because our heart returns to the yokes of our old ways.[237] When Peter entered that boat, he was struggling internally with how he abandoned Christ. His heart stopped following, and his frustrations had brought him back to the beginning. He was standing on a fishing boat, just

---

[235] Matthew 26:69-75
[236] Matthew 4:18-20
[237] Galatians 5:1

as he was when he met Jesus. In the same place and way, Christ appeared to him so that he may follow Him again.[238]

A fall is not always a failure; it is a misstep in your following. Restoration is your ability to follow after a fall.[239] When Peter knew God was calling him again, he clothed himself again and dove headway into the waters. His following restored him before he hit the shore. If we have fallen, we must clothe ourselves with righteousness again and head straight for Christ. He's waiting to call us out of our fall and back into our follow. Following Christ will never make you fail.

> **Prayer:** Father, I appreciate you always picking up the pieces after me when I've messed up everything. Please forgive me for every time I moved ahead of your timing and needed you to bail me out. I will not return to my old habits or viewpoints because your grace is sufficient. Thank you for making me something new and transforming my life, hope, and future in the name of Jesus Christ. Amen.

---

[238] John 21:15-19
[239] Proverbs 24:16

Oil Laid Upon Me

---⁂---

Leviticus 14:18 The rest of the oil that is in the priest's hand he shall put on the head of him who is to be cleansed, and the priest shall make atonement for him before Yahweh.

Sin is a contagion of our fleshly nature, causing insensitivity to God and leading to our death.[240] Leprosy is used as a typology of sin because it does in the natural what sin does in the spiritual. Cleansing the leper required that they come to the door of the Tabernacle, to the altar of sacrifice. The oil on the head was part of the wave offering, and it declared that they were now clean and could enter.[241] Likewise, the oil in the hands of the elders brings healing and restoration and consecrates those in need.[242]

The title Christ means the anointed one. Each time the priest anointed the leper, he rehearsed the future work of the cross where Christ would cleanse the sinner by His sacrifice.[243] Just as the leper, we have stood at the doorway of the cross receiving from Jesus the oil laid upon us, which is Christ Himself. Just as significant events were commemorated by plays dedicated to their reenactment, laying hands with oil commemorates Christ's person and work.

---

[240] James 1:15
[241] Leviticus 14:12
[242] James 5:14-15
[243] 1 John 1:7

The spiritual significance of placing oil upon the head with prayer declared the finished work of Christ. The Old Testament Priest rehearsed it. Jesus performed it, and we commemorate what He performed. Rehearsing the work Jesus would perform empowered the priest to proclaim cleanness. The Old Testament priest rehearsed His work. The New Covenant believer repeats the works of Christ, calling on His name to work wonders.[244] The oil represents the completed work of Chris, which He has laid upon us. We receive when we pray and believe because He is the oil on us.

Prayer: Father, thank you for connecting me to the healing power of the cross. I ask that your anointing break every chain and destroy every yoke from off my life. Every act of intercession leads me back to what you have provided at the cross. I call your healing, blessing, restoration, and freedom into my life. Continue your work in my life and draw me near you, in Jesus Christ's name, Amen.

---

[244] John 16:23-24

Grace Givers and Forgetters

---❦---

Ecclesiastes 7:21-22 Also don't take heed to all words that are spoken, lest you hear your servant curse you; or often your own heart knows that you yourself have likewise cursed others.

We are not to wear our feelings on our shoulders or allow everything people say to get into our hearts.[245] Fake friends are secret haters; they start speaking about you when you stop speaking to them. The truth is we are all perfectly imperfect. All of us have gossiped before, and we have been the offenders speaking out of turn with others when we shouldn't have. Just as we have done, it has happened to us. But God gives us grace.[246]

Do not forget the grace of God.[247] Where there is more grace, there is less judgment. Everyone we meet is fighting some kind of battle. Don't expect from others more than you have given because we all need God's grace. They may have messed up, but we have done so, too. If you want the scales of grace to tip in your favor, you must refuse to take things to heart and forgive. What people say about you is a reflection of them, not of you. When you forgive, you pursue peace; unforgiveness will cause you to fall short of God's grace.[248]

---

[245] Proverbs 4:23
[246] Titus 2:11-12
[247] Ephesians 4:7
[248] Hebrews 12:15

Grace gives us the capacity to accommodate, tolerate, and forgive people. When we remember what God has done for us, it helps us extend grace to others. We expect others to rise to our standard, and when they have done something unbecoming, we take it to heart and hold it against them. We become grace forgetters, not grace givers. Instead of remembering and extending the grace we received, we brush them aside.[249] When we stand before God, we won't regret loving, forgiving, or healing too much. But we may regret not giving the grace we have been given.

Prayer: God of abundance and grace, I come to you for mercy. Please help me express my gratitude by remembering the times I slipped up, and you forgave me. When others come against me, I ask you to fight the battle to vindicate me. I reject every accusation made by the adversary and accept your sacrificial grace. Help me provide the same grace to others so that resentment doesn't take root in my heart. I love you, Lord, and ask that you keep my heart and mind stayed on you. In Jesus' name. Amen.

[249] Matthew 5:44-48

Blame Shift

---⁑---

Lamentations 3:39-40 Why should a living man complain, a man for the punishment of his sins? Let us search and try our ways, and turn again to Yahweh.

It is rare for people to think they may deserve what they are going through. Blaming others for challenges, problems, and unhappiness is easier than dealing with the reality that we are responsible for most of our issues and joy.[250] Complaints are the verbalization of issues that we don't hold ourselves accountable for. Complaints arise when we look outward but have not turned inward to see our part in making the situation what it is.[251] Unless we search ourselves, we will end up shifting the blame on others for our misfortunes.

Spending today complaining about yesterday will not make tomorrow better. Sometimes, it's you; other times, it's what you let others do. We can quickly shift the blame and complain if we don't see ourselves.[252] Complaining is a strategy to manipulate others and strengthen our ego. The answer to complaining is to search out and examine our ways.[253] We must look at what we do and realize the effects of our actions. The moment

---

[250] Job 4:8
[251] Micah 7:9
[252] James 1:23-24
[253] 2 Corinthians 13:5

we take responsibility for our part, we stop complaining and start turning to God.

Complaints find fault; wisdom finds solutions. Many problems arise because instead of turning back to God, we have turned our backs on God.[254] We haven't listened to or sought Him, and we shift the blame when things happen. Instead of spending time complaining, we should do something about it. The complainer rarely takes responsibility, and a responsible person rarely complains. Next time you feel the urge to complain, examine your ways and turn it over to the Lord.

> **Prayer:** Lord, I say I won't complain, but sometimes I find myself doing just that. Today, I turn those things over to you. I take charge of my life to behave responsibly and see my part, and I ask that you fix those things I cannot. I seek healing, not blame, gratefulness, not a complaint. I rid my life of every root of bitterness and ask you to heal the broken parts in Jesus' name. Amen.

---

[254] Proverbs 14:14-15

Contempt in the Divine Court

Nahum 1:14 Yahweh has commanded concerning you: "No more descendants will bear your name. Out of the house of your gods, I will cut off the engraved image and the molten image. I will make your grave, for you are vile."

Finally, the Lord got to the point where He said, "Enough is enough," He will no longer put up with the people's disobedience. He had given the Ninevites a chance to repent back in the days of Jonah.[255] But now, a hundred years later, he sends the prophet Nahum, and they are so stubborn they won't repent no matter what the Lord does.[256] After giving grace, the Lord now holds the Ninevites in contempt as a righteous judge, and their punishment would come swiftly.

Contemptible means able to be held in disdain or scorn. Disobedience puts the Lord in a place where He holds us in contempt for our actions.[257] Unrighteous actions vex the righteous Spirit of God by fighting against His grace.[258] Max Lucado says, "Grace calls us to change and gives us the strength to pull it off." The idols of the people blocked God's mercy by

---

[255] Jonah 3:5-10

[256] Nahum 1:1-9

[257] Psalm 2:4-5

[258] Jonah 2:8

offending His holiness. The people became just like the idols they worshiped, vile and contemptible in the sight of God.

Backsliding begins in the heart by neglecting prayer and bible reading. The distance grows until we have nothing but filthy rags.[259] Like the Ninevites, we also put many things before God. They become our idols, our excuses not to serve God. Our actions often reflect how little we love God and how much we love ourselves. God comes at best, second, maybe even third in our lives.[260] How long do we think the Lord will put up this? Do you want to be vile or victorious? Put down every excuse and everything we place ahead of God, and you will never be in contempt.

> **Prayer:** God the Father, I'm here today to renew my lifelong commitment to you. I appreciate your patience and pray that you keep working in my life. Help me always put you first so I won't disappoint you. I pray for a revival of faithfulness in all those around me. Let us live to please your heart and keep the faith in the name of Jesus. Amen

---

[259] Isaiah 64;6
[260] Deuteronomy 10:12

Let God Have His Way

---⚓---

James 4:1 Where do wars and fightings among you come from? Don't they come from your pleasures that war in your members?

The question was rhetorical: "Where do fights come from." The answer is, "It comes from our selfish pride and desires." One of the most unattractive things about the church is strife and backbiting. The place of the most incredible love is, at times, unloving and lacking in understanding of the needs of others.[261] We preserve peace by keeping our relationships pure. Nothing can change God's love; our love needs to be changed and shaped according to His.

The source of the problem stems from the fact that we haven't won the war within us.[262] We desire pleasures that war in our thoughts, hearts, and will. We quarrel because believers desire to shape the church in their image and style rather than let God shape our love and devotion. If unchecked, the war within us will spill out of us as conflicts within the body of Christ. The solution is for us to gain greater love. Our love should be profound because it covers a multitude of sins.[263]

If we don't have victory over ourselves, we will never have victory with the family of God. The desire to have our way in our hearts, minds, and

---

[261] John 13:34-35
[262] Romans 7:14-20
[263] 1 Peter 4:8

will brings conflict in Christ's otherwise holy and righteous body.[264] We fight our most significant victories in the quiet chambers of our souls. It's a battle between who we are and how we want to be. A cease-fire is declared in the church when our desire for pleasure is defeated.[265] Winning battles in your mind will make you win battles in life. But it starts with getting out of our way and letting God have His way.

> **Prayer:** Lord, make it possible for me to foster love and keep peace. I commit to winning the internal war because He who is in me is greater than everything in this world. Give me the courage to surrender my inner self to your love and grace. I ask for a life that has undergone a transformation that displays your character and offers comfort and healing to your people. I silence the voice of every evil plan and accept your triumph in the name of Jesus Christ. Amen.

---

[264] Galatians 5:17-18
[265] Romans 12:18

Don't Slip

---✦---

Hebrews 2:1 Therefore we ought to pay greater attention to the things that were heard, lest perhaps we drift away.

A Hebrew wrote the Book of Hebrews to Hebrews to tell them to stop acting like Hebrews. Persecution had begun, and many Hebrew converts returned to observing Jewish practices to escape. Instead of practicing their new faith in Christ, they fell out of fellowship.[266] You got it. Hebrews is written to church dropouts, telling them that God doesn't want them out of fellowship with Christ and other believers. Letting them know that a relationship with Christ and His body is better than religious practice they may fall into.

Often, we hope for a victorious life in Christ but neglect to do the things that gave us victory in the first place. At the beginning of our walk with Christ, we exercised our faith, prayed, read scripture, and wanted to win the world for Christ just from our love for Him. Our fellowship and service to the Lord mattered regardless of what we knew or didn't know. However, over time, many of us have drifted away. We have neglected our salvation by not giving heed to the truth.[267]

Perhaps the author could have started the letter, "Dear future church Dropout, God says stay." Remember, a neglected spark makes a great fire.

---

[266] Hebrews 6:4-6
[267] Hebrews 2:3

Neglect of scripture starts as an infection and ends in a disease of sin.[268] Neglecting prayer drains us of protection and provision.[269] Neglecting to serve God leads to a lack of joy and zeal for the Lord.[270] Neglect robs you of victory. God wants us in a church fellowship, but more so, he wants us in fellowship with Him. It's time to pay attention to what we have drifted away from so you don't fall. Because stop, drop, and roll doesn't work in hell.

Prayer: Lord, I ask that you breathe on the spark within me. Help me to hide your word in my heart so I will live accordingly. I pray that your Spirit will lead me in my next steps as I stand up from my prayers. I will do my part and ask for your grace to do the things I cannot. Help me to pay attention to the warnings and lessons I have learned so that I never stray from the love and fellowship of your church. I ask that you keep my family and loved ones from straying too far in the matchless name of Jesus. Amen.

---

[268] Psalm 119:9

[269] James 4:2

[270] Matthew 25:21

Sheep Invasion

Matthew 10:16 Behold, I send you out as sheep among wolves. Therefore be wise as serpents and harmless as doves.

We live in a world that views shrewd actions as a plus. It appears that only in the community of faith is meekness a benefit. Understanding our disadvantages, Christ instructs us to find the balance we need so that misuse or abuse doesn't overwhelm us. Many think of being sheep amid wolves as a flock surrounded by hungry predators. However, Christ's flock isn't gathered but sent out by the shepherd as an invading force where the wolves dwell, taking what they need to grow and sustain themselves.[271]

Amid wolves, we are to be wise as serpents. When serpents invade new territory, they don't make their presence known but check everything out first. They find Safe spots to hide from predators and search out watering places and strategic locations. The serpent sees past the camouflage of deceit. We must discern how the wolves work while depending on our shepherd's voice to guide and protect us through every situation we face.[272] Being wise as a serpent means knowing how the enemy operates; being gentle as a dove means you choose not to operate that way.

---

[271] Matthew 16:17-19
[272] 1 Peter 5:8

People and situations tempt us to act just like the wolves when attacked. We should rise above every situation instead of getting into a dogfight. Doves are harmless but alert because they soar above to get the bigger picture.[273] It doesn't just see the wolf; it sees the wolf pack gathering around. Likewise, we should not be unwise but discern beyond the physical attack and see the spirits working behind the scenes.[274] We can afford to be as kind and empathetic as a dove when we use wisdom and discernment to block enemy schemes. Soar above, but stay alert to defend.

Prayer: Lord, you have commanded us to have a shrewd understanding but be gentle in character. Please help me to distinguish between the two. I need guidance from above to recognize the spiritual assault hiding behind the outward manifestation because I'm not going to fight the person but the spirit driving them. I'll battle smart to keep my heart free of resentment, suffering, and regret. In the name of Jesus, build a wall of protection around me so I can walk in peace beyond understanding, in the name of Jesus. Amen.

---

[273] Colossians 3:1-2
[274] Luke 22:31-32

Rewritten and Redeemed

---⟡---

Isaiah 44:22 I have blotted out, as a thick cloud,
your transgressions, and, as a cloud, your sins.
Return to me, for I have redeemed you.

What a great picture of how God rewrote our story by taking our sins away. He blots out every sin recorded against us. They are not only covered, but they are also totally obliterated. Yet they returned unto the one who destroyed our sin, Jesus Christ. He had to pay for what He erased.[275] He covered our sins with a heavy cloud where they were unseen, and they returned to Him as a mist, resting on Him. He not only took our sin, but He also took our shame. He did this to bring us back unto Himself as our redeemer and a precious people in His sight.

It's a rewrite; the whole story of your sin has been removed and replaced. Removed by the blood of Jesus and replaced by the righteousness of Christ. We are redeemed and given another chance.[276] Through redemption, God turns sinners into saints. God even blots out the mental stain of our guilt. Satan says look at your sins; God says look at my Son. Our past can no longer dictate our future, and our failures no longer affect our success. Through Christ, we are with God, and there is nothing we can't achieve.[277]

---

[275] Colossians 2:13-15

[276] 1 Peter 2:24

[277] Philippians 4:13

Redemption has rewritten our whole life. Your current situation is part of the redemption story that Christ is writing. Redemption removes the lousy part; only what is good remains. Formerly, we were castaways; now, we are near.[278] We can walk with God and be His unique treasure. Our sins have turned into His righteousness, and our faith replaces our faults. When someone brings up your past, tell them that Jesus has rewritten it, blotting out every transgression and redeeming you from them all.

Prayer: Thank you for your Son, Jesus Christ, for providing redemption through the cross and renewal by the resurrection. I acknowledge my sins and thank you for not having to live under its power. By your stripes, I am healed, delivered, and set free. Because I walk in obedience, you have erased the guilt and shame of my past. Please help me to make the best decisions with my faith, finances, and future. You have provided everything I need to be victorious. So, cause me to walk in your favor. In the name of Jesus Christ. Amen.

---

[278] Ephesians 2:11-15

Get Fed

Jeremiah 23:4 I will set up shepherds over them, who will feed them. They will no longer be afraid or dismayed, neither will any be lacking," says Yahweh.

Jeremiah lived in a time when leaders listened more to their own hearts than to the voice of God. They shepherded their own lives and led many astray.[279] We enter dangerous territory when we follow our desires. Through the captivity, God would wipe clean the leadership of Israel and could now start afresh with new shepherds set in place by Him. The closer they were to these shepherds, the safer the flock would be from the wolves. They would feed Israel and bring them back into a place of health, not under compulsion but as a joy to the Lord.[280]

God is always concerned about the health of His people, and therefore, He sets shepherds over them to feed them.[281] A shepherd who serves God will always lead the people closer to the Lord. The shepherd's job is to remove fear, confusion, and lack from the people by teaching them to obey God. Through exhortation, example, and encouragement, the people feed upon the word of God, and as they apply it in their daily lives, they

---

[279] Jeremiah 23:1-3

[280] 1 Peter 5:2-4

[281] Jeremiah 3:15-18

overcome, becoming bold in the faith, sound in reasoning, and built up in every way.[282]

Notice how the scripture connects our provision to staying fed by the shepherds God sends. Bodily exercise does profit some, but your spiritual health is His number one concern.[283] Our spiritual health is proportional to our love of God. Whatever is healthy will grow, and as we grow in the love of God, we become more obedient to the things He has for us. As God feeds us through shepherds and pours His love into us through the Holy Spirit, we will become healthy again, not listening to our hearts or voice but to the voice of God. Get fed, get healthy, and watch God provide.

Prayer: Lord, as one of your flock, you desire to use pastors and mentors to feed me your word and strengthen my soul. I know I am responsible for my spiritual health, but thank you for your spiritual help through your people and the Holy Spirit. I do not stand alone, but within the body of faith, you will heal and grow me. I will lack nothing by staying near your body and obeying your leading. Provide for my home, family, and life in the name of Jesus, Amen.

[282] 2 Peter 4:2
[283] 1 Timothy 4:8-10

Set Your Mind For The Kingdom

1 Peter 3:8-9 Finally, all of you be like-minded, compassionate, loving as brothers, tenderhearted, courteous, not rendering evil for evil, or insult for insult; but instead blessing, knowing that you were called to this, that you may inherit a blessing.

Whenever you see the word "Finally" in scripture, it describes the last action in a list of things to do. It informs us of our responsibility to victoriously walk out our faith. Peter informs his writers to prepare themselves for anything that may come by living holy.[284] Next, he says to love others deeply,[285] to grow in salvation,[286] and to practice submission because of Christ and according to His example.[287] Lastly, he sums it up, letting us know that we can still choose to love and honor others regardless of what we have gone through. Our love should affect how we think, feel, and treat others. It is a mindset of humility to promote the kingdom of God.

Charles Spurgeon said of the committed believer, "God is more ready to forgive than we are to offend." The believer who promotes the kingdom of God has to have a mindset of unity, love, and service. To conquer the world for Christ, we must first conquer ourselves and do what is contrary

---

[284] 1 Peter 1:13-16
[285] 1 Peter 1:22
[286] 1 Peter 2:1-2
[287] 1 Peter 3:13-21

to our carnal nature to embrace a spiritual life.[288] We must go beyond our issues and get involved in the issues of God, which is what it takes to win the world for Christ. God calls us to this, which will cause us to inherit a blessing.

Peter wrote that believers live in such a way that they promote God's kingdom. We begin by living in unity with others in the body of Christ, genuinely loving and treating them with kindness. The final caveat is, what do you do when someone wrongs you?[289] Love and kindness adjust our attitudes and behavior, but are we ready to make the Christ choice and pray? If you want to inherit your blessing, you must live out your calling. Live right and stay blessed on purpose.

Prayer: Lord, you called me to live right and inherit a blessing. Help me in taking the steps necessary to attract favor. I approach you humbly, seeking your strength to overcome my flesh and advance the kingdom. I ask you to do great things which I have never seen. I ask you to increase my well-being, wealth, and joy in Jesus' majestic name, Amen.

---

[288] 1 Corinthians 9:25-27
[289] Matthew 5:44

Wait on the Rock

---✦---

Exodus 17:7 He called the name of the place Massah, and Meribah, because the children of Israel quarreled, and because they tested Yahweh, saying, "Is Yahweh among us, or not?"

Massah and Meribah mean temptation and strife, and it was the location where God brought forth water from the rock. The children of Israel turned a place of favor and provision into a place of tempting and strife by asking, "Is the Lord with us or not." They were thirsty, so the Lord led them to the rock containing flowing waters. But they couldn't wait to see what God was doing and complained.[290] Even after Moses smote the rock so the waters pour forth, strife remained in the people's hearts.

How often do we complain because we can't see what God is doing? With joy, we stepped out on faith, seeing God open doors, but what happens when we get to the other side? Will our inability to see what the Lord is doing cause us to doubt and complain?[291] We can believe in what we don't see because the one we love works in the unseen. We should know that the water is in the rock.[292] The Lord has led you to a place where He will provide for your every need. We have to pray for the Lord to reveal our rock.

---

[290] Exodus 17:1-6

[291] Ecclesiastes 8:17

[292] 2 Corinthians 5:7

Like Israel, how quickly we can turn our contentions into a curse. We are in a place of provision, yet we strive against God and His people because we lack vision.[293] That led Israel into 40 years in the wilderness, where God proved that He intended to care for their needs. God doesn't always do what we want but does what is right. Why tempt the Lord by questioning "if He is with you" and end up for years stuck like they were so that He can prove to you that He is a provider. You may not see where your provision comes from, but God does. If you can't see it, wait for God to provide it.

> **Prayer:** Lord, help me to overcome my perplexity and frustration while I wait for you to act. You said peace would be mine when I keep my thoughts on you, so please aid me in doing that. I will trust you in the dark times and follow you in the light. Please guide me to the rock and pour forth what I need. I ask that you remove temptation and conflict and replace them with your favor and provision in the name of Jesus Christ. Amen.

---

[293] Proverbs 29:18

A Good Answer

---✦---

2 Chronicles 10:8-9 But he abandoned the counsel of the old men which they had given him, and took counsel with the young men who had grown up with him, who stood before him

The people had approached the new king with an offer that they would serve him if he lightened the heavy load of their duties. Seasoned counselors pleaded with Rehoboam to show compassion, saying the citizens would be faithful to him forever.[294] Yet Rehoboam's young friends told him to show strength, threaten them with force, and make them serve. Rehoboam did just that and paid the price by losing over 80% of the kingdom.[295] He ignored his head to satisfy his heart and made a wrong decision.

We often overlook the counsel of previous generations, who gained wisdom through forethought and experience.[296] These men had advised his father, Solomon, and helped him rule the kingdom. Rehoboam rejected their advice not because it was unwise but because his heart aligned with the new young counselors. A relationship is not the best measure when seeking advice; character is.[297] Individuals with an honorable character

---

[294] 2 Chronicles 10:3-7
[295] 2 Chronicles 10:10-17
[296] Proverbs 1:8-9
[297] Psalm 101:6

tend to possess good decision-making skills. However, good advice is hard to accept when there is a problem with the heart.

It's not only greed and selfishness that causes problems of the heart, but sometimes having love and compassion that are not in balance with the relationship's behavior and nature. An unbalanced life in an ordinarily good-hearted person is why we sometimes see people with good advice living a bad example.[298] Good advice promotes godly character and purpose. When seeking counsel for any decision in your life, you need to seek the Lord first, then seek counsel from those who will seek the Lord on your behalf. You will save yourself a world of headaches.

Prayer: Lord, assist me in walking in counsel consistent with your word. Give me people who will push me to change when I feel a certain way. When you elevate me, allow me to use good judgment and avoid using familiarity as a barrier to my development. I am grateful for knowledgeable leaders with the experience and expertise I need to advance and win favor in the name of Jesus. Amen.

---

[298] 2 Peter 3:17

Tune Into God

---✦---

1 Kings 3:2-3 However, the people sacrificed in the high places, because there was not yet a house built for Yahweh's name. Solomon loved Yahweh, walking in the statutes of David his father, except that he sacrificed and burned incense in the high places.

Everyone was doing it, people and kings alike. Yet it wasn't idolatry as some may think. These people went to the high places because David's planned temple construction was not completed.[299] The ark of the covenant was in a tent in Jerusalem; however, the tent of meeting with the bronze altar remained in Gibeon. In the eyes of many, this was the first time the holy place and the holy of holies were in separate locations.[300] The people began to worship where it was convenient for them. Like the heathens, they sacrificed in the high places. This was a warning against them, and they chose the high place over His place.

The Lord gave them many places He consecrated for worship, but regardless, many people who loved the Lord worshipped in the high places. We create a high place when worshipping at the altar of convenience instead of where the Lord has placed His name.[301] We choose the high place over His place. To someone peaking through a window, a believer home

---

[299] 2 Samuel 7:1-13

[300] 2 Samuel 1:2-6

[301] Deuteronomy 12:13-14

watching church on television looks like the unbeliever cheering for their game. We can be in the same place doing the same thing, just tuned to a different channel.

D.L. Moody said, "Church attendance is as vital to a disciple as a transfusion of rich, healthy blood is to a sick man." The right station in the wrong place, messes up the reception. The church is a place God has chosen for discipleship and the molding of believers.[302] Treating worship gatherings as if we were sick and shut-in causes us to lose our vigor and zeal, even if our love remains. It's time to get out of the high place and into God's place. Let's tune into God, where you can get the best reception. Tell a friend to get off the couch and worship where God has chosen to place His name.

> **Prayer:** Lord, form me and put me where you have written your name. Instead of choosing what is convenient, I will do what is right. Help me to serve as an example for those around me to return to where you have inscribed your name. I ask for your grace and peace to be with me. Protect and deliver my loved ones, friends, and colleagues, drawing them nearer to your love, in the name of Jesus, Amen.

---

[302] Isaiah 64:8

A Heart for His People

--- ☙ ---

Zechariah 8:17 And let none of you devise evil in your hearts against his neighbor, and love no false oath; for all these are things that I hate," says Yahweh.

Two aspects are always present in serving God: our actions and hearts.[303] It's easy to discuss people's wicked hearts and lies, but what about the wickedness of not hoping others will have the same transformation you have had? Sometimes, familiarity with people's past failures and flaws causes us to view their present situation with a heart that falls short of God's heart. Most limit their definition of devising evil to those who plot against them. However, our inability to see and accept growth in others and expect their failure during times of struggle also falls in the category of imagining evil in our hearts.[304]

There are many evils in the heart of man. Greed, lust, pride, and selfishness are only a few. However, doubt is the only evil that dismisses growth and God's work in others' lives. When we swear in our hearts that someone will never change, we have made a false oath.[305] Our doubts about others force us to look at their promise through the lens of their past. These are false oaths made in our hearts because they stem from viewing the pressure of life and not the change in their conscience or character.

---

[303] Isaiah 29:13

[304] Acts 9:26-27

[305] 2 Corinthians 4:16-18

The Lord hates actions feigning love from a heart with evil imagination. He hates when His people love false oaths instead of holding on to the truth. This includes wanting good for yourself and others but doubting it will ever happen.[306] If we are to do well in this world, it must start within our hearts. The same heart believes God should love the truth and believe in a turnaround. We can't imagine evil about someone and hope for the good for someone simultaneously. Don't let your heart cancel out your good works. Have hope in their growth and keep the heart of God.

Prayer: Since you are a protector, Father, I implore you to prevent evil thoughts from entering my mind. You can cleanse my thinking by bringing to mind the truth of your word. Change my heart and mind for the sake of the kingdom. I will extend the grace you have given me by praying for and encouraging change in others. Let your favor rest with me, in the name of Jesus, Amen.

---

[306] James 1:5-7

Man's Curse/God's Blessing

Micah 6:5 My people, remember now what Balak king of Moab devised, and what Balaam the son of Beor answered him from Shittim to Gilgal, that you may know the righteous acts of Yahweh."

Balak and Balaam, what a combination these two made. Balak, with his armies, was poised to attack. Yet, he would need more than an army to defeat God's people. He would need them to be cursed.[307] Wherever they went, the prophet Balaam would stand on the mountains and try to curse the unsuspecting Israelites. However, God turned every attack into an opportunity to bless His people. What He has blessed, no one can curse.[308]

Remember what Balak and Balaam tried to do so that you may know the righteousness of the Lord. The Lord became a blessing whenever they tried to curse God's people.[309] There are some attacks that God has protected us from that we never know about because we received a blessing. Unknown devices that the enemy has been throwing, that God has sheltered us from.[310] The enemy is trying to bring us to a place where he can defeat us, but God turns cursing into a blessing.

---

[307] Numbers 22:10-12
[308] Numbers 24:1-11
[309] Deuteronomy 23:5
[310] 1 Peter 5:8

It is not easy to attack blessed people, and the Lord has saved you from more attacks than the ones you had to go through. Some people hate you because, like Balaam, God has empowered them to see you as blessed. Instead of focusing on your struggles, consider your daily blessings and expect God to do something extraordinary in your life.[311] God turned the curse into a blessing when He poured our sins upon Christ on the cross. Before you think your situation is unfair, remember that the Lord turns terrible things into promising futures.[312]

> **Prayer:** Thank you, Father, for the invisible guard you have put up around me. The hits I take don't measure up to the number of attacks thrown at me. I appreciate you thwarting the enemy's plans and those of those who are against me. Please give me your favor and surround me with your hedge. I will rise despite everything they planned to do to me. I am fortunate to be favored and blessed. In the name of Jesus, guard my house, my family, and my life. Amen.

[311] Psalm 121:7-8
[312] Genesis 50:20

Pressed Into Service For Christ

---✠---

Luke 23:26 When they led him away, they grabbed one Simon of Cyrene, coming from the country, and laid the cross on him to carry it after Jesus.

He had traveled from Cyrene to keep the Passover Feast. The word of God may have penetrated his African nation as far back as when the Queen of Sheba returned from hearing Solomon's wisdom.[313] Christ approached being weighed down by the strain of bearing the cross after such a horrid night of beating and betrayal. Tradition says he fell three times before Simon was selected out of the crowd and pressed into service by bearing the cross of the wounded Christ.

This man's name is forever etched into believers' hearts because he didn't resist when pressed.[314] The people in the crowd watched but tried to avoid helping the weary Christ. People often make excuses why it was too hard to bear the cross while simultaneously expecting God's best for their lives. Carrying the cross isn't just about bearing weight but about picking up your life and moving in a better direction. Scripture could have easily skipped over Simon's contribution, but the Lord mentioned him for a purpose. How can we expect to receive all that Christ has for us without being pressed into service for Him?[315]

---

[313] 1 Kings 10:1-9
[314] Matthew 5:41
[315] Matthew 16:24

The crowd claimed to have a relationship with God, but it was never evident in their actions.[316] Simon bore the weight, but he also got the prize. Many of us fall into the category scripture calls the crowd. It takes courage to step out of the crowd. The crowd seeks Christ for their needs, but they are not disciples because they haven't entered into service. Do you want to be part of the crowd or be part of the disciples? Christ first carried the cross we carry. So, what will you answer when asked to serve?

Prayer: You told me to deny myself, take up my cross, and follow, Lord. I don't want to follow in the footsteps of the crowd that does not bear the cross. Please give me the strength to bear up when you call. Please grant me the stamina to endure. My answer is yes and amen, so I plead for you to protect my home and family. Bring us in close, and don't let go of us. In the name of Jesus Christ. Amen.

---

[316] Matthew 7:21

Don't Cut Your Blessings

---⚓---

Proverbs 28:20 A faithful man is rich with blessings;
but one who is eager to be rich will not go unpunished.

Faithful people will continually receive God's blessing, but expecting without investing will lead to a lack. The previous verse says: Tilling the land gives you abundant food, but chasing fantasies breaks you.[317] The faithful are the ones who consistently have given themselves to do work. To Paraphrase: The one who puts effort into work with what the Lord has given them will receive much. But the one who expects to receive blessings without investing labor into what God has given them will go without.[318]

There is a connection between how faithfully you work for the Lord and the blessing you will receive.[319] We all desire blessings to abound, yet are we faithfully using our gifts and abilities for God? Eagerness expects God to do much when they have done little; expecting a blessing without investing in the harvest will lead to nothing but trouble.[320] How many of us consider ourselves faithful because we have a relationship with God yet are not doing His will? Blessings won't come until you are ready to receive them.[321]

---

[317] Proverbs 28:19
[318] Proverbs 6:10-11
[319] Proverbs 14:23
[320] 1 Timothy 6:9
[321] Exodus 23:29-30

Being blessed is not only an action of God; it is a frame of mind that invites God to work. Only those who are truly faithful in their relationship with God and the work He has given them can expect blessings to abound. How much can we lose because we have not labored in service for God? Jesus connects the abundant life to hearing and following Him.[322] How many plans has the Lord placed in our hearts to bring us abundance that we have ignored? The Lord is waiting to pour abundant blessings into the lap of those who listen to His voice. Don't cut yourself out. Serve faithfully and let His blessing abound.

Prayer: Father, help me frame my mind to heed your voice asking me to follow. I pray that I will be faithful and rich with blessings. Empower my labor to bring forth a hundredfold harvest. You know my every need, so I will work without worrying. I declare every seed that I plant will increase with favor. I will follow your Spirit and not chase fantasies, so I ask for the abundance that you give. Thank you for being my God and providing all my needs, in Jesus' name. Amen.

---

[322] John 10:3-7

Empowered By Christ

---✦---

Matthew 10:1 And calling His twelve disciples to Him, Jesus gave them authority over unclean spirits, so that they could drive them out and heal every disease and sickness.

Christ chose and called specific individuals to receive power and advance the kingdom in His name. They would go out, cast out demons, and heal the sick and infirm. Christ is the head of every power.[323] They walked in authority because they walked under His Lordship. No demonic force or sickness would stand before them because Christ stood behind them. As they answered His call, they would receive the power to do what they had never done before.[324]

Christ's uniqueness was seen not just in His miracles. No, rather, it was seen in His ability to empower others. We are empowered to overcome every obstacle and win; no one can empower someone to do God's work without Christ. When the apostles laid hands on them, believers would receive the Holy Spirit that Christ had sent.[325] When Elisha asked for a double portion of Elijah's spirit, it was too great a task for him to accomplish, and he had to trust that God would make it possible.

---

[323] Colossians 2:9-10
[324] Acts 1:8
[325] Matthew 3:11

What sets Christ apart is His power to set us apart. His power to empower is second only to His power to save, and the two work together. When you trust God, he will both strengthen and guide you.[326] Christ's calling may not fit who you are today, but it will fit your future. You have everything you need to fulfill your call, and the only thing most of us lack is the confidence to do it. Believe in Christ's gift to empower you, and you will receive His power.[327] You have been set apart and empowered by Christ.

Prayer: Lord, I need your power, and I ask that you give me the authority to control every obstacle to my destiny. You have called me first to yourself, to walk in your character, and then to the kingdom to use your authority over every defect, deceit, and diabolical scheme. I declare that your hand to heal would rest with me and that no foul spirit affects my family. I pray for your peace and goodness in my life, in the name of Jesus. Amen.

[326] 2 Samuel 22:33
[327] Mark 16:17

Depart From Me

---✦---

Matthew 7:21-23 "Not everyone who says to me, 'Lord, Lord,' will enter into the Kingdom of Heaven, but he who does the will of my Father who is in heaven. Many will tell me in that day, 'Lord, Lord, didn't we prophesy in your name, in your name cast out demons, and in your name do many mighty works?' Then I will tell them, 'I never knew you. Depart from me, you who work iniquity.'

Jesus is discussing people called the workers of iniquity. They claim to know God but have no connection to His Christ. They call Him Lord and seem to operate in His power, but the simple work of faithfulness isn't present. We can't serve God without serving others. When they prophesied and performed exorcisms and mighty works, they sought to bring glory to themselves rather than to God.[328] Professing to serve God, they serve their own interest.

God seeks believers who will serve others, not themselves.[329] He doesn't want us to serve because we want something. He looks for those to serve just because they love Him. It does not matter how many things we do if we are in it for ourselves. These men had outwardly performed many good deeds, and they tried to earn their way into heaven. However, God knows

---

[328] Matthew 7:15-20
[329] Matthew 25:37-45

our hearts, and the heart that departs from the will of God shall not be in the presence of God.[330]

We can live for earthly pleasures or store up heavenly treasures. Basil the Great said, "We know a tree by its fruit and a man by his deeds." The faithful go out on a limb because that is where the fruit is. The difference between works and fruits is that works stem from us, and fruit comes from our roots in Christ. He never knew the workers of iniquity because what they had been doing was not rooted in Him.[331] We shall bear the fruit of righteousness in Christ or be workers of iniquity within ourselves. Will he say, 'I know you,' or depart from me?

> **Prayer:** Lord, I come to you in faith, asking you to help me live the golden rule. I will treat others with equity and justice. Help me live for the spiritual good, not selfish gain. I surrender my life to you and ask that you shape it according to your plan. With your love, power, and grace, I will stand victoriously in Jesus' name. Amen.

---

[330] 1 Samuel 16:7
[331] John 15:5

Press on to Know the Lord

Hosea 6:3 Let's acknowledge Yahweh. Let's press on to know Yahweh. As surely as the sun rises, Yahweh will appear. He will come to us like the rain, like the spring rain that waters the earth."

Some things we will never honestly know unless we first experience them. The prophet Hosea was speaking of knowing healing and restoration not just for himself but also for the nation.[332] Through all His troubles, he pressed on to know the Lord. Avid bible readers will know that Hosea married a woman named Gomer, who was unfaithful to him, and eventually, she left him and ended up as a prostitute.[333] His strength came from his struggles, and he realized he would go through the same things we put God through.

Imagine the embarrassment, frustration, financial woes, and emotional turmoil Hosea endured. Yet through all that he suffered, he pressed on to know God. Hosea felt about what Gomer did the way God felt about unfaithful Israel. No matter how difficult your relationship gets, if you press on to know the Lord, you can be sure He will show up just as the fall and spring rains cause the harvest to grow on the earth. The Lord will bring the comfort and assurance you need to make it through.[334] In a

---

[332] Hosea 6:1-2

[333] Hosea 2:5

[334] 2 Corinthians 1:3-4

sense, God allowed him to feel hurt to bring forth his purpose when He healed the pain.

J.I. Packer said, "There's a difference between knowing God and knowing about God. When you truly know God, you have the energy to serve Him, boldness to share Him, and contentment in Him."[335] If you need healing and restoration, the Lord will bring it, but you must press forward to know Him. If you need peace and focus, it will be there. Eventually, Gomer left her life of prostitution and came back faithful to her husband.[336] It may have cost Hosea a great deal, but he received what he needed because he persevered in seeking to know the Lord.

> **Prayer:** Lord, assist me in dealing with betrayal without becoming resentful. My affection for you will not be altered by any betrayals in which I offered my assistance but wound up being humbled or embarrassed. I am more resilient and forgiving because of you than ever, and I am free to experience your unspeakable joy. I ask that you recognize my scars and grant me healing and grace by the blood and in the power of Jesus. Amen.

---

[335] Daniel 11:32
[336] Hosea 3:1-3

Cultivate It Into To A Blessing

---❡---

Hebrews 6:7-8 For the land which has drunk the rain that comes often on it and produces a crop suitable for them for whose sake it is also tilled, receives blessing from God; but if it bears thorns and thistles, it is rejected and near being cursed, whose end is to be burned.

It's the same ground and rain but not the same blessing. Cultivation is the big difference between a blessing and something rejected. To cultivate means to prepare, encourage, or foster growth. Two parcels of land receive rain, but only the prepared one has good growth. What we put our time into cultivating will grow into something that we call blessed by God.[337] Whether it's our mind, character, or relationships, cultivation causes things to blossom into blessings.

God is blessing us so that our hands may work and bring forth blessings.[338] We have to take what He gives and cultivate it into a blessing. He provides all the resources, but we shape them into what they will become.[339] Without cultivation, what could have been a blessing is instead rejected. Fertile soil, when not cultivated, sprouts enormous weeds. Yet

---

[337] Isaiah 28:24-29
[338] Deuteronomy 28:12
[339] 2 Corinthians 9:10-11

still, we can take what is near to being cursed and turn it around so that instead of destruction, it can receive blessing from God.

God intends to cultivate your life so that you will grow and bear fruit.[340] When the Lord desires, you can bear fruit in any season. Cultivation takes work. You must eliminate things that hinder growth, nurture it, wait patiently, and trust in God.[341] In the end, you will possess something helpful in your life. An uncultivated mind is full of the weeds of wickedness, and an uncultivated life is full of rejection and bondage. Instead of experiencing abundant blessings, a curse is growing in the background. Cultivate your life and receive a blessing from the Lord.

Prayer: Father, you despise the uncultivated life that permits unrighteousness to go unchecked. Please teach me how to discipline my time, thoughts, and mouth. Show me what relationships to cut off and which will foster my growth. I expel anything that seeks to undermine my relationship with you. I pray the spiritual seeds you have given me may bear fruit to harvest righteousness and goodness in my life, in the name of Jesus. Amen.

---

[340] John 15:1-2
[341] Psalms 37:3

Delighting In Mercy

Micah 7:18 Who is a God like you, who pardons iniquity, and passes over the disobedience of the remnant of his heritage? He doesn't retain his anger forever, because he delights in loving kindness.

God delights in mercy. The Hebrew word "Hesed" relates to covenant faithfulness and loyalty that goes beyond all required. That is something that sets Him apart from all the so-called gods. God goes further for us than anyone else would. Though our sins can anger Him, He releases His anger because He delights in showing mercy even when not deserved. Those who have offended Him become restored because faith in Him[342] and mercy toward us bring Him joy.

Sometimes, we can't fix our minds to think about how the Lord can forgive us when we have done so much. That's because we delight in vengeance and not mercy. We're happy when someone gets what's coming, and God is happy to forgive.[343] The passing over of our disobedience relates to the night of the Exodus, which states that when God sees the blood applied, He passes over, placing His presence at the door and keeping the destroyer out.[344]

---

[342] Hebrews 11:6

[343] 2 Peter 3:9

[344] Exodus 12:23

Forgiveness is the ultimate form of love because it requires sacrifice. It sets us as free as the forgiven one. Forgivers are a forgiven people.[345] They have taken on the mind of Christ, for they know what it is like to delight in mercy. If someone has done you wrong, do you delight when misfortune has come upon them, or do you delight in mercy?[346] Sin is not greater than forgiveness because it brings death. Mercy brings healing, restoration, and life. God's mercy is greater than any mistake you have made. Be like Him and delight in loving kindness.

Prayer: Lord, help me delight in the things that you delight in. May I decrease and you increase so I will see your hand in healing hearts, restoring families, and bringing unity for purpose. I pray for forgiveness to remove family dysfunction and bring peace. Show us how to live your ways, considering our words and actions. Please help me improve as you pour out your grace in my life. I can do all things through Christ who loves me. Give me strength, focus, clean hands, and a pure heart to do your will in Jesus' name, Amen.

---

[345] Matthew 6:14
[346] Proverbs 24:17-18

Do You See Them

---✦---

Isaiah 25:4 For you have been a stronghold to the poor, a stronghold to the needy in his distress, a refuge from the storm, a shade from the heat, when the blast of the dreaded ones is like a storm against the wall.

Though He is the God of all creation, Jehovah's acts are intricately woven into the lives of those in need. He maintains the universe and sustains the individual. He is concerned with the oppressed, upholds the needy, and relieves those battered by life.[347] With all the work He has to do, the Lord does not overlook anyone. He sees the individual within their struggles and becomes a provider of their needs, helping us when we cannot help ourselves.[348]

God doesn't forget the needy, and neither should we.[349] Sometimes, we get so busy with the world that we overlook the needs within the world. Maybe we say, "That's their problem; it doesn't involve me." However, the truth is it involves God. We should never be so busy that we can't pause to do some good.[350] God helps those who help others. If we want God to

---

[347] Isaiah 57:15

[348] Psalms 12:5

[349] Psalm 113:7

[350] Luke 10:30-35

rescue us from our problems, we must be willing to let God use us to rescue others from their problems.[351]

Some people create their storms and get upset when it rains. However, sometimes we deal with ruthless and dreaded people. The dreaded ones are those who are a part of someone's storm rather than being a part of their rescue. God will lead you when you are self-sabotaging and protect you from the schemes of others. He always provides us with a clear path to follow.[352] We can be those who God uses to give strength to the poor and needy, to provide refuge from the storm and cover from the heat. In a day when people have so much against them. God is a wall against the storm. Will you stand with Him or walk by?

Prayer: Father, enable me to protect others as you have me. When I don't know the answers, I come to you; when lost, let me point others in your direction. I ask that you alter the habits of the dreaded and drive away the vengeful who bring storms. Keep them from me. Thank you for being my stronghold, refuge, and shade from the wicked. Continue to work your good pleasure in me, in the name of the Lord Jesus Christ. Amen.

---

[351] Matthew 25:34-40
[352] John 14:6

Let There Be Light

Genesis 1:3-4. God said, "Let there be light," and there was light. God saw the light, and saw that it was good. God divided the light from the darkness.

The Lord spoke, and the universe responded. Seven times, Genesis says that what God saw was good, and[353] Scripture suggests that the light had to be separated from the darkness because it was good. Contrary to popular thought, God sees but never speaks of its goodness. Speaking of goodness would have sealed the creation in righteousness. However, before God says it is not good for man to be alone, He gives Adam free will to choose righteousness.[354]

God can see the goodness in any person, thing, or situation, but for us to see it, we must allow Him to separate us from the darkness.[355] The light was good, but not useful until it was set apart from the darkness. We can't influence the world by trying to be like it. Jesus referred to our separation when He called us the light of the world.[356] You were born to stand out, not fit in. You can't shine in the darkness when you are in the darkness yourself.

---

[353] Genesis 1:4, 10, 12, 18, 21, 25 &31

[354] Genesis 2:16-18

[355] 1 Peter 2:9

[356] Matthew 5:14-16

John Hagee said, "A Christian should set the standard so high that the world will want to know where you have been." However, all your good qualities won't amount to anything if you remain trapped within darkness.[357] Just as when the Holy Spirit hovered over the waters, He watched over us to separate us from the darkness so that our light would shine. When the Lord said, "Let there be light," the universe obeyed. Nevertheless, we have a choice.[358] Will you let there be light in you, or are you going to sit in the darkness?

Prayer: Father, I confess my transgressions and ask your forgiveness and cleansing. Please remove any remaining blemishes of darkness from my soul. I won't keep my light hidden; I'll let it shine so that people may know how you changed me. I ask that you grant me a close relationship and that your Holy Spirit gives me the strength to live a life that pleases you. My loved ones struggling with addiction, abuse, and regret are in my prayers. Bring them into your marvelous light so they can experience your presence. The name of Jesus. Amen.

---

[357] Isaiah 64:6
[358] Genesis 49:6

Prophetic Plagiarism

Jeremiah 23:30 Therefore behold, I am against the prophets," says Yahweh, "who each steal my words from his neighbor.

One day, while speaking, Christ rebuked the Pharisees by telling them thieves come to steal, kill, and destroy.[359] Often, He chastised them for prioritizing traditions over the Word of God and following the crowd of religious elites rather than forming personal convictions based on the Holy Spirit and God's Word. However, because of their spiritual blindness, they couldn't realize He was speaking about them.[360] That's just how the prophets were in Jeremiah's days, blind from their acts of stealing God's word from others.

Most of us don't think of ourselves as thieves. However, think of some of the things that we steal from God. We take from Him His glory,[361] embezzle money due to Him,[362] and now even steal His word, repeating what others have said and proclaiming it as if the Lord had spoken it to us. That's prophetic plagiarism, which robs people of God's truth. False prophets in Jeremiah's day told the people what they wanted to hear. There was little conviction to change their character and habits. God's word should have

---

[359] John 10:10
[360] John 9:40-41
[361] Malachi 1:6
[362] Malachi 3:9-10

been a hammer to break up the stony heart; they made it into a field of lying dreams.[363]

Prophetic plagiarism robs God of His ability to speak to us directly, and it is speaking a word that has resources in man instead of receiving its source from God.[364] Charles Spurgeon says, "The Word of God is a lamp by night, a light by day, and a delight at all times." The word of God should be fresh in our lives, not recycled. The written word was given freely to us to compare with what people speak. Don't steal from your neighbor what God gives freely. The word He brings won't be plagiarized or recycled, but will refresh us.

Prayer: Lord, give me an attentive ear to hear your word and the wisdom to spot prophetic piracy. I oppose any dishonesty or deceit that I may encounter. Deal with my selfish ear that tingles at my desires, the carnal ear that lacks faith, and the obstinate ear that won't listen. With a heart of love, reproof, and discipline, please help me to heed your word. I humbly ask that you grant me joy and favor as you lead me to the whole truth, the precious name of Jesus. Amen,

---

[363] Jeremiah 23:25-29
[364] Jeremiah 23:32-36

An Active Word For An Active Life

--- ⚡ ---

Hebrews 4:12 For the word of God is living and active, and sharper than any two-edged sword, piercing even to the dividing of soul and spirit, of both joints and marrow, and is able to discern the thoughts and intentions of the heart.

We are a society on the move, running to and fro, involved in some matter. But everything we do has a motive behind it. Some of our motives are noble, while others are not so gracious. Sometimes, we do the wrong thing for the right reasons and good things for the wrong reasons. God weighs our motives, and His word is the scale of whether the intent is good or bad.[365] Our activities require an active word to focus on what we genuinely need to do and why we should do it.

God's word penetrates deep into man's heart to expose the motives that lie beneath the surface.[366] The word penetrates our hearts to both discern and transform us. Many have never desired to delve that deep into our lives because it exposes what sin has put within us.[367] The active word that penetrates even the hardest-to-reach places reveals every sinister plot Satan and his minions have implanted in our hearts. When we listen and

---

[365] Proverb 16:2
[366] Jeremiah 23:29
[367] John 3:19-21

meditate on what the word speaks to us, the Holy Spirit opens our hearts to receive life transformation.

No matter how active we are, the word of God is heart surgery for the spirit. You don't have to lie down or stop, but cooperate as it enters our hearts to eradicate the cancer sin has placed there. The word is an active remedy for sin; by hiding it in our hearts, our ways become pure before God.[368] Every thought and intent of our hearts is laid bare by the word. Discerning even down to the intents we didn't know. Let's test ourselves, expose our hearts to the word, and receive the power to live for God.

Prayer: Father, examine my heart and show me the places that require repair. Please guide me in how to have grace-based motivations rather than judgmental or egotistical ones. I expel unclean intentions and ideas while asking your Holy Spirit to fortify my resolve to live upright. Identify the strategies and intentions of those who may intend harm and shield me from their schemes. I will always love and praise you, for you are my God. Transform my heart and mind to conform to your will, in Jesus' name. Amen.

---

[368] Psalm 119:9-11

A God Perspective

---✦---

Song 1:5-6 I am dark, but lovely, you daughters of Jerusalem, like Kedar's tents, like Solomon's curtains. Don't stare at me because I am dark, because the sun has scorched me. My mother's sons were angry with me. They made me keeper of the vineyards. I haven't kept my own vineyard.

Written as a duet, the words in the Song of Solomon predominantly come from the Shulamite woman.[369] Some suggest that she may have co-written the book, or that Solomon transcribed her words, just as he had under the pseudonym King Lemuel, using his mother Bathsheba's words to describe the Proverbs 31 woman.[370] The Shulamite was King Solomon's one true love. She was known for her exquisite beauty, but didn't think that highly of herself. Looking in the mirror, she saw her flaws, what the sun had done to her skin, and how taking care of the responsibilities of others caused her to neglect herself.

Even in her splendor, her imperfections stood out as if to make a mockery of her self-worth. Elizabeth Drew said, "The world is run not by thought, nor by imagination, but by opinion." Our opinions shape how we perceive our situations and the world around us. They transform small things into significant thoughts. They determine our habits and cause us

---

[369] Song of Solomon 1:1-2
[370] Proverbs 31:1

to view the same events differently. Everyone has opinions; however, their opinions are often based more on feelings than well-informed evidence.[371]

As the song progresses, the Shulamite woman learns to put aside her opinions and look at herself based on the thoughts of her beloved.[372] Her growth mirrors a God perspective. What matters is not the opinions of others or your own opinion of yourself but what God thinks of you. Your value doesn't decrease because of opinion; it increases because God knows your worth. Our opinions often derive from our emotions, but the Lord's thoughts are truth-based. Gain a God perspective over your life, see yourself from His eyes, and know your worth.

Prayer: Father, help me see myself as the masterpiece you see. You shaped me not to be controlled by my past or a negative self-image, but by your hand. Remove pride and self-abasement from my heart and give me a perspective of respectable humility. Thank you for recognizing my value and helping me avoid selling myself short. I pray that others will see what you see and that your blessing will rest upon me, in Jesus' name. Amen.

---

[371] Proverbs 18:2
[372] Song of Solomon 8:10-12

Salvation is Yours

---✦---

Habakkuk 3:13 You went out for the salvation of your people, for the salvation of your anointed. You crushed the head of the land of wickedness. You stripped them head to foot. Selah.

God has many defining characteristics, yet one that stands out is that God looks to save His people.[373] God wants to give us victory more than we want to receive it. The law of God is His victory plan for our lives, yet because of the flesh, we have a hard time following it. Temptation reveals our worst tendencies and reflects our level of self-control.[374] Trials challenge our focus and commitment, revealing our level of spiritual maturity. Testing shows us the love of the world and proves whether we have a sincere heart for God. The wicked fail when tempted, tried, and tested because they lack a commitment to God and follow their selfish heart and desires.

God's salvation is not only to save our flesh from the day of trouble; it is to save our souls. He helps those He anoints by taking the extra step to help us in our temptations, trials, and tests.[375] He covers His people with His hand and strips the wicked head to foot. The Hebrew phrase "arah yeshod ad tsavvar" describes something laid bare from the foundation it

---

[373] Psalm 68:20
[374] James 1:14-15
[375] 1 Corinthians 10:13

151

stands on to the neck, where they laid the burdens. The wicked are without divine resources because God's hand is against them.[376]

God will crush the head of the land of the wicked and strip them naked. Victory belongs to those who persevere and are preserved by God. We must decide whether it's best to live right and have God go out for us or live according to our ways and have Him against us. Salvation is God freely bringing grace to those who are His.[377] We must ask if we are living as one of His or for ourselves. We will either stand covered by His grace or be stripped from head to foot, ashamed in His presence.

Prayer: Lord, I need your help in tests, trials, and temptations. Keep your good hand on me to prevent me from stumbling into wicked ways. I bare my soul to you and find healing in your presence. Act favorably on my behalf and protect my family. Please save me from trials, temptations, and self. Cause me to follow your victory plan for success, leading to eternal life in Christ. Amen.

[376] Ezekiel 35:3
[377] Ephesians 2:8-9

Lord Send Me

---♦---

Isaiah 6:8 I heard the Lord's voice, saying, "Whom shall I send, and who will go for us?" Then I said, "Here I am. Send me!"

Every believer has a function to fulfill in the grand design of things.[378] We call it purpose, and it derives from a sincere desire placed in the heart of man by God. If we discover what we have an unselfish passion for, then we have discovered that purpose. However, we often see a need that touches our hearts and expect someone else to fill it.[379] The Lord is saying, "Whom shall I send and who will go for us," and few are stepping up and saying Lord, here I am, send me.

Many claim to have a vision from God; however, too few raise their hands and say, "Here I am."[380] When others fill in for work God calls us to do, we will be frustrated when things aren't right. Likewise, when God calls us to work, we shouldn't force our passion on others, thinking they are wrong if they don't do what we do. There will be people with a shared vision and purpose that God places in your path. However, our passions are our own, and we should recognize that not all of us share the same mission.[381]

---

[378] Ephesians 4:16
[379] 2 Corinthians 10:15-17
[380] 1 Samuel 3:4
[381] 1 Corinthians 12:17-20

When God spoke, Isaiah was ready to go. No hesitation, no looking around for others to sign up before him. He knew that God would be with him.[382] It's not the size but the depth of your commitment that matters. What you do will make a difference, and if you have the heart, you will make the time to do what God has made for you. It's time for us to step up to the plate and go where the Lord sends us. Is that your prayer, "Send me, Lord, where you need me to go." He is waiting for you right now to say, 'Send me.'

> **Prayer:** Lord, please give me the patience to handle the demands and difficulties of a busy life. Please guide me in finding a healthy balance between my family obligations, work, ministry, and personal needs. Place me in the company of those who share my vision for serving the mission you have given me so that together, we can carry out your will. As I say, "Here I am, send me," I ask that your serenity, joy, and hand of protection accompany me, in the name of Jesus, Amen.

---

[382] Deuteronomy 31:6

Love Like Never Before

---✦---

1 Peter 1:22 Seeing you have purified your souls in your obedience to the truth through the Spirit in sincere brotherly affection, love one another from the heart fervently,

Dallas Willard said, "Discipleship is the process of becoming who Jesus would be if He were you." However, sadly, not all who believe in God follow His ways.[383] Why? Because their souls are not purified. Some believe according to the word, while others follow their hearts. Those who follow the word from their hearts are disciples. Disciples have committed to becoming more like Jesus through their trust in God and obedience to His word.[384] Believers may trust, and followers may commit, but only disciples have their souls cleansed.

Christian obedience is more than an act of adherence to instruction. It is submission to follow God's truth from sincere love. It is a disciple yielding to the Holy Spirit from a love for Him and the people of God.[385] Love removes our resistance to obeying the truth. It gives us greater strength and allows us to weather the storms, withstand opposition, and refuse to accept anything short of the will of God. When we obey the truth, trusting in the Holy Spirit, our love for others deepens and becomes vibrant.

---

[383] Acts 8:21
[384] John 8:30-32
[385] Mark 12:30-31

Our hearts are to be a loving space, not a living space for the junk of our past. Purifying the soul requires us to rid ourselves of defilement while making room for God's love[386]. When we stop resisting God, it purifies our souls, allowing us to have an avid love for one another. If you struggle to love others, your soul is not yet pure.[387] The more we yield to obey God's truth, the more our love becomes natural. It is a genuine love that God is seeking to extract from all Christians. Obey the truth, purify your heart, and love like never before.

> **Prayer:** Lord, I confess my faults to you at the foot of your cross, Lord, and ask you to help me grow in righteousness. Please assist me in obeying rather than delaying the truth. Purify my soul with sincerity and integrity. Expand the capacity of my heart to love with discernment guided by your Holy Spirit. To become more like your Christ, conform me on the inside. In Jesus' name, Amen.

---

[386] 2 Corinthians 7:1-2
[387] Romans 5:5

Give Me My Vision

--- ✦ ---

Acts 9:10-12 Now there was a certain disciple at Damascus named Ananias. The Lord said to him in a vision, "Ananias!" He said, "Behold, it's me, Lord." The Lord said to him, "Arise and go to the street which is called Straight, and inquire in the house of Judah for one named Saul, a man of Tarsus. For behold, he is praying, and in a vision he has seen a man named Ananias coming in and laying his hands on him, that he might receive his sight."

God spoke to Ananias in a vision, and in that vision, a man named Saul had a vision of Ananias coming to him to restore his sight. It may seem complicated, but Saul lost his vision while having a vision of Christ.[388] He began to pray, and God gave him a vision of Ananias helping him. Then, the Lord gave Ananias a vision explaining Saul's need for Ananias to come and pray for him to regain his sight. The only way Ananias could fulfill what God spoke to him was to fulfill Saul's vision of him. Ananias realized that fulfilling a personal vision happens when seeking to fulfill a larger one.

Saul's vision was only restored when a disciple named Ananias willingly carried out the vision God had given him. God revealed to Ananias the nature of all vision. That is, the Lord only has one vision for the

---

[388] Acts 9:1-9

kingdom of God. All visions we receive from the Lord are only small parts of His overall vision. For Paul to complete the vision God had for his life, Ananias had to complete the vision God had for his life.[389] God connects all visions like pieces of a puzzle. Put the pieces together, and you have a picture of the kingdom of God.[390]

When Ananias fulfilled his vision, Saul regained the natural vision that the Lord had taken away. Though he heard many things about Saul, he overcame his hesitations.[391] Our visions are connected. The Lord's design is unity, achieved by working together to fulfill the kingdom's mandate. Someone sees you in their vision that you will come to help fulfill their vision by fulfilling your God-given vision. Don't hesitate to fulfill another believer's vision because it may help you to fulfill what the Lord has for you.

Prayer: Father, I realize that if I work toward a bigger goal that aligns with my purpose, I will achieve your vision for my life. I'm only scratching the surface now; lead me by your Spirit to serve zealously and complete whatever you have for me. May I obey your heavenly vision and see your kingdom come in power and love, in Jesus' name, Amen.

---

[389] Acts 9:14-19
[390] Ephesians 4:16
[391] Acts 9:13

God Is In Control

---⚓---

***Micah 4:3 and he will judge between many
peoples, and will decide concerning strong
nations afar off. They will beat their swords
into plowshares, and their spears into pruning
hooks. Nation will not lift up sword against
nation, neither will they learn war any more***

God rules all, but He doesn't enforce control over everything. He influences decisions without dictating the outcome. God does not suggest but commands and deals with our disobeying those same commands. He is sovereign over all[392] and has all knowledge and power, but still, He restrains the use of that power to control us. He rules us by handing us the power over our destiny. Yet a day will come when we come to the Lord to learn to do things His way.[393]

Sometimes, God shows us He is in control by putting us in situations we cannot control. We must surrender to God and let Him lead us during those times. The weapons we grab are truth, righteousness, faith, and the word, as God defends us, as His peace rules our lives.[394] When we give God control of our lives, we let Him fight our battles. Our weapons of

---

[392] Jeremiah 32:17

[393] Micah 4:1-2

[394] 2 Thessalonians 3:16

destruction become tools of production. Our former ways of dealing with our conflicts give way to godly thinking and discernment.[395]

Each person who surrenders to Christ continues the process of the nation's coming to Him. When God is in control, His rebuke will change our attitude. You haven't given God total control if you aren't at peace within yourself. Whatever is under God's control is never out of control.[396] Giving God total control means releasing our hearts, minds, and lives to Him and holding nothing back. In exchange, we receive His sovereign will for our lives and peace. Be at peace and make the Lord sovereign.

Prayer: Savior, teach me to remove my hands from things so you will place your hands on them. I now employ the same audacity and persistence I used to knock things down to rebuild them. I enlist your help to mend the harm I have caused by repairing the wounds. Please help me follow your lead so I can honor your name in every circumstance. I ask for peace in my house, family, and life in the name of Jesus Christ. Amen.

---

[395] 2 Corinthians 10:3-5
[396] Proverbs 19:21

Covered, Blessed, and Increased

---⚶---

Job 1:10 Haven't you made a hedge around him,
and around his house, and around all that he has,
on every side? You have blessed the work of his
hands, and his substance is increased in the land.

These are Satan's words when asked about his attempts to come at a faithful man named Job. His faithfulness and fear of the Lord placed a hedge of angels around him, restraining the hand of the enemy.[397] Job didn't have one hedge but three. His personal hedge protected him, his patriarchal hedge protected his home and family, and his professional hedge covered his prosperity and possessions. God covered every aspect of his life, yet he was still concerned about his children's mistakes, just as we are.[398] Satan could do nothing while Job's three hedges were up and needed an entryway.

The release of the hedge opened up a disaster.[399] Even with Job's greatest fears realized, he still trusted God; nothing would shake his faithfulness.[400] It was a lousy season, yet he would regain his hedge because he maintained his integrity. Phillip Yancy said. "The point of the book of Job

---

[397] Psalm 34:7
[398] Job 1:5
[399] Job 1:12-19
[400] Job 2:3-10

is not suffering: or where is God when it hurts? Chapters 1 & 2 dealt with that issue. The book's point is faith, where is Job when it hurts."

Job endured his trial as an example of perseverance, so you don't have to.[401] When we are faithful even in hard times, the work of our hands will eventually produce for us. Faithfully following God's will leads to success. A fruitful season of continual harvest is available to us, where blessings multiply, and the hedges will never again reopen.[402] Because Job was faithful, God was with him, and He can be with you in the same way, healing your pain and blessing your life.

Prayer: Lord, as long as I maintain my faith in you, please plant hedges around every aspect of my life and keep them there. I will follow you in every circumstance and not veer to the left or the right. Pour your love and grace upon me by restoring and multiplying all I have. I ask that you heal the hurts and bless me so that I may be a blessing to others. I pray for a special blessing of protection over my loved ones. Draw each one close and cover them in the name of Jesus, Amen.

[401] James 5:11
[402] Job 42:10-16

Moving Forward

---✦---

Exodus 14:15 Yahweh said to Moses, "Why do you cry to me? Speak to the children of Israel, that they go forward.

It was the time of the Exodus, and God had begun the Israelites' journey to freedom through Moses. God intentionally instructed Israel to turn around and camp where they would seem boxed in by the Red Sea to draw Pharaoh out.[403] Yet when they saw God's plan in action, they wondered if they had done the right thing by venturing out. Fear of the unknown began to grip them, and they spoke from their feelings instead of their faith.[404] Yet God was telling them not to cry out to Him, just move forward.

God has already begun this journey with you, and He will not turn back; therefore, move forward. Every great move starts with a leap of faith, yet sometimes we get so far out there and, like the Israelites, wonder, "Did I do the God thing or my thing?" We can be on the right track and still get run over if we stop. That's what it's like to struggle when moving in faith. Emotions stop us and cause us to speculate whether we have followed the right path.[405] Faith transcends feelings and propels us forward when our emotions attempt to halt and turn us back.

---

[403] Exodus 14:1-4

[404] Exodus 14:8-12

[405] Matthew 9:23-25

Faith follows God's heart, and feelings follow our hearts. A small stop during your walk of faith will cause your heart of emotion to rise and cast doubt on where you are.[406] Moving forward is not about figuring everything out but taking the next step. Faith pushes ahead instead of stalling in fear. We worry about failure, but failure is a bend in the road, not the end of the road. Regardless of how you feel, God says to move forward. Be strong and courageous; don't let your heart hold you back.[407] It's time to move forward and see what God will do.

Prayer: Lord, I will continue to move forward with faith that you will move any mountains in my path. I come to you for strength and courage because I know I can accomplish everything through Christ and your Holy Spirit empowering me. Break every barrier to get me over to the other side. I appreciate you putting my old nemesis behind me so that I can move on. Let your will spring forth in my life and the depths of my soul, in the precious name of Christ, Amen.

---

[406] Luke 9;62
[407] Joshua 1:7

The Blame Game

---✦---

Zephaniah 3:5 Yahweh, within her, is righteous. He will do no wrong. Every morning he brings his justice to light. He doesn't fail, but the unjust know no shame.

The unjust see the Lord's goodness, and their ears hear of His righteous acts, but their hearts fail to respond.[408] There is no chance these events will occur; these are God's openings. However, many things get in our way of seeing what God is doing. He could be right in our midst, providing for our needs and protecting our homes; still, we overlook God. The Lord is active enough in our lives so all can see his righteousness, yet because many lack the insight to discern their faults, they blame God.[409]

The unjust heart is a shame, a reproach to the righteousness of God, and it refuses to see that God will only do what is right. The unjust justify themselves and find fault with God; they blame God for the wrong in the world to their shame.[410] Most who blame God have not done their part in getting their affairs in order. People who don't take responsibility for their well-being do not gain control over it. Though He never fails, they fail to uphold Him as the one who does righteousness.

---

[408] Psalm 145:9
[409] Psalm 19:12
[410] Proverbs 21:2-3

It is a shame that we blame God for what we have done to ourselves. Few appreciate all the help He gives. The righteous accept responsibility and apply their actions to handle what is needed. The unjust give little or nothing in return but expect everything. If they don't get their way, they play the blame game and say that God and not them is unjust.[411] When things don't go our way, the Lord is still just, and when our ventures fail, His justice still shines. When it comes to God, don't play the blame game. His righteous acts never fail.

Prayer: Mighty God, I ask that you keep an eye on my steps. Keep me safe and prevent me from making poor decisions that I will have to live with. God, I see you. Be my strength in the morning, my defense during the day, and my haven where I may rest. Please guide me to all wisdom so that I might live in your kindness and favor. Continue your work in the lives of all those around me, in Jesus' name, Amen.

---

[411] Ecclesiastes 7:29

Pentecost for the Soul

Leviticus 23:15-16 You shall count from the next day after the Sabbath, from the day that you brought the sheaf of the wave offering: seven Sabbaths shall be completed. The next day after the seventh Sabbath you shall count fifty days; and you shall offer a new meal offering to Yahweh

Called the Feast of Weeks, Pentecost counts off seven sabbaths after the presentation of First Fruits during the Passover. While Passover occurs at the time of the barley harvest, Pentecost completes the grain season with the harvesting of wheat. During these 50 days, the Jews would bring grain offerings commemorating two significant events. The Passover began the physical liberation of the Israelites. Pentecost reminded the Jews that their liberation was incomplete without spiritual redemption, which came with the receipt of the Law on Mount Sinai fifty days after the Passover.[412]

Pentecost is the anniversary of Moses receiving the Ten Commandments, and it represents the birthday of Israel as an independent nation and the birthday of the New Testament Church.[413] The disciples were re-gathered and strengthened with each other and the risen Savior for fifty days through encouragement, instruction, and fellowship. However, they

---

[412] Deuteronomy 4:10-13
[413] Accts 2:37-41

needed to receive the power to be His witnesses.[414] Those brought into the kingdom covenant would be incomplete without the Word and the Holy Spirit giving us the instruction and power needed to live as kingdom disciples.[415]

Robert Baer said." Bethlehem was God with us, Calvary was God for us, and Pentecost is God in us." We are incomplete if the Word is without the Spirit of God to guide us. The counting of seven times of gathering ourselves unto God marked the Pentecost of the completion of the promise to give us what we need to serve the Lord. It showed us the prayer before the Spirit works to bring renewal, revival, and redemption to our souls.[416] Let's make our offering unto God personal by living according to what He has given.

Prayer: God of inspiration, move in my life, filling me with your presence. Ignite my fire to be a witness for you, helping me live a holy life before you. Revive my passion for praying alongside your people until a change happens. I ask you to draw me near as your child and in your continued love, in the name of Jesus Christ. Amen.

---

[414] Acts 1:8

[415] John 5:39 compare with John 14:26

[416] Acts 2:1-4

Instruction for Construction

---✦---

Genesis 7:1 Yahweh said to Noah, "Come with all of your household into the ship, for I have seen your righteousness before me in this generation

It was an ark of safety constructed to save lives. The Lord looked and alone favored Noah and found him as righteous before Him.[417] Now, the time had come for God to invite Noah to enter what He had told him to build. It would support not only Noah but his wife, children, all the animals of the earth, and birds of the air. It was constructed according to what God had instructed, and its reproduction would deliver them from destruction.[418]

Rob Hill said we should build a life from which we don't have to vacation. Noah's righteousness did just that; God trusted that what he built would be sufficient for his household. When followed correctly, godly instructions build a sound life. If we reproduce an exact representation that the Lord tells us, we will escape much destruction. The Lord speaks about how we should live and tend to the things in our lives to cause growth and bring favor. Christ is our foundation, so what we build with is as important as how we build.[419] Solid materials such as God's word, integrity, sincerity, wisdom, and love make for a dependable life.

---

[417] Genesis 6:5-8

[418] Genesis 6:14-22

[419] 1 Corinthians 3:10-15

We must ask ourselves whether we are building as the Lord commands or following the flesh's commands. What has purpose should be locked into our home, and everything else blocked out.[420] God instructs us and invites us to live in what we have made. Have we made homes to enjoy or just houses to live in? Have we made fellowships with the right people we can lean on or relationships with the wrong ones that fall apart? By the knowledge of Christ, God has given you all the suitable materials to build with.[421] Build on what He instructs, not how you feel, so your home will stand.

> Prayer: Heavenly Father, I'm grateful you used your divine power to give me all I need to lead a good life. I commit to erecting the proper foundation and demolishing every obstacle to my future. I ask that your Spirit help me comprehend how to put your message into practice and live accordingly to gain knowledge, stature, and favor with God and man. Place my family in your ark of safety so we can withstand storms and emerge victorious through the power and in the name of Jesus. Amen.

---

[420] Genesis 7:13-16
[421] 2 Peter 1:2-3

Break Me Off Something

---⁂---

Lamentations 4:4 The tongue of the nursing child clings to the roof of his mouth for thirst. The young children ask for bread, and no one breaks it for them.

As a church, we must follow the practices that Christ laid forth. We see this in the early church's focus on teachings, fellowship, breaking bread, and prayer.[422] These are the four pillars of practice for the New Testament church. When applied, God caused the church to grow.[423] However, in breaking bread, many limit their understanding to communion, which is one side of the coin in an essential part of spiritual life. That is the common meal called the love feast, which communion sprang and provided for those who lacked.[424]

The Holy Eucharist, commonly known as communion, remembers Christ's sacrifice and shares His life through the elements of bread and wine.[425] While it is true that the breaking of bread allows us to share in God's life, the other side of the coin allows us to share life with others. There are needs in our communities that too few try to help. People are

---

[422] Acts 2:42
[423] Acts 2:47
[424] Jude 1:12
[425] John 6:48-51

asking for bread, but who breaks it if not us? When we help those in need, our light shines in the darkness.[426]

When God saw our need, he broke bread (His body) so we could partake of His righteousness. The breaking of bread meets the needs of humanity both spiritually and physically. Generosity shows that you are blessed.[427] It's as simple as making a sandwich or giving a water bottle, but it shares life with those in need. You don't need deep pockets, but it requires a deep heart to help. As humble servants, let us break bread with God and then with one another, and feed the needs.

> **Prayer:** Lord, thank you for sharing life through the holy sacrifice that renews my soul. Give me opportunities to cross the road and help those beaten by life and left with a genuine need. I will pour out abundantly to be a blessing as you pour abundance into me. As you lead me, I pray for your power, provision, and safety. Fulfill each need with your grace, in Jesus' name, Amen.

---

[426] Isaiah 58:10
[427] Proverbs 22:9

Fight Until We All Win

---◆---

Deuteronomy 3:20 Until Yahweh gives rest to your brothers, as to you, and they also possess the land which Yahweh your God gives them beyond the Jordan. Then you shall each return to his own possession, which I have given you."

The Reubenites, the Gadites, and half of the tribe of Manasseh of the tribes of Israel conquered and divided the land east of the Jordan River, which was not part of the original promise given to Abraham.[428] They had possessed the land they asked for, and the remaining tribes were poised to cross and take the land west of the Jordan. However, even though the struggle east of Jordan was over, they weren't released to rest. Those who had supported their dreams would now need their support so they could possess the land of promise.[429] They had to fight until everyone won.

There comes a time when some may feel that they have achieved their goals and want to sit back and enjoy it. We can get comfortable in our world and ignore the plight of others. God wants us to work together until we win together.[430] Individual victories are not enough because we dwell in a spiritual kingdom. We share success; when one wins, we all win, but until we all win, we haven't conquered. When we arrive at the place we

---

[428] Number 32:1-5
[429] Galatians 6:2
[430] Joshua 1:14-16

want to be, we must remember those who supported us despite having their own struggles.[431]

People who have supported us need help; we must also be willing to step in and give them a chance to possess and live the life God has planned for them. Those who have fought for us by praying, encouraging, and believing in God on our behalf will one day need us to do the same for them. We may have to cross some troubled waters for them to see victory.[432] We can't turn our backs on those who have been with us when they seem down or defeated, even if it is their own doing. Show them your support and fight until we all win.

Prayer: Lord, I appreciate each triumph you have given me, and I can rest well knowing that I won't accomplish my goals alone. I ask that you increase my sense of calm, satisfaction, and devotion. I commit to supporting others who work to overcome the same challenges I once overcame. Thank you for being with me and sending me the help I need. I pray that you cause my family, friends, and church to thrive as we work together for your glory in the name of Jesus Christ. Amen.

_____

_____

_____

_____

_____

---

[431] Matthew 7:12
[432] 1 Corinthians 15:57-58

Victory Verses

---✦---

Psalm 119:98-99 Your commandments make me wiser than my enemies, for your commandments are always with me. I have more understanding than all my teachers, for your testimonies are my meditation.

Whether it is competition or conflict, it is natural to want to gain the upper hand over those who come against you, and it is spiritual to want to gain the upper hand over sin. We wrestle not against flesh and blood, so our most substantial combat is with the influences on this world and the sin within us.[433] The word wiser comes from the Hebrew "Chakam," meaning dealing with better thoughts, words, and actions. We gain an advantage over what comes against us by doing things better or doing them differently than before. Our most significant advantage comes from being equipped with God and His word.[434]

Not having a Bible in front of them, the ancients used strips of parchment containing scriptures, called frontlets and phylacteries, as storage containers strapped to their bodies to pull out and meditate on throughout the day.[435] The most crucial part of meditating on a verse for the day is to meet every obstacle by reciting that verse to give yourself a victory. Meditating on scripture is memorizing, applying, and activating our faith.

---

[433] Ephesians 6:12

[434] Hebrews 13:20-21

[435] Exodus 13:16

Each day, we should take a verse and use it as a weapon to fight our battles.[436]

Taking the verse from your daily devotional and applying it to all situations makes us more effective by proving the verse each day we meditate and memorize it. It is like practicing with a weapon before a fight. Many try to fight using a word they haven't practiced with. When we practice using the day's meditation scripture throughout the day, we won't struggle with it when we truly need it.[437] Gain more understanding than your teachers by practicing using the word you meditate on daily.

Prayer: God, I am grateful that you see me and provide me with the spiritual weapons I need to succeed. I commit to investing time daily to let your word flow through me. I have all I need in you, and I'll beat anyone who challenges me. Give me comprehension through your word and the Holy Spirit to hone my discernment, gain wisdom, and cast off any thoughts that might hinder my knowing you, in Jesus' name, Amen.

---

[436] Ephesians 6:17-19
[437] Luke 4:1-13

Putting it in God's Hands

---✠---

Esther 4:16 Then Esther asked them to answer Mordecai, 16 "Go, gather together all the Jews who are present in Susa, and fast for me, and neither eat nor drink three days, night or day. I and my maidens will also fast the same way. Then I will go in to the king, which is against the law; and if I perish, I perish.

Today, many people believe they must keep the status quo and can do nothing to change our society. Are the problems so big that there are no solutions? Is the system unable to be penetrated and changed even from the inside? These are the issues Esther had to deal with. There were problems within the government and society at large. What could she do in what appeared to be an impossible situation?[438] She put her life in the hands of God.

Rosa Parks said, "One person can change the world." Many have suffered mistreatment and died to make change happen.[439] Throughout generations, people like Esther have had to put their lives on the line to effect change. Most social injustices ended because people's lives were on the line. Yes, change is possible, but who will pay the price? Satan and his minions have so corrupted world systems that only bloodshed will make

---

[438] Esther 4:6-11
[439] 1 Kings 19:10-14

some do what they know is right to do.[440] The book of Esther may not mention the name God, but her confession meant that if her acts led her to death, she was okay because she was in God's hands.

Jesus died to effect change in this world and allow others to live the life God intended for them.[441] Putting your life in God's hands may not be the easiest choice, but it is the best. People need our help, and what are we willing to risk to see them free? We start changing the world by changing ourselves and being good to those who cannot repay us. When we stand for others, we stand for the world. Stand up and be counted, putting it all in God's hands.

> **Prayer:** Father, you know the convictions in my heart that guide my standing. I ask that you give me boldness, and I will put my life in your hands to make a difference. Stir me up in love and good works. I pray for the development of our society's social and economic fabric and that we show mutual concern for all. I appreciate all you gave up to save me, and I ask you to put me in a position to assist others in the name of Jesus. Amen.

---

[440] Ephesians 2:2
[441] John 10:10

Running Into Things

---∗---

Proverbs 4:18-19 But the path of the righteous is like the dawning light that shines more and more until the perfect day. The way of the wicked is like darkness. They don't know what they stumble over.

he walk of the righteous is not like the sun, but compares to the pathway the light takes, which gets brighter as the sun rises to its peak. The same light that appears dim at first shines brightly as more time passes. When we start traveling the road to righteousness, it seems like darkness is all around us, but a little more time with God will reveal our light.[442] People struggle to see the new light because of the darkness of our past. The light is where we fellowship with God; His presence will light our path as we press forward.[443]

The wicked stumble because they don't walk where God brings light.[444] When we live according to our own understanding, we run into trouble. The path of the righteous may seem a little dark at first, but the wicked's way is total darkness. The wicked stagger, seeing everyone else's problems yet can't see the log in their own eyes.[445] When we don't deal with our issues, we will stumble into things and wonder why there is so

---

[442] John 8:12
[443] 1 John 1:7
[444] John 3:20
[445] Matthew 7:3-5

much pain. The wicked are often bolder, stumbling in the dark, than we are walking with the light.

Stumbling is not the same as falling. There is a chance that those walking in darkness will run into Christ and turn on the lights.[446] At times, the righteous may become embittered at the wicked, not considering that they stumble because they don't see. Those who do see clearly should walk the path that gains light as we go. Others will learn they can walk without stumbling when they see our walk. You are the light in the world. Let your light shine like the noonday, so others will follow Christ and see that perfect day.

Prayer: I ask you to lead me in paths of righteousness and watch over every footstep I take. Shine the light of your instruction to prevent me from tripping when I am led into the wilderness or other dark areas to walk. I thank you for always being with me. I proclaim that better days are on the horizon. Strengthen my heart and mind so that I might serve and be a light when the times of blessing and refreshing draw near, in the precious name of Jesus. Amen.

---

[446] Psalm 119:105

Harvest Time

***Galatians 6:9 Let's not be weary in doing good, for
we will reap in due season if we don't give up***

Nothing you do goes unnoticed by God; if you do well, you will reap a harvest. Interestingly, scriptures frequently compare expected rewards to the agricultural cycle.[447] Our obedience prepares the ground. Each God-led deed we perform is like a seed planted. Our faith uproots the weeds that would harm the seed. Our worship and prayers nourish and water the spiritual seed in our souls, and God causes the growth.[448] For a believer, this is our daily well-doing; we cannot afford to grow weary in it.

The phrase "we will reap" means that the time of blessing is the most active.[449] Many believers approach harvest time as a time to sit back; however, harvest reflects the work that has been done in us. Harvest meant you had to reap by cutting the grain from the root (remove the past), thresh by beating it to remove the stalk (watch your attachments), gather it into bundles (fellowship), and then winnow the grain to separate the head from the chaff (sanctify). The head was crushed by grinding to be useful (anointed by trials). This process required considerable effort.

---

[447] Exodus 23:16

[448] 2 Corinthians 3:6-7

[449] Matthew 9:37-38

Some wait on their harvest; others go out to reap it. Each of us has a due season when we can reap the benefits of what we have sown.[450] At this time, you must move quickly to get your work done. The grain may shatter, spoil, or suffer weather damage if harvesting is not timely. Not to mention that birds will steal from your harvest if you wait. We must focus more on the Lord's work while He blesses us. Wake up and encourage yourself in the Lord. Your harvest is waiting. Commit yourself to walking as an obedient servant of God and reap from what you have sown.

Prayer: Lord, help me to know my seasons of preparing, plowing, sowing, watering, nurturing, reaping, and resting. Each has its purpose for my growth and blessing; I declare your favor as I walk in them. I ask you to make my ground fruitful and bring your abundance that supplies me with more than I need. Let charity rest in my soul so others may reap the corners of my field. To you be the glory forever and ever, Amen.

[450] 2 Corinthians 9:6-8

Keep Me In The Right Position

---⟡---

Ezekiel 11:4 Therefore prophesy against them. Prophesy, son of man."

In today's world, many sinners often think of God as harmless. You may ask why. It is because God is quick to forgive and slow to judge.[451] People seem to think that delayed judgment is an escape. God is not naïve or ignorant but is altogether righteous. Delayed judgment is His way of giving us a chance to repent and return to His good graces. He desires that we be drawn to Him so He can help and strengthen us.[452] Nevertheless, many had not learned the lesson He tried to teach Israel before He sent Ezekiel to prophesy against them.[453]

Even within the church, some will perform offensive acts against God and say that because of His love, they will escape judgment.[454] The word stands against them. The word above, translated as "against," is the Hebrew "Leeyhem," which means from above, over, or upon. The word suggests one who is above, lowering the state or position of someone below. Rejecting God's word lowers our position with God, trapping us in the pit of our sins.

---

[451] Numbers 14:18
[452] Isaiah 55:1-3
[453] Ezekiel 11:1-3
[454] Psalm 94:3-10

Ambrose said, "The devil's snare does not catch you unless the devil's bait first catches you." Most of us don't realize how trapped in rebellion we are. Satan loves a compromised walk because it gives false security while, at the same time, opening doors to him.[455] Compromisers hope God will violate His word to judge the unfaithful because of His love. How long will we lower ourselves and fall for the devil's lies before we step out of the trap?[456] Brothers and sisters, stand on the right side of God and don't fall into a trap.

> **Prayer:** Lord, I accept your correction and shut the door to demonic encroachment, being left in the pit of despair. I confess my faults to repair the breaches in our relationship. I ask you to lift me up and not take me down. Restore my zeal and passion for a straightforward relationship with you. I entrust you with my entire life. Lead and guide me to the truth, in the name of Jesus Christ, Amen.

---

[455] Ephesians 4:27-29
[456] Psalm 40:2-4

Enabled to Serve

---◆---

1 Timothy 1:12 I thank him who enabled me,
Christ Jesus our Lord, because he counted
me faithful, appointing me to service,

At its root, an enabler means one who helps another to achieve something. People approach enablers negatively because they often allow vices to continue. However, Christ is an enabler, not of vice but of victory.[457] The Greek "Endunamoo," translated as enabled, means to put dynamic power, explosive ability, or tremendous strength into. Christ offers us the dynamic power to change, the explosive ability to break free from bondages, and the strength to trust Him in all things. Christ has enabled us to live victoriously.[458]

We started by trusting in Christ to enable us, but how many have begun to trust in our ability? People are mistaken in their efforts to fix themselves, thinking they can only begin to dedicate themselves to the Lord's service when they have cleaned up their act. Not realizing that the power to be a Christian does not originate in us, but in Christ.[459] We must constantly trust in the empowerment of Jesus Christ to help us in our daily walk. Without Him, we can do nothing to please God.

---

[457] Philippians 4:13
[458] 2 Peter 1:3-8
[459] John 15:4-5

There is a danger in thinking that we can keep clean by ourselves after God has cleansed us from our sins. That is Satan's tactic.[460] The tendency to lean on our own strength opens the door to disappointment. Then, after we fail, guilt settles in, and we experience spiritual withdrawal, separating ourselves from the only one who can enable us to get right. Paul didn't just trust in His faithfulness. He trusted that Christ accounted him faithful, and as he surrendered, He would empower him to stay that way.[461] Take an active role in showing appreciation, allowing Christ to lead the work. Trust and lean on Him as your enabler.

Prayer: Lord, bestow power that transforms my life spiritually and gives me new abilities and confidence. I pray that you will allow me to overcome my anxieties, shortcomings, and flesh. I always triumph with you. Allow me to stroll in your holy domain, where I have a strong bond of fellowship with you. I commit my entire being to you and ask that you watch over my family, renewing our goodwill and unity. I pray your hand of loving grace be always with me, in the name of Jesus Christ, Amen.

---

[460] Galatians 3:1-3
[461] Psalm 20:7

A Time for Prayer

---------★---------

Esther 1:12 But the queen Vashti refused to come at the king's commandment by the eunuchs. Therefore the king was very angry, and his anger burned in him.

It was a time of peace and merriment, and in his third year as king, Ahasuerus celebrated for 187 days. One hundred eighty days with the princes and the final seven days with the people included.[462] While hosting a celebration for the women, Vashti received a royal summons.[463] People speculate about many things, but we are unsure of her reasons for not coming. Her refusal closed the door for her, yet it opened a new chapter for the deliverance of God's people.

Tradition has the event starting at the Jewish New Year in spring. According to the Jewish calendar, three months had 30 days, and three months had 29 days. That means it was the tenth of Tishri (Yom Kippur, AKA the Day of Atonement) when Vashti refused to show herself before the king.[464] The rebuilt temple is significant for Yom Kippur, as it was the day when the priest would pray and go beyond the veil to make atonement for the people, and the prayer that day provided for their future victory.[465] When you pray to God, He begins to shift things to work in your favor.

---

[462] Esther 1:4-5
[463] Esther 1:9-10
[464] Leviticus 23:27-28
[465] Leviticus 16:11-17

Often, we don't understand our circumstances, but if we could see from God's perspective, we would understand that He is working for our good.[466] Vashti angered the king and opened the door for a new queen four years later, and for the deliverance of all the Jews in the province.[467] The goodness of God shows us how He worked them out of bondage before they even got in. Before the schemes of Haman even began, the way of escape through Esther was made. God prepares a way out of every trial before you go into it. Remember, prayer prepares and provides for your triumph. Pray today and win tomorrow.

> **Prayer:** Redeemer, thank you for working behind the scenes for my favor and deliverance. I thank you for preparing a way out before I get into trouble. Let my trust rest in you, and continue your work of delivering the souls of my family. Grant me favor with people in high places as I follow your plan. In Jesus' name. Amen.

[466] Isaiah 64:4
[467] Esther 2:16

Getting Our Lives in Order
to Receive the Blessing

---⚓---

1 Corinthians 14:40 Let all things be done decently and in order.

Doing things in decency and order starts with being decent and in order ourselves.[468] The word decency is the Greek Eusxemonōs, meaning having good, respectable, modest, or noble form. The word "order" comes from the military term Taksis, which deals with a detailed ordering of rank. Together, they mean that interactions within the church should always be respectful and, in proper turn, allow each person's input to be valued, with consideration given to age, wisdom, or rank.[469]

Dr. Phillip Goudeax once asked people, "Would you put your money in a machine that reads "Out of order?" They would say no. What about putting your paycheck through a broken ATM? Again, the answer was no. If we won't put our money into something that's out of order, how come we expect God to pour His riches and blessings upon us when our lives are out of order with His will and plan?[470] Most of us have been waiting for God's blessing, but are we in a state of readiness to receive it? God is the God of order and will not pour all He has into someone out of order.

---

[468] Psalm 37:23

[469] Job 32:7-9

[470] Exodus 20:6

Many are waiting for many promises and blessings, but the Lord has been waiting for us to line up in our homes, ministries, and jobs. We must align ourselves and our attitudes with God's plan if we expect to receive anything from Him.[471] Belonging to and supporting ministry, paying our bills promptly, and spending time with our families are just a few things we must do. If we are going to reap a harvest, we have to position ourselves under the floodgates of heaven.[472] Line up and get yourself back in order with God.

> **Prayer:** Lord, I ask you to take anything out of order in my life and place it in order. I surrender to your authority and declare that you will order my steps. Show me what I must do to open the floodgates of heaven, receive the promised blessings showered into my life. I pray for order in my life, family, and church, and that you will be pleased and favor us in the name of Jesus. Amen.

---

[471] James 4:3
[472] Malachi 3:10

Finding Yourself

---✦---

Ezra 2:62 These sought their place among those who were registered by genealogy, but they were not found; therefore they were deemed disqualified and removed from the priesthood.

Cyrus, the king of Persia, issued an edict that the people taken captive during the Babylonian reign should return and rebuild the house of the Lord their God.[473] Yet, they could not serve their purpose because some had lost their identity during captivity. The temple registered priests from the time they were three years old and required them to sanctify themselves in holiness.[474] Yet they could not be found. The process of setting them apart had not occurred, so they were priests without a priesthood because they couldn't prove who they were.

We lose part of ourselves when imprisoned by thoughts, habits, or individuals. Often, we don't realize how much of ourselves we have lost until we come out of our situations. The loss of identity prompts us to seek rediscovery, reassurance, or reinvention. Bondage robs us of more than time; it takes custody of our identity and confines our purpose. We must deny ourselves to grow, change, and serve our purpose, but not lose

---

[473] Ezra 1:1-4
[474] 2 Chronicles 31:16-18

191

ourselves.[475] Many find themselves free of bondage and still bereft of purpose and direction.

Christ's priesthood does not concern genealogy, but we must still find our identity in Him.[476] Many operate with a partial identity, knowing they are a child of God but not realizing the portion of identity that identifies their purpose and call.[477] To build the kingdom of God, we must know who we are and whose we are. Often, we discover our complete identity not by seeking it, but by seeking to understand who Jesus is to us.[478] If problems, habits, or people's expectations have robbed you of who you are, find yourself in Christ, identify with Him, and receive God in His name. You will never be lost again.

Prayer: Father, you had a purpose when you created me. Please help me to fulfill the calling you have set for me with integrity and passion. Please send me the perfect partners to work with so that I can achieve your purpose with joy and fulfillment. Set my heart's desire to do your will and help build your kingdom, in Christ's name, Amen.

---

[475] Luke 9:23
[476] Hebrews 7:11-16
[477] Jeremiah 1;5
[478] Matthew 16:16-18

Grateful to Share

---✦---

Acts 2:11 Cretans and Arabians—we hear them
speaking in our languages the mighty works of God!"

It was a miraculous beginning for the church, as the Holy Spirit now empowered the fledgling disciples to be witnesses for Jesus Christ. This event fulfilled the promise given to them before Christ ascended.[479] They would wait, gather, pray, and fellowship for ten days before the Holy Spirit would come. Fifteen languages from three continents, and each understood these Galileans speaking the praises of God in their native tongues.[480] How they spoke was important, but what they spoke was of equal importance because it speaks of their mission to be witnesses to Christ.

We learn from Acts that witnessing is simply speaking to people what you have spoken in praise to God. As the disciples spoke the praises of God, it gave testimony to all those gathered for Pentecost. Witnessing should not be a frightful experience. The church would praise God for what He has done, then share with others why they praised Him. The testimony of our praise directs others to the worship of God, which is the spirit of all preaching and prophecy.[481] Living a life that praises God in all situations before others draws them to ask questions about our faith.

---

[479] Acts 1:4-8
[480] Acts 2:1-11
[481] Revelation 19:10

Thankfulness is essential because gratitude brings joy, and expressing that joy before others attracts them to God. The word of Christ should live richly in our hearts, and we are to share it through speaking our praise.[482] Regardless of our situation, if we take a moment to praise God for what we have and then share that with others, we bear witness to His greatness. We have two testimonies to share: our own testimony and Christ's testimony, which we refer to as the gospel. Sharing our thankfulness to God in both is our witness to save others from sin.[483]

Prayer: Father, give me the strength to continue singing your praise so that others may come to know you. I apologize if I made witnessing difficult. I express my gratitude, and as I witness, I ask you to do marvelous things in my life so that I will have more to say. Let my favor be commensurate with my testimony so both your kingdom and I will be blessed. I thank you and ask you for the power to share, in Jesus' name. Amen.

---

[482] Colossians 3:16
[483] Romans 1:16-17

Blessing Folk

Ruth 2:12 May Yahweh repay your work,
and a full reward be given to you from
Yahweh, the God of Israel, under whose
wings you have come to take refuge."

There is a tradition in scripture that modern believers mostly overlook. That is a pronounced blessing. A blessing would be pronounced over their lives whenever the people encountered great faith through acts or great deliverance.[484] It is good that we praise God in those situations, but what about pronouncing a blessing over the person God has delivered? The pronounced blessing has become something left for altar calls and benedictions in church. Nevertheless, scripturally, it was a powerful tool to strengthen and encourage those with a great faith test.[485]

Pronouncing a blessing over someone encourages the one receiving the blessing and lifts God's presence in the atmosphere.[486] The blessing verbally expresses God's grace and power upon the one blessed.[487] It imparts faith, peace, authority, and grace. The pronounced blessing blesses God so that He will bless you. The hearer's submission to the blessing allows God to penetrate the deepest places of their faith and restore lost hope. It

---

[484] Genesis 15:18-21
[485] Matthew 15:28
[486] Isaiah 65:16
[487] Deuteronomy 1:11

causes doubt, fear, and despair to dispel from their lives. Whenever you notice God doing something in someone's life, you should pounce on it by pronouncing a blessing.

Naomi first blessed Ruth upon her return to Bethlehem.[488] Then Boaz began to bless her after hearing about Ruth's faithfulness to Naomi following the death of her husband and sons. The blessing they pronounce sets in motion the events that transpired in the rest of the book. The blessing became the pivotal point at which Ruth received favor from both God and man. You may not have known, but your future may hinge on the pronounced blessing upon your life. Get with God and start pronouncing blessings.

Prayer: Heavenly Father, from whom all blessings flow, help me recognize the chances to encourage faith and bless others while declaring your favor. You have given us the power to declare grace over individuals, communities, and issues. Wherever I go, I will pray for and proclaim the impending blessing, healing, and deliverance as you fill me with your Spirit and raise me from doubt and despair. I pray for a blessing on my life and family and for faithfulness to your kingdom in the name of Jesus Christ. Amen.

---

[488] Ruth 1:9

A Righteous Return on Sin

Obadiah 1:15 For the day of Yahweh is near all the nations! As you have done, it will be done to you. Your deeds will return upon your own head.

Think about your nation's history. What are the atrocities committed by the government against those who could not defend themselves all in the name of the greater good? The day of the Lord is when nations reap what they have sown.[489] The time we call the great tribulation is when God pours out His wrath on the world. However, the tribulation is not a judgment based upon individual deeds; that judgment happens during the white throne judgment. The tribulation is a judgment of the sins of nations.

You may wonder how the judgments fall in order. First is the judgment of the saints,[490] where the unfruitful and unfaithful are left.[491] Next is the judgment on the nations, we call the great tribulation.[492] Then, after the 1000-year reign of Christ comes the great white throne, where believers and unbelievers are separated to go into judgment.[493] Those of us who have been able to stand in the judgment receive our final judgment at the

---

[489] Galatians 6:7

[490] 1 Peter 4:17

[491] Matthew 24:36-44

[492] Revelation Chapters 5-20

[493] Revelation 20:11-15

seat of Christ, where he rewards us for what we have done as believers.[494] Whether it is the individual, family, community, or nation, the judgment of God will return to them for what they did.

Many think that God's wrath is anger, but it's not. Wrath is the righteous return on our sins stored because of His mercy. His mercy holds back the return on our sins until we are saved or die in them.[495] Christ took the punishment for our sins so that we can deflect the wrath stored against us onto Him through repentance in Christ. Either it will return upon your head, or you will make Christ your head. Whether we stand with Christ in the judgment or against Him, it's our choice.

> **Prayer:** Heavenly Father, I stand with you, repenting from sin and committing to Christ. Show me how to accumulate blessings rather than wrath. I pray for my nation to turn to the righteousness of your word that we do justice, love mercy, and walk humbly with you. Fill my life, family, and home with your grace as I ask you to help me live a life that pleases you in the name of Jesus Christ. Amen.

---

[494] Romans 14:10
[495] John 8:23-24

One Day You'll Understand

---✦---

Jeremiah 23:20 Yahweh's anger will not return until he
has executed and performed the intents of his heart.
In the latter days, you will understand it perfectly.

One thing no one likes to do is suffer. Whether God sends the suffering, or it is stirred up by the devil or caused by our actions, we want to avoid it. Suffering comes from pain with an often unrevealed purpose.[496] Suffering reveals what we are attached to, and if we aren't sure that God is for and with us, it will cause us to question our protection, provision, and the plan of God. When we are in pain from grief, sickness, or distress, we often do not understand why it is happening to us. Yet if we seek God, the reasons we suffer are revealed as our healing occurs.[497]

There are good reasons why we have to wait for the answers. The main reason is that while you are in pain, the reason for that pain never seems justified.[498] Most of us would reject the purpose of our pain because we are still feeling it. The reality of our suffering dims our objectivity as to why we are suffering. Donald Miller said, "Suffering ceases to be suffering when you have a redemptive perspective." Therefore, we often don't accept the reasons for our suffering until we make it to the other side.[499]

---

[496] Romans 5:3-5
[497] 2 Corinthians 4:8-10
[498] Psalm 38:13-15
[499] 1 Peter 1:6-7

One day, we will reconsider why we suffered in the first place. At that time, we will place value on the purpose of what we suffered in the past, allowing us to see our lives in the bigger plan.[500] When we view our situation from the vantage point of heaven, we gain a greater knowledge of how we fit into God's design. Healing is, therefore, the revelation of God's purpose for you to live by and a glimpse of His redemption of the world.[501] Let us fix our minds on Christ, who suffered to make us more like Him.

> **Prayer:** Father, I often don't understand why I go through certain situations. But in the latter days, I will understand it perfectly. I have faith in the arrival of my solutions, and I ask you to uphold me while you mold me into your image and will. I ask you to sustain me as you conform me to your image. Please give me the wisdom and be my shield, strength, and help in times of need. Thank you for your provision and all you have done for me, in the name of Jesus, Amen.

---

[500] James 1:2-4
[501] Philippians 3:10

Walking the Gray Line

— ⚓ —

1 Corinthians 8:12 Thus, sinning against the brothers, and wounding their conscience when it is weak, you sin against Christ.

What is sin? Simply put, it is a transgression of the law.[502] However, certain things not restricted by the law are not sins within themselves but remain on the border of sin. These lay in the area between what you can and should do. They leave us with questions such as, Can a believer smoke, drink, or gamble? They are not virtues because they have no redeeming qualities; nevertheless, they do not transgress the line of vices because they are not wicked when under control. These are potential bondages that the scriptures refer to as weights that can entangle us.[503]

Not everything permissible is good to do. The question remains: where does a believer draw the line? The answer does not lie within you but with those around you. It is an answer to their conscience.[504] First Corinthians chapters 8 through 10 address the gray areas of the faith, where actions may not be directly sinful but may entangle others and lead them to sin. As believers, we are free to follow God and not bound by superstitious

---

[502] 1 John 3:4

[503] Hebrews 12:1

[504] 1 Corinthians 10:23-33

practices. Yet our freedom comes with the responsibility to consider others in our actions.[505]

Being Inconsiderate of the views and thoughts of others is a sin against Christ, who redeemed them. The sin is that we use our freedom with pride and do not consider what may hurt our brethren. It's not that they are weak in faith but weak in conscience, meaning you can draw them into condemnation and bondage. This is why the scriptures say that whatever is not of faith is a sin.[506] If drinking offends a brother around you, you shouldn't drink. If gambling offends them, then don't gamble. Consider others and never use your freedom in a way that can put another in bondage.[507]

Prayer: Father, I thank you for my freedom in you. Please help me to be conscious of the temple of my body, the disposition of my soul, and the conscience of others who stumble at my liberty. Help me stay clear of anything that may lead to future bondage or ruin the faith of others. I can do so many other things that will delight me. I offer you my all and ask that you continue to give me yours; in Jesus' name, Amen.

---

[505] 1 Corinthians 8:13
[506] Romans 14:23
[507] 1 Corinthians 8:7-11

In the Face of Christ

---✦---

2 Corinthian 4:6 seeing it is God who said, "Light will shine out of darkness," who has shone in our hearts to give the light of the knowledge of the glory of God in the face of Jesus Christ.

There is power in the word of God to dispel all darkness. The first thing we know about the voice of God is that when he saw the darkness, he spoke, "Let there be light."[508] The first principle God has taught us is that God's word can go into the darkest places and bring forth Light. We do not have to fear the unknown because God calls light to shine in the darkness. Darkness has neither power over light nor the ability to comprehend the depth of the one called the Light.[509] Darkness dispels wherever there is the Light of God's word.

This same God who spoke Light into the world has shone forth His Light in the hearts of the believer so that we may have the knowledge of His glorious light revealed in the face of Jesus. The more time we spend in His presence, the greater glory we will partake in. This is to unite us with God and bring His presence wherever we go.[510] We discover God's glory when we allow the Lord to shine in our hearts as we seek Christ. It

---

[508] Genesis 1:3-5
[509] John 1:5
[510] John 17:22

is in the face of Christ that the glory of God is shown to us so that we can partake of His divine presence.[511]

The revelation of God's glory comes through illumination. Our hearts must be free from darkness for our minds to perceive God's glory. When Philip said, "Show us the Father," Jesus replied, "If you have seen me, you have seen Him."[512] Jesus knew that His flesh veiled the glory of God, and to see Him was to behold the glory. Those whose hearts have Christ's light and continue in faith find God's glory.[513] Christ lifts the veil, and when you seek Him, you find God's glory.[514] Let Christ manifest in your heart and see His glory.

Prayer: God, fill my heart with the knowledge of your glory so I may know and experience your presence. I ask for your help illuminating my path and bringing light to all the dark places in my life. Let my life serve as a lamp to reflect your light so that others can emerge from their pits of darkness. Thank you for bringing me to the light with your mercy, strength, and healing power, in the name of Jesus Christ. Amen.

---

[511] 2 Peter 1:3-8
[512] John 14:8-9
[513] John 11:10
[514] 2 Corinthians 3:13-15

Maintaining control of your spirit

---✦---

Philippians 2:14 Do all things without complaining and arguing,

Murphy's law says, "If it is possible for something to go wrong, it will." In short, we should expect difficulties to arise, so we had better be ready to face them. However, too often, we face our problems by complaining and disputing. We live as if we believe everything will always go according to plan. If there is little deviation from the plan, we either complain because it's not right or dispute with those who are interfering with it.[515] Complaints and disputes often focus on what isn't working, while ignoring the things that are going well. The answer to your problem may require more effort, but it won't require a complaint.

Complaining and disputing are not constructive but rather destructive acts.[516] They add to the existing strife and confusion. There is never a good reason to worsen a bad situation, but that is what complaining and disputing do. We are to let neither our circumstances nor our environment disrupt our spirit. As believers, we are not mere men and women. We have the power to control the situation by controlling ourselves.[517] As long as we complain, we submit ourselves to contention instead of taking

---

[515] James 5:9
[516] Numbers 11:1-3
[517] Proverbs 25:28

authority over our situation. Every problem we face has the providence of God attached to it.

Venting and complaining are similar, but have a fatal difference. Venting is a quick release to let go of frustration. Complaining is a passive disposition that doesn't act to change things. When we take our complaints to God, we are venting to the one who can do something rather than spoiling everyone's mood.[518] When we stop complaining, we start believing. The Lord is the one who fights our battles, so when we dispute, we step in front of God and mess things up. Complaining and disputing are issues of faith and submission.[519] God's law is more potent than Murphy's. We must submit to letting God handle our problems. If we keep the Lord in control of our lives, we will keep control of our spirit and won't complain or dispute.

> **Prayer:** Lord, help me do all things with a calm spirit. I vent my feelings to you so that you can help me change. Help me stand confident in you when things aren't going my way. Give me joy unspeakable. Erase frustration, anger, and strife from my life and replace them with your unsurpassed peace in the great name of our Savior Jesus Christ, Amen.

---

[518] Psalm 55:17
[519] Numbers 21:5-9

Clever Little Devils

Luke 11:52 Woe to you lawyers! For you took away the key of knowledge. You didn't enter in yourselves, and those who were entering in, you hindered."

C.S. Lewis once said, "Education without values, as useful as it is, seems rather to make a man a more clever devil." That is what the scribes were producing: clever devils who knew God's word but never entered into knowing God. Knowledge became a façade to mask their rebellion against spiritual transformation, holiness, and love.[520] People admired them for their appearance of dedication and consecration to the Lord. However, privately, the word has not penetrated their heart; they were ambitious and sensual. They stole the key of knowledge that could have unlocked the people's hearts for genuine transformation.[521]

God does not desire us to know without receiving the values that the knowledge brings. We are not just to learn about Christ but to learn Christ's ways.[522] His heart, compassion, and attitude are to become ours. Nevertheless, sometimes we are hindered from entering into the life-changing power of God because we allow others' traditions, in the form of opinions and formality, to erect a blockade in front of our hearts.[523] God

---

[520] 2 Peter 3:2-5
[521] Matthew 23:13
[522] Ephesians 4:18-20
[523] Mark 7:13-15

is calling His church to something new so He can do a new thing inside and through us.[524]

Unless you possess the key of knowledge, you may become a clever little devil instead of a loving, Spirit-filled saint. When we learn the word, we should see the purpose, holiness, and love of God in every verse. The key of knowledge still rests with Christ.[525] It is yours for the taking. Clever devils, in the guise of lovers of God, have obstructed the way of God. Woe to them. Nevertheless, as we seek to know God fully, His grace is multiplied.[526] We can enter into a complete and liberating relationship with the Lord. With Christ's love as the key to knowledge, the Lord will continually penetrate our hearts as we learn of Him.

Prayer: Lord, make my life about knowing and experiencing the transforming love of Christ. By your Spirit, grant me wisdom, and keep the cunning little devils out of my thoughts, life, and family. I stand against everything having a form of godliness but denying the power thereof. Keep me in your loving grace, in the precious name of Jesus, Amen.

---

[524] Isaiah 43:18-21
[525] John 5:38-42
[526] John 1:16-18

It's Only For A Season

---✦---

Psalms 126:6 He who goes out weeping,
carrying seed for sowing, will certainly come
again with joy, carrying his sheaves.

Trials come, and that's an indisputable fact. People say life is the cruelest instructor we will ever meet. Sometimes, life slaps you in the face, but it is only for a season.[527] What do we mean by only for a season? Well, the hard times don't have to last. We will go through difficult times; however, what you do during those times will determine how you come out of them.[528] The Hebrew word Bakah, translated as "Weep," deals with someone who laments in hardship or humility but moves forward.

The one who goes forth bearing seed while weeping is the one who still sows in their pain. Life may hurt you, but it does not have to change you.[529] The seeds sown in our poverty or our pain are seeds of promise. No, I'm not talking about sowing money but sowing faithfulness. Money is only a tiny portion of sowing faithfulness to God's word. The one who sows faithfulness even in the most difficult of times will undoubtedly find themselves one day rejoicing because they will force a new season to come.[530] They will have a harvest and a time of rejoicing.

---

[527] Ecclesiastes 3:1-4

[528] Isaiah 61:3-4

[529] 2 Thessalonians 3:3-5

[530] Hosea 10:12

God's goodness forces a change in the seasons of your life.[531] So many people talk about what they don't have to do because it won't affect their salvation. You don't have to attend church, give, or even read scripture to maintain salvation. These are essential for sanctification, not salvation; without them, you will stagnate your growth. In their weeping, they refuse to sow and never see change. Doubtless, they will have no harvest to rejoice over.[532] Life will come at you hard, but it must only be for a season. If you bring seed even in times of weeping, joy and abundance will bring you into a new season.

Prayer: Lord, keep my hand on the plow, moving forward. I won't turn back because blessings are in store for me. Despite my hardships, a fruitful harvest will appear. My times of rejoicing are near. Help me maintain my integrity so that my season of weeping may become a joyous one. Thank you for the good things coming as I release what's in my hand to you in the name of Jesus Christ. Amen.

---

[531] Ezekiel 34:26-27
[532] Proverbs 11:23-25

Great Things In Small Packages

---✠---

Haggai 2:9 'The latter glory of this house will be greater than the former,' says Yahweh of Armies; 'and in this place I will give peace,' says Yahweh of Armies."

It was the time of the temple's rebuilding, yet it was not the same. It looked like nothing compared to the temple that once was.[533] They began to see this new temple as only a shell of the former one. Nevertheless, this was God's doing.[534] The Lord downscaled the temple but would make the glory of the new temple outshine the previous glory. The time of looking at the splendor of the temple was over. Now, God wants us to focus on His presence. He would not give it glory based on appearance but on His peace and presence.

When we look at things with our eyes, we often don't see what God has placed on the inside.[535] We often view downsizing as a curse, so we never see the glory that lies within. We become fooled, thinking we are not blessed unless we increase. A bigger home, a larger bank account, the bigger, the better, has become the motto of our age. However, God puts His glory in small, unassuming vessels, giving us great things in small

---

[533] Haggai 2:2-3
[534] Ezra 3:12-13
[535] 2 Corinthians 4:7

packages.[536] When you don't have as much as you would like, He offers the greater glory you need.

The Lord desires that His people keep their eyes on Him and glory in His presence.[537] The temple's former glory never brought happiness, contentment, or faithfulness to the people. However, the latter glory, the glory of a greater manifestation of God's presence, brings all this and more. We must learn that having great things does not mean God is with you. He is more concerned that you possess the peace that comes from Him than that you possess all the silver and gold this world has to offer. Like children, we sometimes look to things instead of the bringer of all things. The glory God offers in this latter house will outshine all that we have been looking for because the latter glory is the glory of the Lord.[538]

> **Prayer:** Lord, help me to declutter my life and do more with less. I long for better, not bigger, and your presence more than presents. Give me peace as a blessing for my soul. I place the things of the past behind me and reach for your grace and truth. Please help me to keep my eyes focused on you and grant me your favor in removing my doubts, distress, and debts; in Jesus' name, Amen.

---

[536] Job 8:7
[537] Psalm 105:4-8
[538] Revelation 21:23

Headed Toward Death

---⟡---

Ezekiel 18:24 "But when the righteous turns away from his righteousness, and commits iniquity, and does according to all the abominations that the wicked man does, should he live? None of his righteous deeds that he has done will be remembered. In his trespass that he has trespassed, and in his sin that he has sinned, in them he shall die.

In the eyes of the Lord, the death of His saints is precious,[539] but He takes no pleasure in those who turn from righteousness. It is marvelous how heaven rejoices when the saints die. It brings new testimony and fellowship to the heavenly realm. Nevertheless, the wicked are headed toward death, bringing no pleasure or great testimony of God's transforming power.[540] There is only a looking on with pity at how pride, deception, and stubbornness kept another person from the graces of God.

God is the God of near-endless chances.[541] He gives opportunities to repent and come to Him and live. It is sad how unbelievers head toward death. However, the Lord is not only talking about them. Believers sometimes flirt with and get pulled into sin. When believers fall into sin, the world will forget all their good deeds. When we sin, we risk having all our

---

[539] Psalm 116:15

[540] Ezekiel 18:23

[541] Lamentations 3:21-23

righteous deeds removed and dying in sin because we have turned away from the Lord.[542]

The soul that sins shall die.[543] How well we have lived for the Lord will never be questioned. However, sin can tempt the best of us because of its pleasures.[544] The pleasures attached to sin are like the bait for a trap. They allure us to trap us and bring us toward death.[545] Let us consider our ways and the things trying to pull us away from God. Stay on the righteous path and have your deeds remembered and your soul delivered.

Prayer: Keep me under the influence of your Holy Spirit and aid me in avoiding the sin trap. Temptations are continually before me, but I chose you, and I need your strength to continue on the right path. Keep reminding my heart to return to your word and repair the rifts that tempt me to stray. I need your love and presence in my life, home, and family, in the name of Jesus, Amen.

---

[542] Proverbs 21:16
[543] Ezekiel 18:20
[544] Hebrews 11:25
[545] 2 Peter 2:21

The Power to Become

John 1:12 But as many as received him, to them he gave the right to become God's children, to those who believe in his name.

When speaking of time, the present is a moment of transition. It is a state of action and becoming. However, many of us get stuck in activity but never become what we could be. Sometimes, we get so complacent in our walk with God that we stall.[546] We stop seeking more and replace our relationship with the Lord with rituals and traditions, which aren't bad, but can replace our fellowship with God.[547] Yet Christ daily offers us the Power to Become. Have you thought recently of what God desires you to become?

Becoming a child of God speaks to our adoption as sons and daughters through faith, as well as our conformity to His image by faith. As many have received Him and believed in His name, He gave them the power to become more like Him.[548] Nevertheless, many settle for adoption only. He wants to give you the power to be so much more. All we have to do is believe in His name, receive what he brings us, and put it into practice. We can become bold in the faith, evangelists, healers, deliverers, prayer

---

[546] Zephaniah 1:12

[547] Colossians 2:8

[548] Galatians 4:18-19

warriors, comforters, helpers, teachers, and more.[549] If we believe in Christ, He will give us the power to become whatever He has put in our hearts or spoken into our lives.

What hinders our power to become: doubt, feelings of unworthiness, fear, unforgiveness, disobedience, selfishness, and pride. The power to become something new comes to those who will believe and receive it.[550] Becoming means you are on the road to possess all the Lord has for you. As you travel that road by faith, He will give you the Power to Become. God deposits gifts and character in the believer when we focus on Christ. Only then will you realize everything God has called you to be and walk as a child of the Most High.

Prayer: Heavenly Father, creator of all that is good, I ask you to place me on your potter's wheel and mold and shape me back to your image and likeness. I submit to your work in my life and on me. Please help me to leave behind negative thoughts, bad habits, and unfruitful speech. Because your Holy Spirit is still with me, my confidence in you will be strong enough to get me through. Grant me peace, favor, and a righteous heart of love by your grace, in Christ's transforming name and power. Amen.

---

[549] 1 Corinthians 15:10
[550] 1 John 3:21-22

Last Words

---·★·---

Revelation 22:21 The grace of the Lord Jesus
Christ be with all the saints. Amen.

The last words a person speaks often summarize their heart or intentions at that time. Winston Churchill's last words were, "I'm bored with it all." Queen Elizabeth, I said, "All my possessions for a moment of time." Harriet Tubman's last words were, "Swing low, sweet chariot." Though Jesus still speaks His last words from the cross, "Father, into your hands I commit my spirit."[551] Last words can be significant. The final words of scripture were a simple prayer. The grace of our Lord Jesus Christ be with you all, Amen.

John speaks to the seven churches, representing believers of all types, and records this prayer as the last written word of Scripture. God's desire is for us to know His grace. It is His grace that saves us[552] and supplies all we need.[553] God gives grace to the humble,[554] and we are to grow in it[555], and we can fall from it.[556] Grace is God's love in action. It looks to take a lousy moment or situation and make it better. We need God's grace to be

---

[551] Luke 23:46

[552] Ephesians 2:8

[553] 2 Corinthians 12:9

[554] James 4:6

[555] 2 Peter 3:18

[556] Galatians 5:4

who He wants us to be, have what He desires for us to have, and go where He leads us. Grace is to accompany us throughout our lives.

God's Grace changes attitudes, hearts, and desires. Grace shows God's kindness and mercy. His grace is beautiful in its simplicity and tragic in its cost on the cross. It is His unmerited favor and His **G**ifts **R**eceived **A**t **C**hrist's **E**xpense. His grace is what we need to get through our day. It takes our brokenness and mends us back together. Grace gives us favor with God and man. It gets us out of our jams and through our struggles. We need to pray that the grace of our Lord Jesus Christ is with us. May great grace be with you today.

Prayer: God, thank you for seeing me with eyes of grace. You have given me access to great grace through faith and the power of repentance. I need your grace. Deliver me from the evildoers' grasp and lead my mind, soul, and spirit to a good place. Let your presence and guiding touch surround me in every struggle. To heal my family and loved ones, I need your grace. Lead me by your Spirit and love in the name of Jesus Christ, Amen.

Most Blessed Forever

Psalm 21:6 For you make him most blessed forever.
You make him glad with joy in your presence.

When speaking of being most blessed forever, the psalmist focuses on one who is not seeking blessing but is seeking to delight in God. As he seeks God, blessings meet him.[557] He is most blessed forever because God knows that His desire is not for things but merely to seek His face. Like a 3-legged stool, his delight pivots on his trust and commitment, giving the Lord his heart, mind, and efforts. When we seek God, we will find Him and our hearts' desires, and we will become most blessed forever.[558]

When we seek the presence of the Lord, He will make us glad in it. Just as the rich reject those who seek a relationship to get their wealth, God also has standards. God invites us to seek His face and delights when our hearts naturally desire Him.[559] We will see His hand everywhere when we seek God's face in everything. The Lord will do anything for those who want His presence just because they delight in Him. This seeking is what it meant for Enoch to walk with God, why there were no others like Job in his time, and why Abraham was called God's friend.[560] They delighted in the Lord and were most blessed forever.

---

[557] Psalm 21:1-3

[558] Psalm 37:3-5

[559] Psalm 27:8

[560] 1 Chronicles 20:7

Where we are in our journey of faithfulness, delight, and appreciation of God will determine if we are most blessed forever. It is a place where our constant fellowship with the Lord brings us joy and life in its fullness.[561] Being most blessed forever is not only an attitude; it's an attitude that places you in the presence of God. In times when we don't feel the nearness of God, we must check our thoughts and motives, then delight in the fact that our love will draw Him again soon.[562] God is with us and desires to make us glad in His presence so we can be most blessed forever.

> **Prayer:** Lord, I desire the joy of your presence and to be most blessed forever. Teach me the steps to take and extract anything in my heart that hinders our relationship. Make me know what truly pleases you. I kneel at the foot of your throne, just wanting to know you. Continue to draw me near as I seek your kingdom and righteousness in the name of Christ Jesus. Amen.

---

[561] John 10:10
[562] James 4:7-10

What God Seeks

---⊹---

Ezekiel 22:30 "I sought for a man among them who would build up the wall and stand in the gap before me for the land, that I would not destroy it; but I found no one.

We search for a lot, but God seeks only a few things from us. The most well-known is that God seeks worshipers who will worship Him in spirit and truth.[563] We draw closest to God when we reflect God's image during worship. During worship, we release our problems and pick up His character. The second thing God seeks is for us to do right by others, which shows His love.[564] The third thing the Lord seeks is people after His heart who will follow Him wherever He may lead them.[565] The last thing He searches for is the intercessor. One who will build up the walls and stand in the gap before Him to preserve the land.

In Ezekiel's days, God searched far and wide for someone to intercede for the people, but He found none. Not a Priest, not a Levite, or a Prophet who would regularly pray and confess the sins of the people. Neither a King nor a Court Official would offer sacrifices with prayer so that judgment would not come upon the people. Idolatry ruled the land, and those still believing in God didn't pray. A few prophets faithfully warned them,

---

[563] John 4:23

[564] Micah 6:8

[565] 1 Samuel 13:14

but few stood in the gap and prayed.[566] When we intercede, we place ourselves in the shoes of another, gaining the compassion to see their need.

God is looking for us to stand before Him with the passion to pray. The intercessors moved God's heart and the Holy Spirit to avoid destruction and hold back judgment on the earth. We must wake up our minds to think like Christ and pray. The Thessalonian church knew what held back and restrained the man of sin.[567] We also would know if we prayed in the power of the Holy Spirit. God wants His people to pray for nations, churches, and individuals. He is searching for one who will stand in the gap. Will he find anyone there?

> **Prayer:** Heavenly Father, I come today not for myself but for others in my life. I ask you to pour grace on the hurting, heal the sick, and restore sight to those blinded by the world. Prompt the hearts of your people to pray and reach out to the lost. Cause us to meet the needs of people experiencing homelessness, widows, and strangers. I pray the compassion in my heart will reflect your love for people to be set free and restored to wholeness in your presence, in the name of Jesus Christ. Amen.

---

[566] Jeremiah 44:4-6
[567] 2 Thessalonians 2:3-7)

Give Yourself Away

---✦---

2 John 1:6 This is love, that we should walk according to his commandments. This is the commandment, even as you heard from the beginning, that you should walk in it.

How do you express your love for God? It's not just through your presence, prayer, or praise. All of these things can be done even by the God hater, who at times mimics the things of God but in their hearts reject Him.[568] Some will pray and praise God because they want a plate of food. But like Esau, they serve their appetites. Others will speak of Christ as the seven sons of Sceva, but they never knew Him.[569] Some, like Ananias and Saphira, will do great deeds only to gain recognition.[570] These were not expressions of faithful love but of pride. In true love, you give yourself away.

As a virgin bride gives herself to her true love on their wedding night, true love expresses itself to God through our faithfulness to His commandments.[571] Our expression of love for God is walking in His commandments, denying our way, rights, and desires. It is to give of yourself because the Lord has a better way for you. We show God our love by

---

[568] Matthew 15:8
[569] Acts 19:13-16
[570] Acts 5:1-6
[571] John 14:21-23

trusting Him and refusing to walk in our own way.[572] Love is unselfish, bringing us closer to God. We give ourselves away to God so that He can use us for His glory.

David Jeremiah said, "God loves you as though you are the only person in the world, and He loves everyone the way He loves you." The Lord's love trains our souls to obey. To walk after His commandments is to pursue his love. It is to conquer our flesh and to live our lives through the power of God. It is surrendering to His word and allowing it to cover our thoughts, hearts, and dreams. As we have heard, even from the beginning, God is love; those who love him will follow His word.[573] Have you shown God that you love Him by giving yourself to Him? Obedience is love, so let's walk after His commandments.

Prayer: Heavenly Father, you are Lord, and I want you to know me. Please help me to follow your word and your ways. Let your loving kindness draw me, as your Holy Spirit guides me through the paths of life. I know you will lift me when I struggle, so help me hear your voice calling me in difficult times. Keep speaking so my mind stays on you, and you grant me peace, in Jesus' name, Amen.

---

[572] Matthew 16:24-26
[573] 1 John 2:6-7

Total Submission

---※---

Ezekiel 24:16-18 "Son of man, behold, I will take away from you the desire of your eyes with one stroke; yet you shall neither mourn nor weep, neither shall your tears run down. Sigh, but not aloud. Make no mourning for the dead. Bind your headdress on you, and put your sandals on your feet. Don't cover your lips, and don't eat mourner's bread." So I spoke to the people in the morning, and at evening my wife died. So I did in the morning as I was commanded.

Sometimes, God does things that we don't understand. He had Hosea marry a prostitute[574] and told Jeremiah to buy property that the seller would soon lose to the Babylonians.[575] He also told the prophet Ezekiel that he would allow his wife to die. Sometimes, we experience times of confusion when things don't seem like God should be allowing them to happen. We know God does everything for a purpose, but when it happens to you, it is hard to understand that purpose. In these things, the Lord calls us to total submission.[576]

We are sure that Ezekiel did not understand why. God Himself knew that Ezekiel's wife was the desire of his eyes, and He knew how much it

---

[574] Hosea 1:2

[575] Jeremiah 32:6-8

[576] Philippians 2:5-7

would hurt Ezekiel to lose her. Yet sometimes, we are called to submit to His sovereign will without knowing why.[577] God may bring us to that place of total submission where we have to give everything over to Him in obedience. When we are confused, hurt, or left alone, we must submit to the Lord's authority and trust that He has a more excellent plan.

The ultimate cross we can bear is submitting to God when we don't understand. These times, we are like Christ saying, Not my will but yours.[578] They test our faith, obedience, and love for God. Just as Abraham showed total submission when taking Isaac for sacrifice on the mountain,[579] we will come into our own time of total submission. Either we will rebel and blame God, or we will square our shoulders and stand as the Lord knows we can.

Prayer: Lord, when I come to struggling times, be with me. I submit to your plan and trust you will bring order to the confusion in my mind and heal the brokenness in my heart. Help me pass my faithfulness test so that better days will come soon. I trust you in the process and know that later I will understand it, in the name of Jesus, Amen.

---

[577] Job 22:21

[578] Luke 22:42

[579] Genesis 22:9-14

Financial Stability

Proverbs 11:24 There is one who scatters, and increases yet more. There is one who withholds more than is appropriate, but gains poverty.

When it comes to Christians, they say that the wallet is the last frontier. It is the undiscovered country and the final place to hold out when trusting God. Scripture goes as far as to say Where your treasure is, so is your heart.[580] That means sometimes our hearts are in the wrong places. When we track our spending habits, we see what our hearts desire. Some keep their money and still owe; others give liberally and continue to receive. Defeating debt comes from understanding the principle of financial stability and detaching yourself from money. When we stop hoarding and chasing money, it starts chasing us.[581]

We often mistakenly think that holding on to what we have will make us better off. However, holding on to money only means your money has a hold on you. Faithful givers detach from money. It will never be their God, nor will it conflict with their desire to serve Christ.[582] They are free to sow and be blessed. They reap financial stability because they sow from a financially stable mindset. Giving in trust to God, even in difficult times,

---

[580] Matthew 6:21

[581] Proverbs 11:23-25

[582] Matthew 6:24

brings a blessing to your finances, where the Lord will reduce debt and bring financial favor.[583]

Those who give freely will continue to be blessed by the Lord. Those who worry about money will be frustrated. Holding back in our actions has placed many under the curse of lack.[584] A financially stable mind leads to financially stable actions, which in turn attract God's blessing. If we freely give, we will freely receive from God. People don't become financially fit until they achieve financial balance. Have you freed the Lord to act upon your finances by taking the proper steps and giving?[585] God desires to open doors and bless His children who do as He asks and are ready to receive a blessing.

> **Prayer:** Lord, teach me to live with sound financial principles to maximize my potential and keep your blessing of financial freedom in my reach. I want balance in my life and commit to trusting you. I proclaim freedom from debt and waste. As I give liberally, I ask you to open up doors of blessing. Please show me your good hand, so I walk in favor, in Jesus' name, Amen.

---

[583] Genesis 26:1 & 12

[584] 2 Corinthians 9:6

[585] Malachi 3:10-12

Man's Second Image

---⁂---

Genesis 1:27 God created man in his own image. In God's image he created him; male and female he created them.

God made humanity in His image and likeness to reflect God's authority and character to the world. We were to care for the earth and each other the way God would. However, an aspect of our creation did not contain God's image. That is the creation of our bodies.[586] Our flesh has never been in the image of God. Our bodies come from the dust of the ground, molded and shaped by God. The flesh carries the image of the earth and needs to be tended to and nurtured just as the rest of the earth does. Our biggest question is, whose image will you leave this world with?

Do you get it? When sin came, the curse on man's body caused God to say, "Cursed is the earth because of you."[587] It wasn't God who caused the curse; He merely pronounced what Adam had done by his sin. Adam, the first matured authoritative life seed fashioned from the earth, corrupted all physical creation because He carried the earth's image in its fullness. He was of this planet as much as he was from God. Because of man's connection to the earth, the earth was cursed and cannot be redeemed until man is first redeemed.[588]

---

[586] Genesis 2:7
[587] Genesis 3:17
[588] Romans 8:19-20

Man has always carried two images. The struggles in our flesh derive from the temptations of the world in which our flesh carries its image. The redeemed spirit carries the image of God. Humanity's sin marred the image of God and bolstered our likeness to the now-corrupted world. We struggle to erase the world's image in our flesh and bring it back into subjection to the image of God. By crucifying the flesh, we put to death the image of the world in us, allowing God's image to come forth.[589] We will either submit to the flesh and carry the world's image or submit to God and reflect the image of Christ.[590] You choose.

> **Prayer:** Heavenly Father, I commit to tearing down the image of the world ingrained in my flesh. As you gave Adam the breath of life, renew me in your Spirit that I may walk in newness of life. I want to reflect your image in my thoughts, integrity, words, and deeds. I ask that you transform my life and that of my family, friends, church, and neighbors. Help us to walk in godly character, commitment, and compassion in the name of Jesus Christ. Amen.

[589] Galatians 5:24-25
[590] Romans 8:28-30

The Marriage Triangle

---⟶⚓---

Malachi 2:16 One who hates and divorces", says Yahweh, the God of Israel, "covers his garment with violence!" says Yahweh of Armies. "Therefore pay attention to your spirit, that you don't be unfaithful.

How can you put it any simpler: "God hates divorce." With marriage being the first institution the Lord created, you would think people would take it more seriously than they do.[591] Marriage takes work, yet many people refuse to put in the effort. People often want to get married because they have a social or emotional void and long for completion and companionship. They end up divorced because they are tired of the behaviors and the emotional void of remaining in their marriage but not having their spouse.[592] How can the very void that many tried to fill through marriage remain there throughout the marriage?

Marriage is like a triangle, with God at the top and the Husband and wife at the bottom corners. As each person seeks to draw closer to God, it automatically brings them closer to one another.[593] Understand that growth in God equals growth in marriage. Every vice you overcome closes the door to disagreements, discontentment, and distress. A step forward

---

[591] Genesis 2:22-25

[592] Ruth 1:21

[593] Ecclesiastes 4:12

with God is a step forward in your relationship. Consequently, each step you take away from God distances you from your spouse.

What God hates most about divorce is how people who are supposed to love and sacrifice for each other treat one another. It covers your garments with wrong to excuse yourself for your actions.[594] Excuses are a step further away from God. He hates it because we are not taking heed to our spirit but are paying attention to our flesh. In breaking the covenant with our spouse, we violate the covenant with our God.[595] We treat our spouse and God treacherously and justify our actions as right in the sight of God and family. If there's a problem, don't cover it with wrongdoing; grow closer to God and watch how he can fix it.

> **Prayer:** Lord, please bring my family and me closer to you. We heal together as we mature in you. Please help us understand one another and our flaws. I pray for your blessing and forgiveness to surround us and relieve any hidden hurt and bitterness. Make us whole, as you intended, and a blessing to one another. By the grace of Jesus, may we respect one another as we honor your name, Amen.

---

[594] Psalm 73:6
[595] Malachi 2:14-15

For This Reason

---⯅---

Exodus 9:16 but indeed for this cause I have made you stand: to show you my power, and that my name may be declared throughout all the earth,

Abraham Lincoln said, "Nearly all men can stand adversity, but if you want to test a man's character, give him power." Our problems show who we are, but how we handle our authority reveals what is deep inside us.[596] Likewise, the way God handles His power shows us His character. God's revelation of Himself through His power is very intimate and personal. To the unspiritual mind, it can seem that He is showboating. However, the heart of God's revelation is relational. He reveals His power so that you may know Him personally.[597] He reveals His character to us through His power.

Reading this verse in isolation may give you the wrong meaning of its intent. God commanded Moses to speak these words to the pharaoh, who refused to let God's people go.[598] The Lord could have easily destroyed the Egyptians, but instead, He allowed them to stand by, preserving their lives to reveal His power to them. Their resistance to His power caused people

---

[596] 2 Peter 1:5-7

[597] Ephesians 1:18-19

[598] Exodus 9:13-15

to proclaim the fear of God for years worldwide.[599] How much more so would His love have been revealed if they had obeyed His word?

Whether you are obedient to the Lord or resist Him like a pharaoh, God's power will one day reveal who you are. The only question is whether it will cause you to rise or fall. Both His judgment and His grace proclaim His name.[600] Equally, they reveal His character as one who is righteous and must punish wrongdoing and as one who loves and forgives those who repent. He shows His power so that those who desire so may have a relationship with Him, and those who do not desire Him will be without His grace. Realize that God raises you for a purpose. How you stand will determine if you will continue to rise or fall.

> **Prayer:** Lord, I thank you for your delayed judgment. Time after time, you have given us chances to get back on our feet rather than destroy us. I commit to following your lead and will proclaim your name for your faithfulness. I ask that you continue working to save my family and friends who resist you. Help those of us who struggle to commit to your ways and word fully. Thank you for your goodness that follows me, and I ask you to keep me standing, in Jesus' name. Amen.

---

[599] Exodus 12:24-27
[600] Romans 5:16-18

Better to Be Blessed

Numbers 24:10 Balak's anger burned against Balaam, and he struck his hands together. Balak said to Balaam, "I called you to curse my enemies, and, behold, you have altogether blessed them these three times.

They may smite fist in hand, scream and shout, but the Balak's can do nothing against you. Balak's name means "devastator or empty." He had a reputation for laying waste to his enemies. He had confidence that when he would attack, all resistance would fall. To ensure this, he brought out Balaam to speak curses over the lives of those he would destroy.[601] Yet this time, nothing happened. He tried again and again, but still nothing. He could not pronounce a curse because no man can curse the one God calls blessed.[602]

Children of God, the Balak's may have people to come against you, but it won't work. The Israelites knew that the armies of Moab had gathered against them. Yet greater is He who is in us than he that is in the world.[603] No matter the enemy's schemes against you, they will come to no avail. People may try to curse you and plot for your destruction, and yet the blessing will remain in your life. No matter how mad the enemy gets, he

---

[601] Numbers 22:5-6
[602] Numbers 23:8-12
[603] 1 John 4:4

is powerless to do anything to the children of God who stand faithfully under God's protection.[604]

The enemy may come in to try to shake you, but don't move. Bitter trials often hide new opportunities and blessings. Our blessing is a threat to the enemy's security. He has no peace because he understands what God has for you.[605] The more they come at you, the more confident you can be that you remain blessed and that they are powerless against your God.[606] They have called people to curse you, and yet you have been blessed. They have put time and effort into your destruction, but it has only led to praise. To God be the glory for the things He has done. Stay Blessed

> **Prayer:** Lord, I thank you that even when attacked, I know it's because your blessing is upon me. I pray that you grant me so much favor that no one can curse. I submit to you, for you have made me unstoppable. Do not hide your face from me or remove your hand. I ask that you extend your protection over my loved ones, home, and church so they will know your goodness in the name of Jesus Christ. Amen.

---

[604] Psalm 91:1-8
[605] Numbers 22:2-4
[606] Proverbs 26:2

It Won't Work

---†---

Zechariah 3:1-2 He showed me Joshua the high priest standing before Yahweh's angel, and Satan standing at his right hand to be his adversary. Yahweh said to Satan, "Yahweh rebuke you, Satan! Yes, Yahweh who has chosen Jerusalem rebuke you! Isn't this a burning stick plucked out of the fire?

There is a reason why God does not listen to Satan's accusations. That is because Satan was a giant screw-up.[607] Imagine you were back in elementary and the biggest goofball kid who, after being held back for years and couldn't read, laughed because you misspelled a word in front of the class. Would that work against you? Would you care? He missed 10 of 20 words on the test and laughed because you missed one. Wouldn't you point out His mistakes and lack of a promising future?

Why do we let the enemy get us down? The biggest failure history is mocking us for our failures, and we are beating ourselves up. He knows that people often don't repent when they feel unworthy. Instead of getting it right with God, we get stuck in what we did and can't find our way out. However, the devil's schemes won't work on those who know the power of God's forgiveness.[608] Satan messed up and stayed that way, but we don't have to be like him because we are brands plucked from the fire.

---

[607] Ezekiel 28:13-18
[608] 2 Corinthians 2:10-11

The worst kid in the angelic class wants to accuse you, but it won't work. Even when you are guilty of sin, God rebukes the enemy. There is no condemnation for those in Christ Jesus.[609] All we have to do is be willing to stand before a holy God with repentance in our hearts. God plucked us from the fire that Satan will fall into.[610] Through guilt and shame, Satan is trying to drag us into the fires of hell, but it won't work. Whenever Jesus ran across a devil, He would rebuke them.[611] Let's stand in repentance, for the Lord rebukes devils.

Prayer: Lord, though I may feel unworthy when I mess up, you love me as your child. You are always there to pick me up and brush the dirt off so I can be clean again before you. Please help me make more right decisions than wrong ones and avoid situations that threaten my prospects. I renounce friendship with the world and stand in faith with you. I pray you stop the devil's schemes against my family and life so that we can live in grace and walk in favor, in Jesus' name. Amen.

---

[609] Romans 8:1-5

[610] Revelation 20:10

[611] Mark 1:25

Thrive or Survive

---·---·— ⚜ —·---·---

Hebrews 5:13-14 For everyone who lives on milk is not experienced in the word of righteousness, for he is a baby. But solid food is for those who are full grown, who by reason of use have their senses exercised to discern good and evil.

W ho wants to eat the same thing repeatedly, like babies, because they can't digest anything else? They are stuck on a basic diet of milk that sustains their life while showing their lack of growth. Many believers get stuck because they desire only elementary things like baptism, healing, and escaping judgment but avoid things that test their faith.[612] We want our feelings encouraged but avoid challenges to radically change our lives for the gospel, leaving our comfort zones and living a life that does not mix the kingdom with the world.[613]

Milk is about entering the kingdom, like a baby entering life by coming out of the womb but unchanged from what they were inside it. When we look for the teaching of the word to encourage us but not change us, we miss three of the four primary reasons of scripture that challenge, correct, and condition us to live righteously.[614] Knowing what scripture says means little if we don't apply its teachings. Even a babe can mimic the words they

---

[612] Hebrews 6:3

[613] Luke 9:23

[614] 2 Timothy 3:16

hear without understanding their meaning. When we don't put the word into practice, we are unskilled in righteousness and treat the word as milk, not meat that will make you grow.

Understand that it's not that part of the word is milk; another part is meat. It's all meat if you understand and apply it, and it's all milk if you are using it only to survive. Without understanding, you will neither thrive nor, by use, have your senses exercised to discern and live the will of God.[615] If all the word is to you is learning doctrine, you will fight over spilled milk. When the word becomes meat to chew on, it leads to a thriving life in righteousness.[616] Those feeding on milk will stagnate in who they are. Those who chew the meat are not yet what they will become, but they are growing toward it.

Prayer: Heavenly Father, thank you for your word, which has become meat to my soul. I appreciate all the occasions when the milk has encouraged me consistently, but I yearn for the meat that will challenge and transform who I am into who I need to be. I pray for the guidance of your Holy Spirit to implement your word and develop in righteousness. Transform me by your word so I will reflect your glory, in Christ's name, Amen.

---

[615] Proverbs 4:7
[616] Psalm 1:3-4

Sleeping In

---⚓---

Ezekiel 22:8 You have despised my holy things, and have profaned my Sabbaths.

Have you ever thought about what happens when you sleep in instead of getting up to meet God in corporate worship? Not only do you miss out on something God desired to give, but when done consistently, you might find yourself in opposition to the Lord. The question is not whether we need to attend church to receive sacraments, worship, or fellowship, but whether we have rejected God's holy things and profaned His times.[617] No one goes to hell for missing a church service, but rejection of God's holy things reveals a problem within our hearts and opposes God's ordinances.

To despise God's holy things means to reject what God has given for our blessing and growth. We have despised the place where He chose to manifest His glory and rejected the holy vessels through which He gives grace.[618] This rejection of God's most holy place and His statutes grieves the heart of God. We have rejected the holy things of God and replaced them with our desires. However, it's not only that we have rejected the holy place and articles of God; we also have profaned His holy times.[619]

---

[617] Ezekiel 22:26
[618] 1 Thessalonians 4:8
[619] Ezekiel 20:16

The Sabbath was a holy time set apart for God. When we do our bidding during God's selected time, it becomes profane.[620] To profane the time means that we make it unclean. We do what we desire and don't give the Lord the time He requires. Shouldn't we realize that, as servants of God, we must be where and when He wants us to be? By despising His holy things and profaning His Sabbaths, we despise Him as being Lord over us. We become guilty of shedding the blood of Christ into the streets because we treat His sacrifice as not being noteworthy.[621] We lift our time and desires as idols because they rule over us, not God. We aren't just losing community with the brethren; we are losing unity with God by treating what He gives as profane.

Prayer: Lord, forgive our guilt for treating your holy things as mundane. You desire to invest your loving grace in us, and I apologize for every time I may have missed it. Please help me hold what you have given as holy and to foster love with every interaction we have. Draw me near your presence and shower me with your grace, in the name of Jesus, Amen.

---

[620] Jeremiah 17:26-27
[621] 1 Corinthians 11:27-31

Destined For Greatness

---✦---

Esther 10:3 For Mordecai the Jew was next to King Ahasuerus, and great among the Jews and accepted by the multitude of his brothers, seeking the good of his people and speaking peace to all his descendants.

Have you noticed how God keeps blessing skilled, faithful, and humble people? It's as if God destines those who possess these qualities for greatness. Look at it. Mordecai went from standing outside the gate to the High Minister of the kingdom.[622] He was committed to God first, then to God's people. Mordecai overcame even with the deck stacked against him. He was a foreigner. Leaders hated his people and attacked him.[623] Yet, He still ends up next to the king, positioned to protect and bless the Lord's people.

Did you notice the exact requirements and conditions that happened to Joseph in Egypt[624] and Daniel in Babylon?[625] Yet they both became second in command in the kingdom. They were faithful and skilled men who humbly served the Lord. They had the right mix for God to use them mightily. What about the apostle Paul and others with this ability, desire, and character mix? God used them. The same is true of Jesus, who was

---

[622] Esther 8:1-2

[623] Esther 5:9-14

[624] Genesis 41:38-44

[625] Daniel 6:1-5

not of this world and was despised and rejected by men but sits at the right hand of the Father.[626]

God is looking for someone destined for greatness whom he can place His people in their care. He is looking for people with the right skills who know what to do. For faithful people, so that they know who they serve, and for humble people, so that they will know how to treat others.[627] Each of us must ask ourselves, "Is that me?" Am I on the path to greatness, or will I sit in the gate's shadows, watching God bring up someone else? How will you answer?

> **Prayer:** Father, I want to be someone you can use to stand and protect your people. Please help me be faithful to where I am as I develop the right mix to operate in your call and destiny. You make the ordinary extraordinary, so I ask that you keep your hand and Holy Spirit with me. As you lead, I will follow. Place your protection around my family, even those who hate me, and deliver them by your grace, in the matchless name of Jesus Christ. Amen.

---

[626] Colossians 3:1

[627] Isaiah 66:2

Led by His Love

---✦---

Philemon 1:8-9 Therefore though I have all boldness in Christ to command you that which is appropriate, yet for love's sake I rather appeal to you, being such a one as Paul, the aged, but also a prisoner of Jesus Christ.

There is a difference between having authority and appropriately expressing your authority. Just having the right to do something doesn't make it right to do. When people use their authority unruly or inordinately, we think of them as bitter and tyrannical.[628] Yes, they have the privilege to do as they please. However, what they please can cause harm to others. When we use our authority as a right instead of an opportunity to promote another's growth and express love, we misuse our rights.[629]

Though Paul was confident he could tell Philemon what to do, he refused to dictate. It had to come down to Philemon's own choice. Instead of demanding, he appeals to Philemon to do what is right by forgiving Onesimus and setting him free.[630] Likewise, even though God has the authority to make us serve Him, He appeals to us to do what is right. He doesn't force anyone to follow Him. He will step away and leave you to

---

[628] Luke 22:24-27
[629] 2 Corinthians 10:7-9
[630] Philemon 1:15-20

yourself until you seek him.[631] The Lord will direct you, but won't make you do anything you don't desire.

It is for love's sake that the Lord directs, and for love's sake, we follow. Not under compulsion but under His grace, He lovingly directs our paths.[632] You can run out of many things, but you will never run out of God's love.[633] His love points the way for us to follow. It's not only the authority of the Lord's power that leads us, but also the presence of His love. God loves the incomplete completely and the imperfect perfectly. God is appealing to us right now with His love.[634] The question is, "Will you follow"?

Prayer: I thank God for your loving presence that leads and guides me to all truth and righteousness. Even when things are difficult, I understand all your acts are acts of love towards me. I was hoping you could help me do the right thing, even in bad situations. Shower me with your love and shelter me from all harm. I appeal to your sufficient grace to guard my family and life. In the name of Christ, Amen.

---

[631] Hosea 5:15
[632] Philemon 1:10-14
[633] Romans 8:37-39
[634] Isaiah 46:3-4

The Mark of a True Believer

John 13:35 By this everyone will know that you are my disciples, if you have love for one another.

What is your mark and claim that you are a disciple of Jesus? Is it in what you say you are or the authority you walk in? No, instead, the mark of a true believer is simply love.[635] The most incredible testimony that Christ is in your life is not in how well you pray or how much scripture you know; it is in a heart filled with love for God's people. Speaking about the problem with church folk is popular, but it pleases God to love those same folk. What pleases the Lord is when we come together in love and unity.[636] The love we have sets us apart and reveals to the world who we are and whose we are.

In Christ's day, Pharisees, Sadducees, and zealots claimed to be faithful disciples of God. They sat in the places of authority and seemed very pious. Nevertheless, at the same time, they resisted God's work in their lives and promoted themselves rather than promoting the Lord's Messiah.[637] Today's believers often are not so different than those who lived in Christ's times. We have some who have the mark of a true believer and others who don't. Some resist God's work in our lives, seeking to change our hearts

---

[635] 1 John 3:13-16
[636] Acts 4:32
[637] John 5:39-43

and actions. We promote our self-worth instead of humbling ourselves as unworthy of the grace given to us.

True disciples stand in love and let their light shine.[638] When we show love, it is apparent to everyone everywhere that God has touched our lives. They may not know why we are different, but they can't deny our differences. Love is part of the unseen man renewed in the image of God and shed by His Spirit in our hearts.[639] Love is the stripes on the uniform of the new man, and the emblem on our spirit marks us as belonging to Christ. Love is the identifier of a life changed by God and the mark of the true disciple.[640]

Prayer: Lord, help me to withstand the challenges of doubts, disappointments, and distractions that try to extinguish the love in my heart. By the power of your Holy Spirit, pour new love into my heart to rekindle my fire. I pray my passion and love of Christ will be contagious wherever I go, causing love to ignite in the hearts of those around me; in the name of Jesus, Amen.

---

[638] 1 John 1:7
[639] Romans 5:5
[640] 1 Peter 1:22

Seven Calls of the Believer

Romans 1:7 to all who are in Rome, beloved of God, called to be saints: Grace to you and peace from God our Father and the Lord Jesus Christ.

Did you know that all believers have at least seven callings? The apostle Paul greets the church, reminding them of their call to be saints. This call means we are to act differently from the world because we are to respond godly to all situations. Being called a saint is recognizing who we are to be in God, one of His. It follows our call to salvation by entering the kingdom. [641] Everything starts with salvation. After which, God calls us to sanctification. Which is the process by which we begin to form kingdom character?[642]

God also calls us to supplication, by which we communicate with God, forming the basis of our relationship. Supplication forms our ability to follow the Lord's leading as we speak to and hear God.[643] The Lord builds all ministry on the back of supplication to Him, in Christ's name, as the Holy Spirit leads us. The call to sacredness is stepping away from what is familiar into the holy presence of God.[644] Sacredness is our call to walk

---

[641] 1 Corinthians 1:9

[642] 1 Corinthians 1:2

[643] 1 Timothy 2:1

[644] John 4:24

with God on holy ground. It is the Lord's place and methods to manifest Himself to us, and we commune with His presence.

The God-given call to service[645] and the call to suffering round off our list.[646] Service is God working through you, and suffering is the devil working against you. All are called to serve, but not in the same position. Likewise, our suffering connects us to the cross of Christ. Operating in your call will create resistance. But as saints of God called to salvation and sanctification, we supplicate to God and reach Him in the sacred as we serve. If we suffer, He will supply all our needs. Shalom.

Prayer: Lord, help me to operate in all you have called me to do. Your call disturbs the carnal nature, and as I commit to further answering your call, crucify my flesh. You have called me near, so keep your presence with me every place I go. I ask that you grow and help me to understand how to live in my calling and bring me victory. In Jesus' name. Amen

---

[645] Acts 13:36
[646] 2 Timothy 3:12

The Welcomed/Unwelcomed Spirit

Ecclesiastes 12:7 and the dust returns to the earth as it was, and the spirit returns to God who gave it.

When people die, questions loom about what becomes of them. Some say that the dead are merely sleeping, while others proclaim that if we are absent from the body, we are present with the Lord.[647] In a sense, both are true in very different ways. When God created man, He formed the body from the dust of the earth and breathed the breath of life into man, thereby creating the spirit. As a result, man became a living being.[648] However, death entered the world through sin.

The purpose of death is to counteract God's work in bringing life. So when we die, we return to what we were before creation. The body becomes inactive and returns to the dust of the earth. It can be said that we all sleep because the body is part of us. The spirit, however, was created by God.[649] When we die, the spirit shall return to God, who gave it. So, as our bodies rest and decay, our spirit is welcomed into the presence of the Lord. Believers are thus alive with Christ and dead in the body, both simultaneously.

All human spirits return to God, yet not all spirits can stay with God. Everyone will go to heaven because before the great white throne, every

---

[647] 2 Corinthians 5:8

[648] Genesis 2:7

[649] Zechariah 12:1

knee shall bow, and every tongue will confess to God.[650] However, unbelievers who will one day go there will not stay there. They are unwelcome spirits. Those whose spirits die in the sin of rejecting God's saving grace through His son, Jesus Christ, are separated from God by their sin. They are ushered into the presence of God to confess, then dismissed from His presence forever. Being unwelcome, they will see heaven, be separated away from God, and then be cast into the pits of hell.[651] Make sure you hold on to Christ, for He is our ticket to staying in heaven.

Prayer: Lord, help me to hold on to your love and grace. I do not want to be lost or to lose treasures stored in heaven. I strengthen my resolve to follow you and remain in your favor. I pray that you draw my family and loved ones to the waters of Your salvation so we will unite in heaven one day and remain in the new kingdom built in the sky forever, in the name of Jesus. Amen.

---

[650] Romans 14:11
[651] Matthew 25:41-46

Victory Commanded

---※---

Psalms 44:4 God, you are my King.
Command victories for Jacob!

Have you ever prayed to God to command victory for you? Have you ever thought of how a sovereign God can speak on your behalf, and you win? During our struggles, God speaks words of triumph. Deep in our pain, He speaks healing and deliverance. Even our troubles must submit to the voice of God. When God speaks, things come back into order.[652] Therefore, knowing how to cause God to speak up on your behalf is essential. There are three things the Psalmist mentions to receive the favor described that commands victory. These are the favor of God's hand, arm, and face.[653]

We must do three things to secure these. The first is to battle in the name of God.[654] We must give the battle to the Lord's hand so it's no longer our struggle but His. Let God own the battle; we merely participate by following His commands. The second is to humble ourselves, not fully trusting our abilities.[655] The more we are sure we have what it takes to get a victory, the less we tend to lean on God's arm. If we are not dependent

---

[652] Genesis 1:2-4
[653] Psalm 44:3
[654] Psalm 44:5
[655] Psalm 44:6

on the Lord, He has no reason to command victory, since we will take the glory on ourselves.[656]

Lastly, you should maintain a state of praise.[657] Through praise, we seek God's face. Our praise and thanks are not dependent on our victory; our victory depends on our praise. Even through the worst places in our struggle, God is our praise.[658] Because He lives, we can praise Him in the most challenging times. Regardless of how things look, if you can praise Him in the darkest times, He will ordain success for you. Know that when you seem defeated, God will command victory right where you are. Seek the favor of the Lord and let Him command your victory.

Prayer: Lord, I surrender all control of my life over to you. You are the one who causes me to triumph. In your name, I have victory. When I don't know what to do, you fight my battles. I will yet praise you in all things and seek your favor. Do your good pleasure in my life for your name's sake. I pray for victory in my family, home, and life in the name of Jesus Christ. Amen.

---

[656] Deuteronomy 8:16-18

[657] Psalm 44:8

[658] Psalm 147:1

An Opportunity to Obey

---✦---

***Hebrews 5:8 Though he was a Son, yet learned
obedience by the things which he suffered.***

No matter what you call it, affliction, suffering, hardships, or pain, they teach us the lesson of obedience through patience.[659] Times like these cause us to wait on the Lord to do His work. We prefer the easy road; however, a burden-free life doesn't reveal our obedience. How we stand through the fires of adversity shows who we are.[660] We tend to obey when there are no burdens because it is convenient. In short, it says I will listen because it suits my needs. That's not obedience; it's opportunity.

Understand that we must use wisdom to make the most of every opportunity.[661] However, God has not required us to be opportunistic but obedient people. There is a big difference. Opportunity is simply taking advantage of doors that have been open to you. You have a chance to do what you want and do it. Obedience, however, requires us not to make the decisions we want but the ones God wants. Not every door that opens to you is good to walk through. We are to give up our desires and opportunities and take the ones God wants, even if it causes suffering.[662]

---

[659] James 1:2-4
[660] Daniel 3:16-18
[661] Colossians 3:5
[662] 1 Peter 2:21

We acquire obedience through challenging situations. Amid sorrow and conflict, we develop and mature when we submit to the Word of God that the Holy Spirit teaches. Many of our problems have come to teach us obedience, yet when we face trials, some turn to their own way instead of leaning on God. No matter who you are, God will allow suffering to teach you. Though Christ was the Son of God, he had to suffer to experience obedient humanity.[663] The same goes for each of us. We will learn obedience if we stop exerting our will during difficult times. Next time you suffer misfortunes, learn how to obey God in it. So you won't have to repeat your trial.

> **Prayer:** Lord, help me to learn the lesson of my trials so I won't keep circling back to the same situations of infirmity, scarcity, and adversity. I believe your word, so when I am weak, you make me strong. You supply all my needs and will fight my battles. I dedicate myself to stand on your word and be led by the Holy Spirit. Come what may, I will trust you and obey through the power of Christ and your grace, Amen.

---

[663] Isaiah 50:4-5

Superpowered Faith

Psalms 8:6 You make him ruler over the works of your hands. You have put all things under his feet:

One thing that strikes me in all Hollywood superhero movies is that they all have unrealized power. The storyline usually goes that fate has chosen an individual to receive power, and they must learn to wield it effectively. To say the apple doesn't fall far from the tree is an understatement. God made man in His image and has given believers the superpower of faith to have dominion over the works of His hands.[664] That extends to the universe of all created things. We only bow down to the Lord and His Christ Himself.[665]

We have unrealized power that God gives us to take authority over all creation. This authority is based on faith and includes situations, demonic forces, and our lives.[666] Many of us have never come to the true power of faith. It is a power that dominates our troubles and controls what goes on in our world. Humanity has authority over everything God has made. Our enemies are fear, doubt, guilt, instability, and anything hindering our

---

[664] Genesis 1:26-28
[665] 1 Corinthians 15:26-28
[666] Mark 16:17-18

faith.[667] Trusting the Lord, who has put everything created under our feet, empowers us to control what comes and goes in our lives.[668]

When a king would conquer another kingdom, he would place his foot on the neck of the conquered king. When God places things under your feet, he gives you the authority to conquer. That's why we must meet problems with faith. This unrealized power allows us to regain control in all situations. Your faith in God is superpowered to defeat the enemy.[669] The god of this world, Satan, will be brought under our feet through faith. Believe in God unconditionally, and He will give you dominion over the works of His hands.

Prayer: Lord, I come to you in faith, asking that you hear my cry. You have given me authority and have waited long enough for me to walk in it. I declare the ceasing of storms, the casting out of wicked plans, and my prayer of faith will see the sick raised. I can do all things through Christ, so I ask you for your strength in every righteous cause. Move by your Spirit in my home, family, and life until we all see the devil under our feet, in Christ Jesus' name. Amen.

---

[667] 2 Timothy 1:7
[668] Romans 16:19-20
[669] Hebrews 11:32-34

Possessing with Honor

1 Thessalonians 4:3-4 For this is the will of God: your sanctification, that you abstain from sexual immorality, that each one of you know how to control his own body in sanctification and honor

It is the will of God that we would be sanctified and that we will know how to possess our bodies with honor. We need to recognize that our bodies carry honor because God designed them to contain the divine presence of God's Holy Spirit within them.[670] Each of us needs to understand how to maintain the honor of the temple God gave us. People who honor their bodies won't just sleep around with anybody willing. The question becomes: How much is God worth for us to reserve our bodies for Him and our spouses alone?[671]

The key to knowing how to possess your body in sanctification and honor is abstaining from fornication.[672] Fornication is possessing the body in a sexually immoral or unchaste capacity. The word for fornication in the text is the Greek word "Porneia," from which we derive our English words porn and pornography. Porneia, therefore, begins as a mental or emotional

---

[670] 1 Corinthians 6:18-20

[671] Hebrews 13:4

[672] Colossians 3:5

259

picture that leads to a physical act. Jesus said if a man looks upon a woman with lust, he has committed adultery with her already in his heart.[673]

Fornication begins with a picture of the flesh in our mind. If you desire to possess your vessel with honor, you must abstain from and give up the pictures and false narratives that lead to the act. Fornication is a process where the mind receives an image, and the heart desires to possess what the mind sees, leading us to act upon that desire.[674] We must stop receiving the picture in our minds to stop the act. Then, because it is His will, we must allow God to heal us from the lust of our hearts. We should know how to possess our bodies with sanctification and honor, and serve God's will.

Prayer: Lord, please continue to strengthen my resolve to obey your word. Despite what the rest of the world claims, I must be unique. I make a covenant with my eyes to not objectify others or look at them for my comfort or pleasure. I won't take part in anything that draws them away from you since they are valuable as a vessel you want to set apart as sacred. Help me take ownership of my thoughts and remain self-controlled and faithful, in Jesus' name, Amen.

---

[673] Matthew 5:28
[674] James 1:13-15

The Image of Your Faith

---⸸---

Habakkuk 2:18 What value does the engraved image have, that its maker has engraved it; the molten image, even the teacher of lies, that he who fashions its form trusts in it, to make mute idols?

There is no profit in an idol that man has shaped.[675] Its creator is always superior to the creation. Even though computers receive complexity from the people who create them, the human brain is the most incredibly complex supercomputer ever conceived. No matter how good the creation may be, the creator will always be better. So, it is with God. He will always be greater than us. He is the image and measure of our faith. However, some have created idols and treat their manufactured products as if they were gods.[676]

What image does your faith bear? Today, many people are still carving out their religion; they have remade God to fit into their cast and based their faith on what they think or feel. God has become to them one who is speechless and cannot disapprove of their actions.[677] The maker has formed an idol and called it God. He trusts in a god of his own making and thus

---

[675] 1 Samuel 12:21
[676] Isaiah 40:18-20
[677] Psalm 115:4-8

relies on the work of his own hands. But his faith is a teacher of falsehood. The image it bears is not that of our creator but that of things created.[678]

What we create will be subservient to us, but the one who created us is the master of all.[679] Our man-made religion reflects our image. Our sinful desires and permissiveness mar manmade religion, allowing us to continue in certain vices. Idol makers place their faults on the idol, and anyone who worships an idol will gain its faults. The Christian faith, however, is based on a relationship because God made us in His image.[680] This means that He made us so that He could relate directly to us and so that we would become like Him. He is then the giver and measure of our faith, made not in our image but in His.

Prayer: Lord, I have frequently wanted things to go my way and adhere to my preferences. However, I put my faith in you today. Keep me from lies and putting anything else above you in life. I will abide by your word rather than man's assumptions. Please protect me from all harm and evil. Let your love fill my life with light and grant me peace beyond understanding in the name of Jesus Christ. Amen.

---

[678] Exodus 20:4-6

[679] Psalm 24:1-2

[680] Genesis 1:26-27

One and Done

---✤---

Genesis 1:1 In the beginning, God
created the heavens and the earth.

We learn something about God and our universe from the scripture's first sentence. The first thing is that there was a beginning. Everything made has a start.[681] Therefore, nothing created can claim all power and glory. The second thing is that God was already there before time began. Yes, even time had a beginning, so by inference, we understand that the Lord is before all time and anything known.[682] Lastly, we learn that God created everything above and below us. He created the heavens and all that fills them. Likewise, God created everything on, in, and under the earth.

Even if we had no other scripture verses, this verse contains enough to prompt us to seek God, learn from Him, and worship Him as the greatest.[683] It shows us that everything is under God's hand and control. Without the rest of Scripture, we would struggle to understand His character and will, but regardless, we would still know Him as God. Without a promise of heaven or hell, we would have enough to desire God and to seek Him wherever He is found.

---

[681] John 1:1-3
[682] Romans 8:38-39
[683] Revelation 4:11

Think about it. Our primary focus in life and study area would be knowing God. We would discover his attributes by looking at what He created and retaining knowledge of God in our hearts, even if we struggled in our minds.[684] The imprint God leaves on the heart could change the world. We would do great works simply because, in knowing God, we would know ourselves.[685] When you lose yourself, start from the beginning and know that God controls everything.

Prayer: Lord, in my struggles, I will hold you as before all things and in control of every situation. I seek to know you in my heart, soul, and mind. Grant me your love and favor as your Spirit guides my soul in self-control. Renew my mind so that distractions and fruitless thoughts find no place. I thank you for the blessings of following my great savior and ask you to show me mighty things, in Jesus Christ's name forever, Amen.

---

[684] Romans 1:18-19
[685] Daniel 11:32

Self-Guided or Shepherded

---✦---

Psalms 23:1 Yahweh is my shepherd;
I shall lack nothing.

Nobody desires to be in want. A desire for increase, blessing, and provision is in our hearts; however, not everyone trusts God as their shepherd long enough to see lack removed.[686] Whoever leads and guides your life has become your shepherd. Many have self-shepherded their lives because they have chosen to become their own guides. They have made themselves masters of their destiny; nevertheless, they always end up at the wrong destination.[687]

If anyone knew what it was like for a shepherd to lead a sheep, it was the Shepherd-King David. As he looked upon his life, he realized that no one had guided him like God,[688] from his time as a shepherd to becoming a minstrel for the king, from his time as a soldier to becoming a general, even from his time of being an outcast until he became a king. God was his shepherd all the way. No matter the situation, David would trust in God to lead him.

Jarrid Wilson said, "The closer you are to the Shepherd, the safer you are from the wolves." The level of trust you place in God will determine just how much provision you will receive. When we stray from the

---

[686] Lamentations 3:25
[687] Luke 6:39
[688] Psalm 25:5

shepherd, we may wander upon fields and streams on our own, but we will consume all of our time in the search. The Lord invites us to follow Him because He has searched out all our needs and has provided the solution.[689] When we trust in God, even amid troubles, we always arrive where we need to be.

Prayer: Lord, I declare, you are my shepherd, and I shall not be in want. Slow me down when I rush ahead, leading me to refreshing and restorative places. Keep me on the narrow path where the righteous walk. I know you will answer when I am in trouble and bring forth your hand of healing and blessing. I pray your goodness and mercy continually follow me and that your presence is with my going out and coming in. Thank you for your protection, love, and grace, in the name of Jesus, Amen.

---

[689] Psalm 23:4-6

Close, But No Cigar

---✦---

Deuteronomy 32:52 For you shall see the land from a distance; but you shall not go there into the land which I give the children of Israel.

Moses was right on the brink of all he had been hoping for. He had come to the top of Mount Nebo and stared across into the Promised Land. Yet he saw the land, but he never entered it. Moses lost it while representing God in front of all the people at Kadesh.[690] Moses was instructed to speak to the rock to provide water. God wasn't angry at the people's request, but Moses was frustrated. He stuck the rock God said to speak to and misrepresented the Lord before His people.

How many of us have gotten so close to our blessing but have been unable to touch it?[691] There it is, everything God has reserved for us: the land of milk and honey. Some are just on the border but will never get to enter.[692] They can only see it with their eyes but never possess it because, like Moses, they did not respect God while they were in the midst of others. What we do amid others can snatch the blessing right out of our hands. How many parents admonish their children to be on their best behavior in public? God wants your best behavior all the time.

---

[690] Numbers 20: 7-12
[691] Hebrews 10:35-38
[692] Deuteronomy 1:37

Sometimes, we can get in our own way. When we look to people instead of our God, we rob ourselves of blessings.[693] You don't want to see your blessing and cannot take hold of it. There will always be things that trouble you. It is better to lose count naming your blessings than to lose your blessing counting your troubles. To maintain your blessing, you must always remain right with God. Be your best, and then you will possess the land.

> **Prayer:** Lord, help me to get out of my own way. I desire to go beyond seeing to live in your vision. Please help me maintain my integrity and self-control during pressing times. Greater pressure reveals my time of rising, so I ask that you be with me every step of the way and at each opportunity. Thank you for transforming my life and future through my hope in you, in Jesus' name, Amen.

---

[693] 1 Thessalonians 2:4

Too Legit for God to Quit

---⟊---

*Hebrews 12:11 All chastening seems for the present
to be not joyous but grievous; yet afterward
it yields the peaceful fruit of righteousness
to those who have been trained by it.*

N o one enjoys chastening. Corrections can be embarrassing, time-
out stifling, and spankings hurt. Whatever form of chastisement
you may have received was not pleasant. All discipline hurts, no matter
what form it may come in. Chastisement is a necessary correction to show
us when we have done wrong.[694] Just like every loving parent, God disciplines those whom He loves. If He has ceased to chastise, then you are
illegitimate.[695]

For legitimate children, God won't quit disciplining you when you're
wrong. Discipline derives from the word disciple, which means a learner
or trainee.[696] Discipline should never be from anger or cruelty. Discipline
is not to punish children for their acts but to disciple them in their character. All disciplining should train us how to or how not to behave. Those
who have received disciplines training should become more righteous as a

---

[694] Revelation 3:19

[695] Hebrews 12:6-8

[696] Luke 6:40

result.[697] Why? Because our behavior has changed, and the fruit of righteousness has been manifested.

John Maxwell said, "Motivation gets you going, but discipline keeps you growing." There is no testimony without a test. Those who have learned the benefit of discipline will discipline themselves for an increase.[698] You are too legit for God to quit correcting you. When you go through troubles, God is only pruning you to bear the fruit of righteousness in your life. For the one who bears fruit, the Father prunes so that they will bear even more fruit.[699] When God sees fruit, he does what He can to make you more fruitful. Let yourself be trained by your problems so the fruit of righteousness can be in your life.

> **Prayer:** Lord, I thank you that your Holy Spirit doesn't make us timid during trials but gives us a mind of power, love, and self-discipline. I need more discipline to transform my physical and mental health for a sound body and mind. I need discipline in spending, saving, and investing to promote financial security and disciple in my spiritual life to destroy the devil's schemes. Please help me in every area so that abundant life comes to me in the name of Jesus Christ. Amen.

---

[697] Isaiah 32:17
[698] Proverbs 10:17
[699] John 15:2

Servant Authority

Hebrews 1:13-14 But which of the angels has he told at any time, "Sit at my right hand, until I make your enemies the footstool of your feet?" Aren't they all serving spirits, sent out to do service for the sake of those who will inherit salvation?

In speaking of the angels, the word reflects not on their authority but on their servanthood. There is a key to authority that we must understand. Actual authority and power come from being a servant first.[700] People may attack your authority, but anyone attacking your service makes themselves an enemy of God. The angels are ministering spirits sent here to the earth to serve those who will inherit salvation. Therefore, angels seek out those who have not earned salvation but will inherit it because they fear God, have received Christ, and become children of God.[701]

Jesus turned everything upside down about what we thought authority was supposed to be. He came not to be served but to serve.[702] He now sits at the Father's right hand while the Father serves Him by making a footstool of His enemies. Many falsely think that God became a servant in Jesus. However, God has been serving His creation from the very beginning. Everything made was for our benefit. That's service. God brought all the

---

[700] Matthew 20:25-27
[701] John 1:12-13
[702] Luke 22:26-27

animals to Adam so he could name them.[703] That's service. In like manner, the authority the child of God manifests depends on their faithful trust and service to the Lord.

Just like the angels, God has not called us to rest in authority but to serve with His authority. The angels serve God by serving humanity; in like manner, we serve God by serving everything He has placed under our authority.[704] They serve the heirs of salvation, and we win heirs to salvation. If they do not rest on their job, neither should we rest until we have won the world for Christ and serve as God makes our enemies Christ's footstool.

> **Prayer**: Lord, thank you for the ministering spirits sent out to encourage, strengthen, and minister to my needs. I pray that your angels would be a hedge of protection, and as I serve you, they guard my family, home, and life. I trust you through the storms, knowing you will cause the enemies against me to bow down. Yet I will not be exalted in pride but humbled in service. I need you, Lord, and ask that you continually be with me, in Jesus' name, Amen.

---

[703] Genesis 2:19-20
[704] Genesis 1:28-30

Working with the Right Things

---✦---

Deuteronomy 22:10 You shall not plow
with an ox and a donkey together.

D o you realize what you have been working with? Being yoked with someone should mean that you both agree with God. On the right hand is an ox, and on the left hand, a donkey. You keep trying to move forward, but the competition between the two hinders your progress. Similarly, working with people who have conflicting ways will slow you down. Separately, each has its value, which makes them assets to you. However, since they are inflexible, they can't get along and are a catastrophe waiting to happen.[705]

An ox and a donkey have different strength levels. The oxen are much stronger, and to yoke them with the donkey would wear the donkey out. The donkey is more versatile and walks in rough terrain; the ox won't walk in. It can pull a plow in dryer environments and on uneven ground that would cause the ox to falter. The spiritual significance is that the ox is a clean sacrificial animal, while the donkey is unclean because it doesn't chew the cud.[706] Putting them together would cause them to hurt each other and harm the work they are to do.

---

[705] Romans 12:16-18
[706] Leviticus 11:26

The New Testament carries this Ideal forth, saying, Don't yoke together with an unbeliever.[707] Yoking with someone not committed to God reveals our lack of trust in God's ways. We think differently about things than the unbeliever. Like the oxen, you are clean, but the unbeliever is not.[708] Like the donkey, unbelievers walk in ways that make us stumble. If we involve ourselves in relationships or service with them, we may initially draw them along because the Lord is our strength. Yet, in the long run, they will weigh us down. Be careful who you hook up with. They might pull you in the wrong way.

Prayer: Lord, I pray my discernment overrides my emotion so that I will link up with the right people. I want to keep moving and need those who will press forward with me. You are full of constant love to all those who trust you, so help me when I am weak and weary. I come to you as the fountain of living water to refresh my soul. Continue to show me your good hand and bless my life, in Jesus' name. Amen.

[707] 2 Corinthians 6:14-16
[708] John 13:10

Too Many People In Your Life

---✦---

Judges 7:4 Yahweh said to Gideon, "There are still too many people. Bring them down to the water, and I will test them for you there. It shall be, that those whom I tell you, 'This shall go with you,' shall go with you; and whoever I tell you, 'This shall not go with you,' shall not go.

S ome of us have just too many people in our lives. Everyone you come in contact with has a purpose in your life.[709] Some come for a reason, and once it's over, they have no part in your life. Others come for a season and are to walk with you for only a specific portion of your life, and then they are to leave. Still, others come to stay and become an integral part of your destiny.[710] We have to learn to lose some folks because they aren't stayers. When we try to hold onto those in our lives for reasons and seasons, we may hinder our destiny.

The story of Gideon is very well-read. He started with an army of 32,000 people who came to him for a reason, but couldn't stay because of fear.[711] The 10,000 that stayed were only there for a short season, but they, too, had to leave because their character made them unalert for battle.[712]

---

[709] Proverbs 20:5
[710] 1 Samuel 14:6-7
[711] Judges 7:3
[712] Judges 7:5

Only the 300 were there for destiny. Most people from your past have no place in your future. They are distractions to destiny. There are just too many of them that do nothing to assist you in achieving your destiny.

You can know who is there for a reason, a season, or to stay because you let God judge them. He will lead you to the waters and show you who you should remove from your life, starting with those who can't stand with you and concluding with those who distract you.[713] Sometimes, people will pop in and out of your life, and that's okay.[714] The 300 may have been unusual, but they always kept alert. They took courage and believed in victory. Those are the ones that are here for destiny.

> **Prayer:** Father, I ask you to see me in the crowd and bring me close. I will not fear, for you are present to guard and guide me. Help me keep my heart focused on doing what leads to my kingdom destiny. Show me who to release and who to hold on to. My battles are yours, and I trust that you have great things in store for me. Lead me to my destiny and victory, in Jesus' name. Amen.

---

[713] Acts 15:36-38
[714] 2 Timothy 4:10-12

Not Falling Away

---✦---

1 Chronicles 28:9 You, Solomon my son, know the God of your father, and serve him with a perfect heart and with a willing mind; for Yahweh searches all hearts, and understands all the imaginations of the thoughts. If you seek him, he will be found by you; but if you forsake him, he will cast you off forever.

With all his years of experience as a shepherd, a worshipper, a general, and 40 years as a king, it was time for David to invest the secret of his success into his son. What wise Counsel King David gave to his son Solomon, who would rule in his place. To be established, you must know the LORD God and serve Him with your whole heart and a willing mind.[715] If we seek God this way, He will manifest Himself to us. Nevertheless, if we forsake Him, He will cast us away from His presence and our position forever.

Could you say you serve God wholeheartedly and with a willing mind? In all that the Lord calls for us to do, He searches our hearts to see our devotion and our minds to know our service.[716] Sometimes, people wonder why it seems as if the Lord is not with them. When he peers at us, he notices our reluctance, half-heartedness, and rebellious thoughts. In this

---

[715] Luke 10:27
[716] Jeremiah 17:10

way, we will never find Him. Only when you search for Him with your whole heart will He be found, and He will establish you.[717]

At the beginning of Solomon's career, he sought God, and the Lord established him as the richest and wisest king ever. Nevertheless, as time passed, he became unfaithful to the Lord, causing God to reject him. The merciful Lord would not take the kingdom from Solomon for David's sake. However, He would wrest the kingdom from the hands of his son.[718] This loss serves as a warning to all of us to keep our hearts devoted to God and our minds focused on Him. If we let things enter our hearts and minds that draw us away from the Lord, He takes notice. Seek Him with your whole heart and mind lest you become cast away.

Prayer: Heavenly Father, help me know my life's direction and how to achieve great success. I declare my dedication of heart and mind to you, so help me grow in my devotion. Keep me in your love, and I ask that you never cast off my family for generations to come. I pray that they all seek and find you and that you will establish them in your grace, in the name of Jesus Christ. Amen.

---

[717] Jeremiah 29:13
[718] 1 Kings 11:4-12

Piercing, Tattoos, and the Lord

Leviticus 19:28 You shall not make any cuttings in your flesh for the dead, nor tattoo any marks on you. I am Yahweh.

W e can use many scriptures to address things we place on our flesh.[719] Leviticus has stirred up considerable controversy regarding the extent, if any, to which tattoos and piercings are permitted. People who pierce are not making cuts in their bodies for the dead, but they still need to consider what is appropriate.[720] However, what about tattoos? Ancient warriors tattooed themselves to invoke fear in their enemies. Over the generations, perceptions have shifted from tattoos being something for sailors and criminals to becoming a form of body art. But what does the Lord say about it?

The passage's context and historical records prove that when the bible talks about cuttings in the flesh for the dead and tattoos, it speaks of idolatrous practices performed to serve false gods. Leviticus displays the holiness of God and how He is to be served and approached. Some Israelites desired to copy the practices of their neighbors and worship God the same way.[721] Idolaters showed their devotion by marking themselves to

---

[719] 1 Corinthians 6:19-20

[720] 1 Peter 3:3-5

[721] Deuteronomy 12:30-31

false gods believed to preside over death and the grave, and Jehovah would have nothing of it.

You can't take the worship of devils and apply those practices to God. When we repeat what idolaters have done and dedicate those same acts to God, He is not pleased. Render to God what is God's and to Caesar what is Caesar's. God desires worship to be in spirit and truth. Are tattoos and piercings wrong? The answer is a combination of no and yes. The what and why matter because what comes out of the heart makes us unclean.[722] In all you do, make sure your heart is right, and you know God, for He was pierced[723] and perhaps even tattooed for us.[724]

> **Prayer:** Lord, my faith is in you, so help me keep my motives pure in all I do. My body is your temple, and I want to honor you. I pray that my life doesn't reflect a temptation to be like others but a testimony of being like you. I pray that for healing from grief in all those around me, we will not carry the pain of loss, hurt, and the past. Continue to cover me and let my light shine so all will see you in me, in the name of Jesus Christ. Amen.

---

[722] Mark 7:14-22

[723] John 19:34

[724] Revelation 19:16

Don't Look Inside

---❀---

1 Samuel 6:19 He struck of the men of Beth Shemesh, because they had looked into Yahweh's ark, he struck fifty thousand seventy of the men. Then the people mourned, because Yahweh had struck the people with a great slaughter.

Every believer wants the presence of God in their life. However, many want to treat God as common and do not honor His presence.[725] We want to look inside things and double-check to ensure God is true. We are more curious than consecrated, and our unclean hands offend God. Instead of accepting His presence through the Holy Spirit by faith, we want to peek inside the ark to see God directly. Instead of looking into the things of God, we want to look into God Himself.[726] Ultimately, we put ourselves at risk because we did not respect His presence.

The Philistines had captured the Ark of the Covenant, but death and disease struck their nation as soon as they touched it.[727] Knowing that Jehovah had judged them for their audacity, the Philistines returned the Ark with a trespass offering to Israel by placing it on a cart pulled by two milk cows.[728] The people of Bethshmesh rejoiced in the ark's return;

---

[725] Isaiah 29:13-14

[726] Ecclesiastes 8:5-6

[727] 1 Samuel 5:2-7

[728] 1 Samuel 6:5-9

nevertheless, they did not respect the presence of God. Though the men of Beth Shemesh were not priests, they lifted the lid to the Ark, called the Mercy Seat, and peered inside.

How often have our doubts caused us to look further than we should? God had shown Himself through creation, yet it is not good enough for some.[729] The lesson for us is, " Bad things happen when you don't respect God's presence." If the Lord is in your life, honor Him. Live life and conduct your behavior according to His presence in it. You don't have to look in if you know the Lord is with you.[730] Rejoice in faith and receive the gift of God's presence inside you.

Prayer: Father, forgive me for all the times I did not honor you in word, action, or faith. I consecrate my heart and life to you and desire to worship in the beauty of your holiness. Please help me to teach others respect for your name and house. Lord, I ask that your mighty work of favor watch over me and my loved ones, in Jesus' name. Amen.

---

[729] Romans 1:20
[730] Matthew 1:23

A Thriving Vision

2 Chronicles 26:5 He set himself to seek God in the days of Zechariah, who had understanding in the vision of God; and as long as he sought Yahweh, God made him prosper.

King Uzziah had a great testimony: "As long as he sought the Lord, God caused him to prosper."[731] Regarding guidance, the only thing better than having a godly vision is knowing where to go to understand it. Even the king needed a covering not just from a visionary but from a visionary who understood the moves and plans of God.[732] As the king sought God, he gained a reverential fear of the Lord and thus submitted himself to receive an understanding of God's requirements for him. As he continually sought God, he prospered in whatever He did.

Nowadays, it seems like everyone claims to have a vision from God, yet we don't always see the visions prospering. We must order our steps in the Lord's ways and ask ourselves if we are continuing to seek God so we can prosper within the vision we do have.[733] Whether your vision is great or small, without proper guidance and understanding, it becomes dreams deferred that dry up and wither away, leaving only shadows of

---

[731] 2 Chronicles 26:3-5
[732] Esther 1:13
[733] 2 Chronicles 27:6

thoughts. A vision without an understanding of how to implement it will not flourish.[734]

Your ability to comprehend the desire of God will feed your vision. Each step we take in seeking the Lord will bring new awareness to what we must do to accomplish God's vision.[735] John Maxwell said, "Vision without passion is a picture without possibilities." Vision is more than just dreams. They are divinely inspired and revealed plans to prosper you.[736] Vision and understanding prosper as we acknowledge and seek the Lord. A thriving vision equals a successful life. May it be said that you prospered as you sought the Lord.

Prayer: Father, I need you in my life. Please help me to seek you and prosper continually. Link me with my Zechariah, who can help me understand how to operate in my purpose and bring forth the vision. I know you have great plans for me, and I ask for clarity of the vision for my life, family, and ministry. Lead me by your Holy Spirit, renewing my mind, heart, and passion for you, in the name of Jesus Christ, Amen.

---

[734] 1 Chronicles 12:32

[735] Proverbs 16:3

[736] Jeremiah 29:11

Evangelizing the Found

---✦---

Galatians 4:17 They zealously seek you in no good way. No, they desire to alienate you, that you may seek them.

Have you ever seen someone try to recruit people to their ministry who are already actively participating in ministry? Why would someone try to evangelize those who are already serving the Lord? You become a notch on their belt.[737] It is another personal victory for them, but it does nothing to give Christ victory. In Galatia, they were trying to persuade the people to turn away from the grace of God and return to the law, so that they would gather disciples after themselves. Why try to win someone over if it's not for God?

The spirit of the Nicolaitans remains alive in the church.[738] The word "Nicolaitans" is derived from two words. The word Nike means to rule, and laity means the people. Some want to rule over God's people not to benefit them but for their own gain. Sometimes, believers act like they are building personal kingdoms within the kingdom of God. Christ came to set us free, but they only want to place us into another type of bondage under them.[739] They say that we will be more blessed by following them.

---

[737] Matthew 23:15
[738] Revelation 2:16
[739] Luke 4:18-19

When will we learn that the sheep do not belong to the church or the leaders; they belong to God?

They are wolves in sheep's clothing, for only wolves steal sheep.[740] Lost shepherds scatter the sheep. The person with the heart of God wins people to the Lord because it is best for the person they are reaching out to. There are too many lost people in the world for us to waste our time evangelizing those whom the Lord already calls His own. We should bring those who have left the church fellowship back in; however, those in fellowship should be encouraged to continue growing where they are.

> **Prayer:** Father, help me to stay grounded and grow in your grace. I want to follow those who follow your Christ, not those who follow themselves. Give me discernment to not lead myself but be led by the Spirit of Christ. I pray for those who have lost their way. That they would return to the fold and follow our good Shepherd. Help us to be one in Christ and follow His voice, in Jesus' name, Amen.

---

[740] Matthew 7:15

Taking Power Over Your Storms

---✦---

Philippians 4:7 And the peace of God, which surpasses all understanding, will guard your hearts and your thoughts in Christ Jesus.

In all our getting, we are to get an understanding,[741] but if peace and understanding were to have a footrace, peace would win out every time. Understanding reveals truth and purpose. It informs us why things have been going the way they are. Understanding helps us accept our situation, but doesn't change our circumstances. However, God's peace protects your faith by guiding and guarding the heart and mind through everything. No matter what may come, the peace of God is there to stand with us.[742]

The Greek word Phroureó, translated as "guard," deals with something preemptively posted to secure and protect you. God's peace is a preemptive strike against the devil's plans. Consider when the disciples were at sea, and a sudden storm arose.[743] Everyone was scared, but Christ was at rest. Jesus could quiet the storm because he had to have peace within himself. God's comfort guards his heart and mind. That peace didn't leave when the disciples awoke Him in a panic.[744] Instead, it spoke to the storm and made it peaceful, too.

---

[741] Proverbs 4:7
[742] Isaiah 26:3
[743] Matthew 8:24-26
[744] John 14:27

You can't minister anything you don't have. Only those at peace in heart and mind can calm the storms that come their way. When you release your fears to the point where you can trust God and pray, thanking Him in your situation, then His peace will rest upon you.[745] Whatever you may understand about your problems won't matter because God's peace will shield you from them. Others may not understand how you can rest in the storm like the disciples. Nevertheless, they will see the storm dissipate when you continually believe and speak peace. Let His peace surpass your own thoughts so you can take power over your storms.

> **Prayer:** Father, your peace gives me confidence in my heart and mind, so I will not be confused or shaken when troubles come my way. Instead of worrying about why the storms arise, you have given me peace to maintain my faith and see the storms cease. I rebuke every storm in my life and declare your Holy Spirit's power to take control of all situations. I come against the storms of doubt, depression, and dependency in my loved ones and ask that you deliver and show them your peace, in Christ's name. Amen.

---

[745] Philippians 4:6

Praying the Vision of God

---⚜---

Romans 8:26-27 In the same way, the Spirit also helps our weaknesses, for we don't know how to pray as we ought. But the Spirit himself makes intercession for us with groanings which can't be uttered. He who searches the hearts knows what is on the Spirit's mind, because he makes intercession for the saints according to God.

One of our most significant weaknesses comes from not knowing how we ought to pray. We must ask ourselves: "If the Holy Spirit came to reveal all truth, why do I still not know how to pray"?[746] When we intercede for someone, we often pray that the Lord will bring them out of the situation. That's praying from a man's perspective. We never see Christ or the apostles praying to remove the situation, but rather to use it.[747] They prayed that the external situation would build internal faith in the individual.

God searches our hearts and knows what is on the Holy Spirit's mind.[748] We often don't know how to pray because instead of searching for what's best, we search for what's easiest. The groanings of the Spirit mind are in our hearts, waiting to be heard by the one searching for them. God's will

---

[746] John 16:13

[747] Luke 22:31-32 compare with Acts 4:29-31

[748] Jeremiah 17:10

for you is the vision He has for your life. So when the Holy Ghost prays, He calls forth the vision to break through your problems. Our storms are vision blockers that come to distract us from our purpose. But God said, 'You will get to the other side if you pray. The vision is that the storm will have to pass.'[749]

Christ told Paul that he must testify of Him in Rome.[750] So when Paul was in a storm, he didn't have to pray to survive the storm. He prayed for the completion of God's vision for his life, which brought him through the storm.[751] We pray as the Lord prays when we intercede for others according to God's vision. Examining situations while praying can reveal a weakness because we are not praying according to God's vision. When you intercede for someone, pray according to the will of God and seek a vision breakthrough.

Prayer: God, I pray that you use this storm to take me to greater levels of faith, strength, and purpose. You have called those who use the storm to help those who have tried to escape it. I ask that your vision and good plan for my life come forth. Pour your love and protection on my family and cause me unspeakable joy, in the name of Jesus Christ, Amen.

---

[749] Mark 4:35-40
[750] Acts 23:11
[751] Acts 27:23-26

An Appointment with the Sword

---✦---

Jeremiah 43:7 They came into the land of Egypt, for they didn't obey Yahweh's voice; and they came to Tahpanhes.

Are you going places, or are you a growing place? People are on the move, but if they haven't used their trials as a place of growth, those same troubles will follow. We think moving to a new place will make things alright, yet we can't outrun our problems.[752] Problems are rooted in who you are and who you connect to. Running doesn't work because the root problem grows again in one form or another. Trials are appointed times to bring you growth through God's instruction, peace, and comfort, but if we leave His counsel, we set ourselves an appointment with trouble.

The people had come to Jeremiah and pleaded with him to seek God so that they would know what to do.[753] Yet they did not like what the Lord had to say to them. The Lord wanted them to remain in the land under the Babylonians and trust Him because the Babylonians would do them no further harm. He warned the people not to flee to Egypt, but the people would not listen. Instead of heeding the Lord's words, they listened to their fears and feelings. Their refusal to obey the Lord made an appointment with destruction.[754]

---

[752] Jeremiah 43:4-6
[753] Jeremiah 42:2-13
[754] Jeremiah 25:7-9

They thought they could escape their situation, but Nebuchadnezzar's armies would follow them. When we disobey God's word, we surrender the protection and provision that could have been ours.[755] They made an appointment with destruction. Through their disobedience, some were destined for death, others for captivity, and others for the sword.[756] God made them an appointment for peace. He desired to bless them after their troubles, but through their disobedience, they received an appointment they couldn't afford. That was the appointment with the sword.

Prayer: Heavenly Father, forgive all the times I failed to operate from my faith and ran from the problems I was to embrace and grow through. Instead of separating myself from troubles, I want to separate myself unto you. Draw me near in understanding, so fear and the rapid attacks of the enemy don't overwhelm me. Place your protective hedge around all I have and cause me to rise in the name of Jesus. Amen.

---

[755] Numbers 14:9
[756] Jeremiah 43:10-11

Don't Fear But Fight

---✦---

Nehemiah 4:14 I looked, and rose up, and said to the nobles, to the rulers, and to the rest of the people, "Don't be afraid of them! Remember the Lord, who is great and awesome, and fight for your brothers, your sons, your daughters, your wives, and your houses.

All Nehemiah wanted to do was to rebuild the walls so that his people would live securely. But here comes Sanballat with his cronies, causing trouble. People laughed at the rebuilding, saying, "If a fox were to jump on it, it would fall."[757] Their taunts discouraged the people. Nehemiah stood up because they had to be secure that God was with them. When you feel alone, remember that God is with you. We must learn to trust God and build with a sword in one hand.[758]

Like Nehemiah, sometimes we must encourage ourselves to deal with the Sanballats.[759] Sanballats are those who try to intimidate you or distract you from the work God has for you. They are on our jobs, in schools, in churches, and in our homes. They try to blow out your candle so theirs will shine brighter. No one can make you feel inferior without your assent and consent. The Sanballat will come up against you; don't be afraid of them, but fear the Lord and fight.

---

[757] Nehemiah 4:1-3

[758] Nehemiah 4:17-20

[759] 1 Samuel 30:6

We have nothing to fear but the Lord.[760] Remember, you have much to fight for, no matter what enemy comes your way. Fight for your brothers; fight for your sons and daughters. Fight for your marriage and fight for your home. We have too much to lose. We must stand and fight, for our sacrifices will eventually pay off.[761] As we seek to do the will of God, He will be with us through every trial. The Sanballats can't harm you because God is on your side. Be encouraged and turn your fear into a source of strength.

Prayer: Lord, You have not given us a spirit of fear, but of power, love, and a sound mind. So, I stand against the enemy's manipulation and intimidation tactics. Give me the skill to build and battle at the same time. Help me to be alert and lead by inspiration, not intimidation. I come against the confusion that tears families apart and stand under your protection in the name of Jesus Christ. Amen.

---

[760] Matthew 10:28-31
[761] 2 Chronicles 15:7

Declaration of the Doorkeeper

Psalms 84:10 For a day in your courts is better than a thousand. I would rather be a doorkeeper in the house of my God, than to dwell in the tents of wickedness.

The worst, lowest person in the house of God is better off than the best person in the world of wickedness. Just one day with God is better than a thousand without Him. People who don't know God may seem like they have things going their way, but they are like the chaff that the wind drives away.[762] They won't last forever. We see it portrayed in the parable of Lazarus' reward and the rich man's suffering.[763] It is better to be a humble doorkeeper in the house of the Lord than to have all the pleasures of this world without Him.

Today's church ushers take pride in being derived from the temple doorkeeper. However, unlike the modern usher, the doorkeeper was the lowest and most menial position held in the temple. Not only did they guard the door and take offerings,[764] but doorkeepers were also penile inspectors. Yeah, that's right, whenever a man who was not known to them came into the temple, they would have to see if they were circumcised. Men would lift their robes to prove they were either Jews or converts. If

---

[762] Psalms 1:5

[763] Luke 16:19-23

[764] 2 Kings 22:4

not, they would be responsible for circumcising the person on the spot or ejecting them from the temple grounds.

Recognizing that it's better to be the lowliest in God's house than hanging with the wicked is a declaration of surrender to the Lord.[765] People who love God will desire His presence in their lives more than things. They will not compromise God for the world or submit themselves to wickedness to gain comfort. The humble person relinquishes pride and acknowledges their strengths and weaknesses before God. This kind of humility is genuinely for the God lover and those who pursue God. It is the declaration of those who walk humbly with our Lord. As a gate for the sheep, Jesus Himself is the doorkeeper of our souls, bringing us to salvation.[766] So, being a doorkeeper isn't so bad after all.

> **Prayer:** Lord, make me a keeper at the open door of your grace. Inspect my heart as I enter with thanksgiving and praise. Take me where your favor flows and renew my passion for your presence. I pray your hand of peace and blessing upon my life. Work out your will and good desire for me and my family in the name of Jesus Christ. Amen.

---

[765] Matthew 23:10-12
[766] John 10:7-10

Knowing God

---✦---

1 Timothy 3:16 Without controversy, the mystery of godliness is great: God was revealed in the flesh, justified in the spirit, seen by angels, preached among the nations, believed on in the world, and received up in glory.

If there was any uncontroversial truth that the early church stood on, it was the fact that God came to earth in the form of a man.[767] He proved he was righteous through His deed. The angels confirmed that He was God and had the power to conquer sin even in the flesh. He sent His servants to preach even to those who did not know Him, and when they began to believe, He returned to His position of authority in Heaven.[768] This codex of truth rests securely on the work of Jesus Christ so that we would know God for ourselves.

The indisputable facts remain that the early church confessed that Christ was God manifested in the flesh from the beginning.[769] The deity of Christ was not something the church came to believe over time, as some think. Instead, it was the hallmark of the Christian faith from its very inception. At no other time has the Lord allowed Himself to be judged by

---

[767] John 1:14
[768] Acts 1:8-11
[769] Philippians 2:5-6

His creation as was in the days of Christ.[770] God, who is the measure of all holiness, lowered Himself to a position that man could judge for himself what true righteousness was. It was a revelation for man to know God.

The mystery of godliness is great because it revealed God's coming in the flesh so we would know Him. Read the scriptures and judge that Jesus is not only the greatest, most righteous man that ever lived, but also God wrapped up in the flesh. On this truth, we rest knowing God. No other faith can say they know and have a personal relationship with a God who knows them.[771] Without a doubt, God wants us to get to know Him better. Not only to know His ways but also to know His heart. He was manifest, justified, witnessed, preached, believed, and received so that you could know Him.

Prayer: Lord, thank you for revealing yourself in the flesh so I can see myself in you. You revealed your power to break the flesh, so I will know your power to walk in the Spirit. Shower me with your love and grace so that I may walk out a transformed life. Cover me under your hand of protection, in the name of Jesus. Amen

---

[770] Luke 23:13-15
[771] 1 Corinthians 8:3

100 Fold

Genesis 26:12 Isaac sowed in that land, and reaped in the same year one hundred times what he planted. Yahweh blessed him

No one said favor was fair. One touch of God's favor can shift you into something greater. However, the cost of favor is faithfulness. Faithfulness takes sacrifice, submission, and surrender on our part.[772] Nevertheless, after you have served God faithfully, He faithfully grants you favor.[773] What is favor? God's goodwill causes benefits to flow into your life. Having favor means that the Lord's goodness rains upon you. You become drenched in it, and His favor attracts what you need and opens doors that would otherwise be closed off.[774]

Favor doesn't mean money. But it means you go beyond your circumstances and live in the overabundance of the Lord. God's favor caused Isaac to sow grain during a famine[775] and reap a hundredfold harvest. God's favor in your life will dramatically change the circumstances around you. While everyone else was hungry and could not find water, Isaac would find water wherever he went.[776] Favor made him prosper in recession, thrive in

---

[772] Isaiah 58:11-12

[773] Genesis 24:1

[774] Leviticus 26:8-12

[775] Genesis 26:1-3

[776] Genesis 26:18-22

inflation, and survive when the market crashed. Isaac was blessed, even though those around him were lacking.

Instead of getting discouraged, we must remain faithful and declare God's favor during hard times. No matter what you call your famine, the Lord will bless the faithful to survive and prosper.[777] Even if you must wait a season, you should expect to reap the same year you sow. Some look for 30, others 60, but still others 100-fold on their return. What is sown in faith, watered in hope, and nurtured by love will spring forth a harvest. Our job is to plant and remain faithful to God as He blesses us with what we need.[778]

Prayer: Lord, I thank you for your favor. I will not sow in fear but in faithfulness to you. Every time people counted me out, you brought me back. My sowing is not a sacrifice; it's a setup for your favor. Please grant me the ability to reap in good times and trouble. With you, I always win. I pray for favor to pour into my church and family and that we all prosper together in the name of Jesus Christ. Amen.

[777] Psalm 37:18-19
[778] Colossians 2:6-7

No Fear in Their Hearts

Exodus 10:20 But Yahweh hardened Pharaoh's heart, and he didn't let the children of Israel go.

Sometimes, we look at life and wonder why we never get to take the easy road out. Why would God harden someone's heart so that we have to stay in a situation that we have been praying to God to get us out of? God reveals himself to us during these times so that we may know him.[779] We learn that God builds our spiritual life on faithfulness, not convenience.[780] Another reason is so we would take courage and be strong. Still, yet another reason is that He may judge and take vengeance upon those who oppressed His people, causing them to reap what they had sown.[781]

Critics declare how unfair it was for God to force Pharaoh to refuse to let the Israelites go and then judge him for doing what God made him do. It may appear that is what happened; however, it's not. The Hebrew word Chazaq, translated as hardened, means "to aid or to make courageous." It deals with how the Lord strengthened Pharaoh's heart by providing relief and letting him seem to get away with things. This allowed what Pharaoh decided not to be, out of fear, but his own judgment.[782] God gave him courage, but the decision was totally Pharaoh's.

---

[779] Exodus 7:3-5

[780] Habakkuk 2:4

[781] Galatians 6:7-10

[782] Exodus 7:13 & 22

Just as God gives courage to those who oppress you, He is building it in you. Look at the world. They despise God, and there is no fear in them. Why would God, who is greatly to be feared,[783] allow or encourage people not to fear Him? The reason why is that pride must precede a fall. People lift themselves against you and come against you without the slightest fear or remorse. Oh, how far they shall fall, but you shall stand.[784] The more they refuse to release their mouth and hands from God's people, the more trials they will endure; nevertheless, you shall be made strong and free.

Prayer: Lord, thank you for building me through the storm. I understand you harden my Goliaths so they fall at my feet. I stand humbly before you in faith, for my confidence in you gives me victory. I ask you to set free my loved ones from every bondage they have endured, and that they will know it was your hand to deliver, in Jesus' name. Amen.

---

[783] Nehemiah 4:14
[784] Proverbs 16:17-20

Preparing For A Sacrifice

---⋆---

Leviticus 25:20-21 If you said, "What shall
we eat the seventh year? Behold, we shall
not sow, nor gather in our increase;" I will
command my blessing on you in the sixth year,
and it shall bear fruit for the three years.

The Lord had commanded the Israelites to take a Sabbath year for the land to rest. For six years, they were to sow and reap, but in the 7th year, they were not to sow but let the ground lie fallow to regain its fertility. It was a festive year to honor the Lord, where the wild harvest of the unattended trees and vines would be available for any strangers.[785] Yet some questioned what they would eat in this year of Sabbath rest. The Lord responded that He would provide a blessing to carry them through before the time of their need came.

Every Sabbath year, the Lord cared for every drought, famine, or sacrifice beforehand. Just as Joseph stored up grain in the seven good years to prepare for the seven bad,[786] the Lord would provide three years' harvest to prepare the Israelites for the Sabbath year. Abraham once said, "The Lord will provide Himself for the sacrifice."[787] Whenever God intends you to sacrifice, He provides for it before He requires you to give it. We never

---

[785] Leviticus 25:4-7
[786] Genesis 41:35-36
[787] Genesis 22:8

have to worry about not having enough to give to God. If we follow God's words, He will give us what we need to do His desire.[788]

For 490 years, the Israelites did not keep the Sabbath year, which became the standard of their 70-year judgment.[789] It comes down to the issue of whether we will trust God. Are we intending to follow the Lord, or are we waiting to see if circumstances make obedience convenient? God expects us to trust Him. He always prepares before a sacrifice.[790] As we follow His word, He provides for us according to that same word. He will command a blessing upon us to prepare us for our fallow days. Then return us once again to better days.

> **Prayer:** Father, I adore you, for you have given me salvation, hope, and love. Help me to obey the hard things without worry, doubt, or fear. I trust you for your season of overabundance and await my festive year. I pray for a 3-year overflow to supply more than my needs. Thank you in advance for the goodness coming my way as I hold steadfast to your word, in the name of Jesus Christ. Amen.

---

[788] Leviticus 25:22
[789] 2 Chronicles 36:21
[790] 2 Corinthians 9:9-12

Much Forgiveness, Much Love

---⚓---

Luke 7:47 Therefore I tell you, her sins, which are many, are forgiven, for she loved much. But one to whom little is forgiven, loves little.

When she heard that He ate in the house of the Pharisee named Simon, the woman who came to Christ was desperate to be forgiven.[791] She had risked rejection and public humiliation because she wanted more than the life she had. She was genuinely sorrowful, yet the Pharisee could only see her past. Christ looked at her and saw her future. He saw the dedication that she would have because she recognized her sin. Yet, in the same place, the Pharisee could not recognize his shortcomings.

When we compare ourselves to others, we may have a false feeling of superiority and righteousness, while in truth, we have only loved God a little.[792] It's easy to recognize the faults of others and overlook your own.[793] Especially in cases where they have committed such highly publicized sins. You know those who sinned without remorse. In comparison, our sins are tiny next to theirs. We thought that they were the ones who deserved hell, but not us, but those whose sins are many love God much.

You are mistaken if you think you have only been forgiven a little. Our own recognition of our sins will cause us to love little or love much. We

---

[791] Luke 7:36-39
[792] Luke 18:10-14
[793] Matthew 7:1-5

see other people's sins clearly, but we often make excuses for our own.[794] If we ever wish to be great lovers of God, we must first recognize that we, too, have great sin. We, too, have rejected His will for our lives. We have offended His Holiness with how we lived, but we have now come to His feet seeking forgiveness.[795] Great lovers of God realize that no matter how good we seem in man's eyes, we fall short in God's eyes. God forgives us of much, so we should love Him much.

Prayer: Lord, only you know the depths of how much you have forgiven me. Thank you for loving and accepting me through all my faults and failures. You have shown great love through your sacrifice, so I declare today that you have all my heart, mind, and strength. Help me be known for leaving my sins behind because I love you immensely. Renew my life and strength in Jesus' name, Amen.

---

[794] 1 John 1:8
[795] Psalm 25:11

Ouch, That Hurt

---✦---

*Matthew 7:4 Or how will you tell your brother,
'Let me remove the speck from your eye,'
and behold, the beam is in your own eye?*

C hrist is speaking of hypocrisy in pointing out the speck in someone's eye while hitting them with the log in your own.[796] We often try to correct others' problems without first addressing our own issues. While others' sins are more apparent to us, ours are the ones that matter.[797] Most of the time, we address others with their problems; we try to correct them without hearing the correction for ourselves. Christ wants us to help, not just correct. However, we first must help ourselves if we are to be effective in the lives of others.

True correction comes from a heart that acknowledges its faults and possesses the clarity of vision to guide others through their situations with gentle understanding.[798] Removing the log in our eye is important because significant wounds must be dealt with delicately so that we don't increase injury. You can't help somebody and judge that person simultaneously because you wound them all over again. No one with a major medical condition wants a crude Doctor who injures them emotionally while

---

[796] Matthew 7:5
[797] 1 Timothy 5:24-25
[798] Luke 6:42

fending to care for their needs. We desire someone who can help us and is sympathetic to our condition.[799]

What if we saw ourselves as an eye instead of an "I"? We would take an introspective look inside ourselves and eliminate the beams because they hurt.[800] We would confess our mistakes before someone pointed them out to us. We would see someone with issues and not forget our own issues. Each time we seek to help others is an opportunity to reflect on the goodness of God. Avoiding the beam in our eyes doesn't remove it. We must address it and eliminate it. Only then will our vision be precise enough, and we will be caring enough to remove the speck in the eye of another.

Prayer: Lord, help me to deal with myself by drawing near to you, confessing my faults, and surrendering to your Spirit of grace. I want to see your mighty works in me and those around me. Remove hypocrisy and give me an eye of discernment to see my problems and know how to fix them. I pray that those I help see the hand of our heavenly Father with me. Thank you for removing my faults and any bondages and changing my life in the name of Jesus Christ. Amen.

[799] 2 Corinthians 1:3-5
[800] 2 Corinthians 13:5

Lock Them Out

Isaiah 22:22 I will lay the key of David's house on his shoulder. He will open, and no one will shut. He will shut, and no one will open.

Locking, unlocking, binding, loosing, releasing, and retaining are all connected to the one with the keys. Keys represent free access to and authority in the house. Eliakim had the key to the house of David laid on his shoulder, meaning he had the authority to use the keys. Still, Christ owned them.[801] Christ lent the apostles the keys to the kingdom of God.[802] Jesus has the keys to death and Hades.[803] The Lord has the keys to the floodgates of blessing in heaven.[804] These keys represent kingdom authority, ability, and advantages that we can faithfully bring into our lives.

Jesus Christ gives us the keys to bind and loose things. We are to open the doors to what He wants in our lives and close the doors, keeping out what isn't good for us. The keys God has laid upon our shoulders will fix every problem we encounter and provide a way of escape when we need one.[805] We are given the keys of binding and loosing as stewards of His

---

[801] Revelation 3:7

[802] Matthew 16:19

[803] Revelation 1:18

[804] Malachi 3:10

[805] 1 Corinthians 10:13

good will. When someone comes to you with something unclean or defiling, it's up to you to lock it out or let it in.

We must ask ourselves what we are doing with our keys. How many keys do we have that go unused? What you open the door to is open, and no one can shut it out but you. Sanctification involves evicting anything that is unlike God and closing the door. Sin is often crouching at the door, waiting to get in, but you have the power to master it.[806] We can let in peace, goodness, favor, and mercy while simultaneously locking out confusion, backbiting, and hatred. Are you locking out the nay-sayers, the doubters, and the unfaithful? Be careful how you control the keys Christ has given you.

> **Prayer:** Lord, I bind the hand of the enemy away from my mind, family, and health. We will stand firm in your blessing. Lead me by your Holy Spirit in using the kingdom keys. I declare a legacy of salvation and wellness in my home. No weapon formed shall succeed against us. Through faith and faithfulness, I open the floodgates of your favor in heaven and will see your goodness follow me; in Jesus' name, Amen.

---

[806] Genesis 4:7

Waiting For A Word

Luke 10:16 Whoever listens to you listens to me, and whoever rejects you rejects me. Whoever rejects me rejects him who sent me.

In sending out the seventy disciples to go ahead of Him and preach in the cities and towns to which Christ Himself was going,[807] Jesus made a sobering statement. If they hear you, then they hear Him. If they reject the seventy, they reject Christ and the Father. Many people claim they want to hear the voice of God, but they refuse to listen when God speaks through a person. Whether it is the written word of scripture or the spoken word of the gospel, to hear the sent word is to hear Christ, who is the word made flesh.[808]

Jesus speaks to those who receive His word, no matter its form. God sent someone before Christ to prepare the way. He did that with the woman at the well.[809] Christ did it with John the Baptist, the twelve apostles, and the seventy disciples. If the people refused to listen to His emissaries, He would skip over that town and move to the next town. Some have missed God's visitation by not heeding the announcement of His expectation. Christ is telling the seventy that those who listen to what Christ says through them are faithful enough for Christ to instruct

---

[807] Luke 10:1-9
[808] John 1:14-18
[809] John 4:27-38

directly; those who reject them will miss out because listening to the word draws God's presence.

How we respond to the word determines whether we are in a religion or a relationship with God. The principle of drawing near to God and He draws near to you applies when hearing God's voice.[810] He first gives the word to us through others; if we receive it, the Lord seeks to come to us directly. Do you want God in your home? Respond to the light He has given, and more light will come. When we heed the word given, we will receive the word we have been waiting for.

> **Prayer:** I have been waiting for you, Father, but you have waited longer for me to heed you. Draw me closer to your presence so I will hear your will for my life more clearly. I will conquer all my fears and stand in faith, for you are with me. I ask you to send help to minister to my loved ones who struggle to hear you. Bring us all near so we can walk together in your kingdom, in the name of Jesus Christ. Amen.

---

[810] John 10:25-28

Kingdom Fit

Luke 9:61-62 Another also said, "I want to follow you, Lord, but first allow me to say good-bye to those who are at my house." But Jesus said to him, "No one, having put his hand to the plow and looking back, is fit for God's Kingdom."

Every believer desires to enter into the kingdom of God. There is no better place for us to be. However, many aren't fit to go in.[811] Many of us make excuses for not participating in the Lord's work. Others put conditions on their obedience to God's word, saying, "If you do this, Lord, then I will serve you," or "Let me do what I want to first, then I will follow you." The truth is that Christ looks at them as unfit for the kingdom of God.[812] The only time we are to look back is to see how far God has brought us.

The plowman had to look ahead to do his job.[813] He would not only guide the plow but would have to rest his weight on the plow for it to burrow deep. The oxen would pull, and the plowman would push down. For the plowman to look behind them, they would have to remove pressure from the plow, causing the furrows to become shallow and crooked. They would have to replough the entire field because he was distracted.

---

[811] Matthew 7:21-23

[812] Luke 9:57-60

[813] Philippians 3:12-14

The plowman wouldn't be worthy because he ruined the field every time he looked back.[814]

Similarly, those who look back are unfit for God's kingdom.[815] God's desire has always been to be first in our lives, and all those who put things before Him are not suitable for the kingdom of God. You're on the right track when you have no interest in looking back. When following the Lord, ask yourself, Is there anything you place before Him? Are you looking back at your life and saying, 'Let me get this done first'? If so, change your mind and go forward so we are fit for the kingdom of God.[816]

Prayer: Lord, help me to resist the conflicted emotions, shakiness, and fear that tempt me to turn around. I'll have confidence in you and not veer to the left or right. My heart yearns to discover how to become nearer to you. Help those who are unable to move forward because they are still struggling with the pain from their past. Provide them the clarity and direction they need to find freedom and begin working the land, in Jesus' name, Amen.

---

[814] Luke 17:32-33
[815] Hebrews 12:1-3
[816] 1 Kings 19:19-21

A Good Heart

---✦---

Zechariah 7:10-11 Don't oppress the widow, the fatherless, the foreigner, nor the poor; and let none of you devise evil against his brother in your heart.' But they refused to listen, and turned their backs, and stopped their ears, that they might not hear.

At the end of the seventy years of captivity, the people of Bethel went to the prophets to seek God's favor. Yet before God would restore them, He reminded them why they needed His help.[817] God had sent prophets to ask the previous generations to be fair, forgiving, and loving, to help those who cannot help themselves, and not to take advantage of others.[818] But they had not listened. Therefore, during the captivity, they became the very people they would not help.

It's possible to believe in God with your heart but refuse Him because your heart remains hardened.[819] Fairness relates to our general goodness of heart and does not even go as far as personal holiness. Even unbelievers can do these things, yet His people had not listened. During the captivity, those who ignored others became widows, orphans, foreigners, and the poor. How many would do more if they realized their families would later be victims of the problems they refused to address? The truth is that even

---

[817] Zechariah 7:2-7
[818] Micah 6:8
[819] Jeremiah 17:9

today, families are dealing with ignored problems while often seeking God to restore them from those same situations.

We are like clay on the potter's wheel; God's word is the sculpting tool He uses to remake our hearts. When we submit our hearts to God's word, the word begins to transform our hearts into the heart of God.[820] We can't say we have a heart for God if we don't have a heart for people. God loves people and wants us to love and consider them as He does.[821] Refusing God's word stops the movement on the wheel that God would have used to mold your heart. We must let God shape us because what we ignore may be what we become.

Prayer: Father, show me those with authentic needs that I can help physically, mentally, and spiritually. Expose the youth in my family to giving to those less fortunate, so they not only appreciate what they have but will not go down the wrong paths that lead to their misfortune. Make my heart sensitive to their need and cause me to walk in your favor without reproach. Thank you for your grace and provision in my life, in the name of Jesus Christ, Amen.

---

[820] Deuteronomy 30:6
[821] Philippians 2:3-4

Get the Want by Fulfilling Needs

---❖---

Philippians 4:19 My God will supply every need of yours according to his riches in glory in Christ Jesus.

What a promise! God will supply every need, not based on what we have but on what He has. It is His riches that supply our needs. Paul speaks to his faithful supporters in Philippi, assuring them that God will meet every need because of their faithful assistance.[822] Paul believed their needs were first spiritual, then physical. When lack occurs, do we address our spiritual poverty and determine if it is something we desire because we see everyone else with it, or do we desire it because it's what God wants for our life?[823]

The world feeds our wants with every imaginable new fad, gadget, and possession. They call it advertising, but it is social programming and manipulation designed to affect the center of our desires by producing cravings for what they suggest.[824] The power of suggestion implants desires inside us, causing many to spend more than they have, leading people into debt, distress, and depression. Even with all our needs supplied, our wants ruin people's lives because we desire what the world craves instead of being fed from a heart and mind desiring God.[825]

---

[822] Philippians 4:15-18

[823] Matthew 6:31-33

[824] Proverbs 19:2-3

[825] 1 John 2:15-17

What we want is not always what we need; what we need is not always what we want.[826] The enemy desires us to break our spiritual discipline and replace our fulfillment in Christ with the world's cravings. God supplies our needs according to His riches in glory, and He does this through Jesus Christ. If we stopped spending on wants, we would realize we have everything we need.[827] The spiritual comes first to discipline us to beat back pride, lust, and the world's cares. Then comes the physical, where we pay off debt, start saving, and build wealth.

> **Prayer:** Lord, I thank you that what I have doesn't matter. You supply all I need from your wealth. I ask that you move on my spirit first, giving me the discipline, discernment, and self-control to stay unattached to the world. Then, move on to the physical pouring out your anointing, blessing, and healing. Keep my mind Christ-centered and heart Spirit led as I faithfully follow you in the name of Jesus Christ. Amen.

---

[826] Joshua 21:45
[827] Psalm 23:1-2

I Need to Reschedule an Appointment

*Proverbs 10:27 The fear of Yahweh prolongs days,
but the years of the wicked shall be shortened.*

Does scripture give a key to prolonging or shortening our lifespan? Many people wonder about when their time on this earth will be up. Many believe that God has set the time of their death in stone and that nothing you do can change it. Scripture says, "And as it is appointed to men once to die, but after this the judgment."[828] Tragedies do happen for some, and nothing we do can change them. We all have an appointment with death, which we shall keep. However, most of us can reschedule the date and time just as we would any other appointment.

We see biblical examples of how we can lengthen our days by fearing the Lord or shorten our days by behaving wickedly.[829] King Hezekiah was near death. He had served the Lord faithfully for years, so when he turned to the wall and prayed, God extended his life for 15 years.[830] King Saul, however, was full of life and potential. His disobedience led to God cutting his reign and life short.[831] Our actions or lack of action either prolong or will shorten your appointment with death.

---

[828] Hebrews 9:27
[829] Job 22:15-16
[830] Isaiah 38:5
[831] 1 Chronicles 10:13

We can eat, smoke, drink, take, or do whatever we desire; however, it will cut years off our lives. Living wisely in the fear of the Lord and listening to what His word says about our behavior can lengthen your life.[832] Reschedule your appointment. Eat right, rid yourself of harmful things, remain sexually pure, avoid bad company, and pray; all of these can extend your life. Nevertheless, if you think your time may be years away, neglect, worry, and recklessness may shorten your years. Let's live long and prosper.

Prayer: Father, help me to live a life of goodness. I pray for prolonged days in good health while serving you in my purpose. Keep me away from excess, distractions, and things that place me in danger. I pray for wisdom in all my dealings, that I will live faithfully, and that you hear my prayer when I call. Lord, I ask that you do the miraculous in my life and turn around every situation that goes against me in the name of Jesus Christ. Amen.

---

[832] Proverbs 3:1-2

Purpose of Financial Woes

Deuteronomy 8:16 who fed you in the wilderness with manna, which your fathers didn't know, that he might humble you, and that he might prove you, to do you good at your latter end;

In today's world of haves and have-nots, pyramid and get-rich-quick schemes, people are consumed with the prospect of being rich. Many have struggled financially at some point in their life. Yet God has a purpose in our financial woes. It's not that God doesn't want you to have money; he doesn't want money to have you.[833] The Lord wants to teach us to increase our wealth without compromising our faithfulness and good heart. That is why He humbles us and tests our hearts to teach us that we do not live off of bread alone and will follow Him so He may increase us.[834]

The Lord did not promise everyone riches, but He laid out His plan for financial increase. We are to increase in wealth as we build, and He teaches us to follow His word and depend on Him every step of the way.[835] The hard times the Israelites suffered in the wilderness, where God provided every need to prepare them for their increase in the latter days. Their clothes

---

[833] 1 Timothy 6:9-11

[834] Deuteronomy 8:3-4

[835] Deuteronomy 8:5-10

did not wear out. He gave them manna from heaven, and they drank from the flinty rock when there was no water.[836]

We must learn to handle what little we have and take our time to grow faithfully.[837] Don't worry about financial setbacks; they are opportunities to bounce back stronger. Financial woes and struggles will train you for success. Have the hard times trained you to organize and steward what you have correctly? God gives us the power to increase wealth to confirm His covenant, but many forget Him as they grow financially.[838] Have they humbled you to the point that you still depend on the Lord for everything, regardless of what you have now? If not, then you may still need to learn the lesson.

Prayer: Lord, I know every seed needs time to grow, and I thank you for caring for me and allowing challenges to develop me. As I grow in faithfulness, empower me to acquire wealth with patience, joy, and a generous heart. Help me overcome every struggle and keep my family in peace and contentment. I ask you to do this in Jesus' name. Amen.

---

[836] Exodus 17:5-6

[837] Matthew 25:20-23

[838] Deuteronomy 8:18-19

Have You Found What You're Looking For

John 10:9 *I am the door. If anyone enters in by me, he will be saved, and will go in and go out and will find pasture.*

The way of the gospel is so simple a five-year-old could explain it, yet many refuse to enter. Christ gives His life for the sheep, but thieves and robbers try to climb in another way.[839] They steal the truth and sell a lie. They depend on following the rules without compassion or balancing their evil deeds with good ones. They act like wild sheep in love with the thorns and brambles they run into, and they won't listen to the Lord and simply enter through Christ.[840] No matter how much you tell them, people keep trying to find their way into heaven.

Many people will try, but not all will enter because there is only one door to the kingdom of God.[841] Entering by Christ will not only save you, but it will save you a lot of heartache from trying other ways. The closer you are to the shepherd, the safer you are from the wolves.[842] The sheep hear His voice saying, "Come follow me." The fulfillment we seek is in our shepherd. The great shepherd of our lives will save and protect us. He

---

[839] John 10:1-3
[840] John 5:38-40
[841] John 14:6
[842] John 10:11-15

will guide us for His name's sake because we have entered the door and made Him ours.

We should ask people, "Have they found what God wants for them, or are they settling for an imitation that's a limitation"? Those who enter by the door can move freely because the shepherd guides them. God creates the green pastures, still waters, and restoration for our soul, then brings us to where they are, much like He created the garden and brought Adam to it.[843] However, many continue to try to find their way. They rob themselves of true joy and salvation because they wouldn't accept Jesus as the way. Don't get lost, but find yourself in Christ. He has what you are looking for.

Prayer: Lord, I enter your gate with a faith that hears and follows you. Continually supply my needs, lead me to peace, and protect me from harm. Call to this next generation who isn't raised in the church and lacks the foundation to learn your voice. Save my family and loved ones so we will enter your gates with thanksgiving. I ask that you draw us into your promise and save our souls, in the name of Jesus Christ, Amen.

---

[843] Psalm 23:1-3

What Kind of Harvest

---***---

Galatians 6:7 Don't be deceived. God is not mocked,
for whatever a man sows, that he will also reap.

Wherever you are today is a result of the decisions you made in the past. Some of us are content to sit back and let life happen to us. Others take life by the horns and end up enjoying where they land. If you're sitting back, then you haven't invested in your future.[844] Sowing is a labor-intensive activity. It's more than just giving a check. It is working for a harvest. It is living your life with expectations of the future. Whatever you sow into your life now will bring either future blessings or repercussions.[845] The question is, what are you sowing?

Many of us have just given up. We've given up on relationships. We've given up on school. We've even given up on church and God. What have we sown? We sowed a pattern of giving up and will reap a life of wasted potential and lost dreams. Sometimes, we sow distrust and doubt, and we reap insecurity. We can also sow sinful practices and reap a carnal life. Whatever you sow, you shall receive back in kind.[846] So, if we don't like what we are reaping, we must change what we are sowing.

Sowing hard work will reap success. You will accomplish your heart's desires if you diligently apply yourself to school, work, or growth. Working

---

[844] 2 Corinthians 9:6
[845] Proverbs 13:4
[846] Hosea 10:12-13

hard now will pay off in the end.[847] Stop living for now and prepare yourself for the future. To bear fruit, you must go to the one who called everything to reproduce after its kind. Get ready to reap from what you have sown. Or decide to start working for your success now. Whatever you believe God has for you, pursue it with all diligence. He blesses what He gives, but if you will reap in the future, you must sow now.[848]

Prayer: Heavenly Father, I thank you for sowing new seeds in my life, and that some things I reap are there because my unity with you taps into what you have sown. My new season starts with what I am sowing, so guide me into the right thoughts, decisions, and actions. I commit to following you and uprooting every bad seed as you cease its growth. Today, I plant new seeds of faith, hope, and love that will grow into a divine harvest, in Jesus' name, Amen.

---

[847] Proverbs 12:24
[848] Psalm 90:17

Simon Says

---᛫---

Acts 8:22-24 Repent therefore of this, your wickedness, and ask God if perhaps the thought of your heart may be forgiven you. For I see that you are in the poison of bitterness and in the bondage of iniquity." Simon answered, "Pray for me to the Lord, that none of the things which you have spoken happen to me."

Since the beginning of the church, believers have offered prayers to intercede for those who should be praying for themselves. Most prayer requests Christians receive are reasonable, especially from those who are dedicated to God. They pray and want someone to touch and agree with them because there is power in unity.[849] However, other prayer requests may wear you down. They come from those who refuse to pray for themselves yet expect you to spend hours praying for them.

Simon Peter dealt with such a person. Though they shared the same name, their conduct was very different. Though Simon the sorcerer had become a member of the Samaritan church, his heart wasn't right. The miracles he saw were greater than anything he had pretended to do, and his ambition caused him to want the spotlight back on him.[850] Yet, for all his bravado, Simon was in bondage to iniquity. He wanted to be an authority but had an unrepentant heart. When Simon Peter told him to pray and

---

[849] Matthew 18:18-20
[850] Acts 8:9-19

get right with God, the other Simon asked, "Will you pray for me?" and went on his way.[851]

People need to pray more than they need prayer. Praying themselves draws their heart and soul near God, so their life and decisions are influenced by His presence. It is a sin not to pray for others; however, we must also tell them what is right when we pray for them.[852] Prayer protects them from harm, but won't do further good if they aren't willing to get right with God. Believers who don't pray often lack vision, purpose, and power, and may require more prayer than others. Simon says to pray, so what are we doing about it?

> **Prayer:** Lord, I understand that wickedness begins in the thoughts of my heart. Help me to deal with my disagreements and doubts so my heart will be pure before you. Let no root of bitterness or bondage remain, so your love, acceptance, and mercy will remain with me. Ignite my prayer life and halt the hand of the enemy. Keep filling me with the Holy Spirit daily, so I may see Your power working in my favor. Thank you for working in and on me, in Jesus' name, Amen.

---

[851] Isaiah 55:6-7
[852] 1 Samuel 12:23

The Breakfast of Conquerors

---✦---

Psalms 5:3 Yahweh, in the morning you will hear
my voice. In the morning I will lay my requests
before you, and will watch expectantly.

We are told, "It's not how you start the race but how you finish it that matters." We all know people with lives riddled with unfinished business. Finishing is what's most important.[853] However, how you start something often determines how you will finish it. Starting your day with the breakfast of conquerors will help you conclude your day in victory. You may say, "What is this breakfast?" Well, it's an affirmation and prayer.[854] By seeking God early in the morning, your spirit will rise so that you are elevated above your problems when issues come.

Breakfast is what it says: a break in our fast. Have you considered that you fast every day? Late-night eating is the only reason we may not get a short 12- to 14-hour fast daily. However, will you break your fast with food, or will you break through with prayer, affirming God's control?[855] Morning prayer is essential because our body and spirit are in a state of fasting. These are powerful prayer times because God reveals things in

---

853 Ecclesiastes 7:8
854 Psalm 59:16-17
855 Psalm 118:24

fasting and prayer.[856] Prayer is the breakfast of conquerors that energizes our spirit for the day.

God wants your spirit and faith to be bigger than your problems, so you stand firm in faith.[857] Did you start your day the right way? Not just praying and walking away, but affirming God's presence and waiting in expectation for the voice of God to speak back to you. Early in the morning, the Lord will refresh and feed the spiritual person inside you so you can handle your day.[858] Starting the day right will help you to complete your day in victory. Let your voice be heard in heaven early in the morning, strengthening your day.

> **Prayer:** Lord, I come laying my request at your throne with expectancy in my heart. I know that you will not disappoint. I affirm your presence and stand in faith as I pray. Please help me to continue to seek you each day. Make me more than a conqueror, and give me victory for what I attempt, in my attitude and over my attackers. Place angels around my family and lead us by your Holy Spirit to be champions in faith and love, in the name of Jesus Christ. Amen.

---

[856] Mark 9:28-29
[857] 2 Chronicles 20:20
[858] Lamentations 3:22-25

Come and Get It

---✦---

Ezekiel 18:31 Cast away from you all your
transgressions in which you have transgressed;
and make yourself a new heart and a new
spirit. For why will you die, house of Israel?

There is hope in God for all. The Lord speaks to Ezekiel about what happens when a lifelong sinner changes their ways and comes to Him.[859] It's a crime how many people are headed unnecessarily to death. Coming before the Lord without the right heart and spirit isn't wise. God knows your offenses, but looks at your heart when you approach Him. We refuse to surrender entirely to God when we hold on to our transgressions. God desires to allow all who repent to come to him, for He takes no pleasure in the death of the wicked.[860]

Getting right with God is up to you. The iniquity of our thoughts connects our transgression to the disposition of our hearts and spirits. The more you sin, the greater your propensity to become in bondage to that sin.[861] Actions bring a reaction in our hearts and spirits, creating a disposition of defilement. If you are bound by sin and troubled by transgression, cast them away. The answer is that we must dethrone ourselves

---

[859] Ezekiel 18:21-23
[860] Ezekiel 33:11
[861] 2 Peter 2:19

and enthrone Christ.[862] Get rid of the things you transgressed in and make a new heart and spirit for yourself.

We can't acquire a new heart and spirit by walking in old ways.[863] The old heart and spirit long for old ways and familiar things. Henry Brandt said, "You would think that everyone would leap at the chance to get rid of sin, but not so. They want relief, not a cure." Our refreshing only happens after we let those things go. We need a new heart and a new spirit to approach God.[864] Don't just cast iniquities away; keep them away. Get right, get renewed, get refreshed, and get God.

Prayer: Lord, whatever transgressions remain in my walk, I cast away and ask you to help me walk with a refreshed mind and renewed spirit that keeps me from evil. Empower me to stand upright and with clarity of purpose. Not only will I be self-controlled, but Spirit-led. I ask that you bring joy into my heart, the right attitude into my mind, and my soul set on worship. Continue to work your will in my life, home, and family, giving us your grace in the name of Jesus. Amen.

---

[862] Colossians 3:15
[863] Ezekiel 36:25-27
[864] 1 Samuel 16:7

Women of Power

---✦---

Luke 8:2-3 and certain women who had been healed of evil spirits and infirmities: Mary who was called Magdalene, from whom seven demons had gone out; and Joanna, the wife of Chuzas, Herod's steward; Susanna; and many others who served them from their possessions.

Christ went about preaching the gospel of the kingdom of God, healing all those sick and afflicted by the devil.[865] Yet few showed their devotion and appreciation in giving as the mighty women who provided for the needs of Christ and the apostles. Men gave their lives to God, but there are no mentions of men providing for Christ personally from their resources. So, these women stand out. Through their dedication, the ministry became a powerful tool of healing, deliverance, and salvation, ultimately shaping the New Testament Church.

The church still receives much of its support from women Christ has healed. Modern-day Mary Magdalenes who have been set free. Women like Joanna use what resources they have to further the kingdom. A myriad of women used their power to support Christ's mission.[866] Their giving was a way of recognizing and giving thanks to the Lord, paying forward for what He did so that others would receive the same help. God takes this

---

[865] Matthew 4:23
[866] Mark 15:41

break in scripture to salute their deeds. Let's acknowledge the women who serve Him in many different ways.

Women share the image and likeness of God men have.[867] Scripture is full of women of power and influence who put themselves at risk for the kingdom of God. Their giving and work allowed Christ and the apostles to do their work. All men of God should appreciate the sacrifice of the women who, though they were silent, were often the backbone of ministry. These women of power stand as equal to men in the service of our God.[868] God saved and healed many because of these women, so let us appreciate all they do.

> **Prayer:** Lord, I thank you for the heart of giving and support in those who sometimes seem underappreciated. I ask that you help us spread healing through our words, prayers, deeds, and attitudes. Show those who feel undervalued their worth and how we can bring hope to the hopeless. I pray the miraculous power of God's works wonders in my home, family, and life, in the name of Jesus Christ. Amen.

---

[867] Genesis 1:27
[868] Galatians 3:28

Who is He

---✦---

Matthew 16:15-16 He said to them, "But who do you say that I am?" Simon Peter answered, "You are the Christ, the Son of the living God."

Jesus Christ is undeniably the most influential figure in history. Every word and act recorded of Him carries significance.[869] Some believe in the miracles God performed through Him, and others don't. Some even call themselves spiritual, but, at the same time, doubt His nature and character. Yet, some don't know who He is. We all know those who think Jesus is just a good teacher or a prophet sent by God.[870] What the world calls Jesus doesn't matter. What matters is what you have to say about Him. So, who is Jesus to you?

Peter was the first to answer. He exclaimed You are the Christ, meaning anointed one, the only son of the living God. Peter believed that Jesus was the culmination of all the hopes of Israel.[871] He was not only a prophet and teacher; He was the manifested presence of God Himself, the only true son of God Almighty, and the savior of the world. I'm not sure we understand all this entails, but we know we can only know Him through God's revelation.[872]

---

[869] John 21:25
[870] Mark 8:27-28
[871] Jeremiah 17:13
[872] Matthew 16:17

Blaise Pascal said, "Not only do we know God through Jesus Christ, we only know ourselves through Christ Jesus." God revealed who Christ was to Peter so that Christ could reveal who Peter was to God.[873] People knew God's law and His acts, but never knew the heart and person of God. Many struggle to accept their identity and value because they don't understand their place in God. The Father can only be known and reached through His Son. Without Christ, there is no proper knowledge of who the Father is.[874] Who do you say He is?

Prayer: Lord, creator of the universe, you are enthroned in heaven and have all power and authority. I want to know you more. Help me tap into your image inside so I understand my strategic placement in the kingdom. Remove all worry, anxiety, doubt, and depression that fixate on what the world is doing rather than who I am in you. I pray your hand of victory is always with me, and your grace is on my household, in the name of Jesus Christ. Amen.

---

[873] Matthew 16:18-19
[874] John 14:8-10

Watch Your Step

---◆---

Psalms 37:23-24 A man's steps are established by Yahweh. He delights in his way. Though he stumble, he shall not fall, for Yahweh holds him up with his hand.

Car chases, crashes, and falls. The world loves to watch them. The more spectacular, the more sensational it becomes. Similarly, people are waiting to see you fail. When a believer falls, it confirms the secret gossip they say behind our backs. Failing is not a complete fall because the Lord holds on to you. It's when we stop delighting in God that we fall. As the saying goes, "You can't keep a good man down." Sometimes, we fail and sometimes fall, but we will not be utterly cast down because the Lord upholds us.[875] We look up, get up, and never give up.

Picture yourself scaling the ledge of a mountain, one wrong move, and it's over. The word translated as "established" means to erect upright. It is only because of God that any of us walks upright.[876] God is your mountain guide who keeps you walking the right path. Living a life submitted to God will make you stand. Have you ever wondered why good men and women fall? We become sheep who go astray when we neglect to delight in God's ways.[877] We tumble downward when we refuse or remove God's guidance.

---

[875] 1 Samuel 2:9

[876] Romans 14:4

[877] Psalms 119:176

If you slip, the Lord won't let you stay down. When someone falls, people will kick them while they're down. Sometimes, believers become critical, judgmental, and dismissive of brethren who fall. We often forget that they are our brothers and sisters, but God never does.[878] The arm of the Lord is upholding them. If you have fallen, let the Lord order your steps again. If you see someone fall, don't talk about them, but be the hand God extends to lift them back up.[879] They may fall, but if we cast them down, we have fallen with them because we stop delighting in God's way, which is to uplift the one who has fallen. Let the Lord order your steps.

> **Prayer:** Lord, thank you for not giving up on us when we fail. You have been there to lift me every time. I ask that you draw me to you and silence every voice against me. Continue to do your work, building and shaping me. Please strengthen me and give me the right words to help others when they are down. Thank you for your love, favor, and mercy guiding me, in Jesus' name, Amen.

---

[878] Proverb 24:16
[879] Job 5:18-19

Getting Back on Track

---✦---

Hebrews 12:2 looking to Jesus, the author and perfecter of faith, who for the joy that was set before him endured the cross, despising its shame, and has sat down at the right hand of the throne of God.

In the Tokyo Marathon 2011, Natsuki Terada experienced a heartbreaking end to his race after he made a wrong turn 0.2 miles before the finish line. He turned right by following a camera car, while those behind him followed the signals of race officials and stayed straight to the finish line. We think training for so long is terrible, and then losing position because he got off track. However, like Mr. Terada, we can quickly stray from God by taking the wrong turn.[880]

Natsuki Terada made the wrong turn because he was looking at the wrong thing. He followed the camera car as if it were part of the race and turned off course when the car had to turn so it would not break the finish line tape. Though he had lost ground, as soon as he noticed the wrong turn, he straightened up and returned to the race, finishing in 10th place. We are not in competition with others, but with ourselves. So, where you finish is not as crucial as finishing the race.[881] When we don't look to Christ, the author and finisher of our faith, we can find ourselves off track.

---

[880] Deuteronomy 5:32-33
[881] 2 Timothy 4:7-8

When some get off course, they drop out of the race because they neglect getting back on track.[882] Few remember who won the marathon, but everyone there remembers the man who turned and got back on track. If you're lost, you have to look to Jesus. He is your course corrector. When you see your zeal wavering, He will give you the stamina to continue. When you get complacent, Christ will cause you to stand. If you sin, He will forgive and make intercession for you.[883] If you fall, He will lift you. Only Christ can put you back on track with God. He's standing at the finish line waiting.

> **Prayer:** Lord, I thank you that I am still in the race. You have given me the Holy Spirit as the officiant of my Christian race and scripture as a signpost to show the way to the narrow path. When I lose focus and veer off, bring me back to you. Help me stay the course, keeping my mind on Christ, who finished first for me. I ask that you draw my family and loved ones to the right path and deliver us from self and the selfish actions that arise on the broad path, in the name of Jesus Christ. Amen.

---

[882] 2 Corinthians 11:2-3
[883] Hebrews 7:24-25

You Control the Flow

Luke 6:38 Give, and it will be given to you: good measure, pressed down, shaken together, and running over, will be given to you. For with the same measure you measure it will be measured back to you.

The principle is simple. Whatever you give will return to you multiplied. The immediate context of this verse is about forgiving and helping even an enemy when they stumble.[884] Judgmental people condemn when others make mistakes, but forgivers give the same grace they walk in. Reciprocity pours into all aspects of giving. Each seed grows and reproduces after its kind, leaving you to harvest what you have sown. God is the one who blesses us, but we control the flow of what kind of blessings we receive by what we give.[885]

Israelites stored grain by pressing it into a container, then moving it around so the grain would be displaced closer together, allowing more grain to be poured in. In the same way, you control the flow of your blessing. How you nurture what you sow causes growth in the measure you receive back.[886] We get more in return when we put more effort into our education, work, or spiritual development. If you give begrudgingly or in doubt, not trusting God, your actions manifest in your harvest. However,

[884] Luke 6:27-36
[885] 2 Corinthians 9:6-7
[886] Proverbs 11:24-25

when you sow your seed in faith, you release faith and favor into your finances. It comes back to you multiplied.[887]

You can provoke God to open up the floodgates of heaven, or you can cause Him to keep them closed.[888] Why? Because He gave you the power to control the flow of your blessings. If you sow frustration in a relationship, that frustration or anger will press down, shake together, and come back to you as resentment and strife—the overflow of peace, healing, and blessing results from how we treat what we put in. Control your blessing by sowing in peace, faith, and forgiveness; you will reap abundant life, favor, and understanding.[889]

> **Prayer:** Lord, I ask that you keep my heart clean and my motives pure, so I may be a generous and happy giver who trusts and obeys your instructions. I will get a harvest in return, but I want to be a good seed in your kingdom first and foremost. Help me distinguish between genuine need and deceit so I sow in the right places. Thank you for the blessings coming my way, in Jesus' name. Amen.

---

[887] Proverbs 22:9
[888] Malachi 3:10-12
[889] Galatians 6:7-10

Voice of A Stranger

---◆---

***John 10:5 They will by no means follow a
stranger, but will flee from him; for they
don't know the voice of strangers.***

We always tell our kids, "Do not talk to strangers." Why? Because it can be dangerous. The stranger could be someone who has come to do them harm. So why do we listen to the voices of strangers? Strangers are thieves, robbers, and hirelings who have opinions about the fold but don't surrender to be cooperative members of the flock.[890] The complaints, conversations, and convictions of those outside of the fold can be convincing, but the voice of Christ is convicting. It challenges you to be a better version of yourself by following something outside yourself with a definite plan for your good rather than just gathering you to their way of thinking.[891]

Do you know those thoughts that pop into our heads that try to keep us from following Christ by faith? They are competing voices that try to drown out what Scripture says about us and our responsibility to serve God with all our heart, mind, soul, and strength.[892] They don't come from the good shepherd of our souls, Jesus Christ, and try to lead us out of the

---

[890] John 10:8-13
[891] Psalm 40:4-5
[892] Deuteronomy 10:12

sheepfold. The voice of the stranger is any voice that attempts to convince you of anything contradictory to God's word for your life.

Too many of us have let other people and even demonic spirits place thoughts in our minds that hold us back.[893] We even incorporate those thoughts so much into our lives that they become our thoughts. It is the stranger's goal to make their thoughts yours. How many abuse victims have blamed themselves for what happened to them? The stranger causes harm and blame, but we should not listen to them. Stop listening to strangers and hear what the word of God says. It will teach, correct, redirect, and train you to walk righteously.[894] It is the voice we are to listen to.

> **Prayer:** Lord, thank you for your Spirit of truth guiding me to an abundant life. As I seek to listen for your voice in my heart, in prayer, and through the word, provide the correction, guidance, and instruction I need. I know I have further to go on my journey, but I will achieve all my goals with hard work and your leadership. I bless you for making me an overcomer and giving me an open door to your favor and blessing, in Jesus' name. Amen.

_____

_____

_____

_____

_____

_____

[893] John 13:2
[894] 2 Timothy 3:16-17

A Good Reason to Give Him Praise

*Job 34:14-15 If he set his heart on himself,
if he gathered to himself his Spirit and his
breath, all flesh would perish together,
and man would turn again to dust.*

Most people will never realize how much we depend on God to sustain our daily breath.[895] How easy it would be for the Lord to call back His Spirit and His breath and end it all. Without God, there is no humanity or any other kind of thing. We are dependent on him for life and everything we receive. By the breath of God, man became a living soul,[896] and if God were to draw back his breath, we would be a pile of dirt. His Spirit gives us life; in the end, our life in the flesh will not be so important.[897] For all He does, we have a reason to praise Him.

Praise God for His love and patience with us, because if He set His heart against us, we would all disappear. God Himself is the only one who truly knows all God has done for you. He has invested His breath and Spirit into us to give us life.[898] Time and time again, when we have messed up, His longsuffering covered us. Many of us would have missed salvation

---

[895] Job 12:7-10
[896] Job 33:4
[897] John 6:63
[898] Genesis 2:7

if He had set His heart against us and shortened our time. That's a good reason to give Him praise.

We must get it right now, for we live off borrowed breath and Spirit.[899] You already know what would happen if God wanted them back. We would die. Some would enter the Lord's glory, but others would face eternal shame. It's good to thank him for paying for sins He didn't owe and letting us keep the breath we borrowed.[900] The Lord sustains and keeps us. The Lord holds our lives in His hands. Without Him, we would return to the dust. That's a good reason to give Him praise.

Prayer: Father, I praise and thank you for giving me life and ask that you continue to breathe upon me until I overflow. I will bless your name in the hard times and in times of abundance. I ask that you lift my soul from worry, sadness, and life traumas. Keep the joy of your salvation in my heart, and extend your grace towards me. I pray your hand rests on my family and that your Spirit continues to flow in our lives in the name of Jesus. Amen.

---

[899] Ecclesiastes 12:6-7
[900] Romans 8:10-12

The Resting Place

---✦---

Psalms 132:13-14 For Yahweh has chosen Zion. He has desired it for his habitation. "This is my resting place forever. I will live here, for I have desired it.

It is beautiful to think about how God desires a place to rest. The Bible refers to it as the mountain of God's inheritance.[901] When we think of a resting place, we often think of weariness. A resting place is somewhere we go to replenish. However, that's not why God has chosen a resting place. He can never tire out or become weary. The resting place is where God manifests His presence to replenish His people.[902] It is the place that He will inhabit forever so that others can partake of His presence, provision, protection, and power.

The resting place is where we can be alone with the Lord and spend quality time with Him. No matter how loud or crowded Zion would get, there was always time to be intimate with God.[903] When we meet God at His resting place, He empowers and places His desires within us. It is the believer's refill station where the Lord fills us anew with His presence so we can receive His strength. The resting place is where God chooses to meet you so that you can receive what you need.[904]

---

[901] Exodus 15:17

[902] Psalms 132:15-18

[903] Psalms 132:7-9

[904] Psalms 48:1-3

With the outpouring of the Spirit, we have also become His resting place.[905] The Lord has desired to rest in us so His presence will live in us. We no longer need to travel to Mount Zion because Immanuel (God with us) has come. The resting place is within the believers. Because we struggle within ourselves to obey God's commands, He works in us instead of resting in us. Surrender to His will, and you will find the resting place. Have you had your morning refill? Have you taken the time for God to replenish you?[906] Blessed is the one who ceases from their labors and lets the Lord reign in them.

Prayer: Lord, thank you for my resting place in you. Pour your power upon me, revitalizing my strength and encouraging my soul. Please fill me with your presence daily and show me where to recharge and refresh. Remove sickness, infirmity, and the cares of this world so I can serve you freely and without fear. I thank you for every blessing in my life and ask that you show me how to care for all you have given me in the name of Jesus Christ. Amen.

---

[905] John 14:16-17
[906] Acts 3:19-20

Expect to Win

---✠---

1 Chronicles 18:10 He sent Hadoram his son to King David to greet him and to bless him, because he had fought against Hadadezer and struck him (for Hadadezer had wars with Tou); and he had with him all kinds of vessels of gold and silver and bronze

The enemy of my enemy is my friend. People who share mutual enemies should be motivated to work towards a common goal. Tou had an enemy that he could not defeat. So when he heard of David's victory, he celebrated and sent his son to bless him.[907] David's victory became a victory for Tou. So, what should you do when you can't defeat our mutual foe, satan? You link up with someone who has, can, and expects to do it again.

People are attracted to winners. We root for them, hold up signs with their name, and stand up for them when they don't even know it. The difference between David and Tou is that Tou hopes for victory. David expected it.[908] If you are hoping for victory, you're not fighting with assurance. When you pray, do you hope for an answer or expect it to come? Each victory increased David's confidence in God. The Lord told him when to fight and when to withdraw. He made it so David's enemies would have a slim hope for victory but never expected it because David always won.[909]

---

[907] 1 Chronicles 18:5-10

[908] Deuteronomy 20:4

[909] 2 Samuel 8:1-6

The devil shouldn't expect victory over you.[910] He should expect defeat. When you trust God fully and never back down, the enemy is afraid to go into battle with you. Satan should be surprised, not expectant, if he wins. As a child of God, you should expect to win. If your faith falters, link up with your brothers and sisters who can speak faith into your life. Don't shake when the battle comes; shout out for victory.[911] Join with other winners and praise God, knowing you have the victory. Always expect to succeed; your winning attitude will carry you through.

> **Prayer:** Lord, help me always to have an attitude of victory. I cast out worry, fear, and every negative thought that says I cannot have what you say I can. I shall conquer the land of my promise and walk in the inheritance you have reserved for me. I will not see myself as a grasshopper but as one who can do all things through Christ Jesus. Place me among believers where we can mutually assist, encourage, and pray for one another. I prepare for and expect victory in mine, in Jesus' name. Amen.

---

[910] 2 Corinthians 2:14-15
[911] Psalm 47:1-4

Reset Your Attitude

------ ❧ ------

Isaiah 46:9 Remember the former things
of old; for I am God, and there is no other.
I am God, and there is none like me.

When considering all that God has done for us, we should consider two definitions of 'remembering'. The first means to bring back to mind. That is, we are to bring God back to the forefront of our thinking so that we can readjust our thoughts.[912] The second is an etiological definition derived from the prefix "Re," meaning again, and the word "Member," representing a person. As to say, bring a person (God) back into your situation. Remembrance brings God into both your mind and situation. In trying to win the discouraged, the defeated, and the backslidden back, God instructed them to reset their attitude by remembering His person and works. [913]

Whether for good or bad, your memory serves as the reset button for your attitude. When you remember events in a negative light, it leaves you with a bad attitude. If you think of all the things that say you can't make it, you won't prosper, that things will never go your way, you will grow an attitude of defeat. However, if you think about the Lord God and all He has done, your mind resets to a winning attitude.[914] Your mind will believe

---

[912] Isaiah 26:2-4

[913] Isaiah 46:10-13

[914] Romans 12:2

you can do everything through Christ because He strengthens you. You will approach life as a victor, not a victim, and it all comes from resetting your attitude by remembering God.[915]

Your ability to remember is a kind of instantaneous attitude reset button that God gives you. Scripture instructs us to focus our minds on righteous, positive, and worthy things so that we can put them into practice.[916] If you change your thinking, you change your life. God wants us to reset our attitudes so that we can walk in victory and peace. Do you want the peace of God? Rid yourself of the lies about yourself and reset your attitude for victory.

> **Prayer:** Lord, prepare me to walk in your favor with a cleansed heart and renewed mind. When I consider your love for me, the lies fade away. I invite you into my mind and situation, declaring I will submit my heart and see your power to work in my favor. I pray that your peace surpasses my understanding and that you lead me by your Holy Spirit. Father, I ask for special protection over my family and life, and that we shall see your goodness, in Jesus' name, Amen.

---

[915] 2 Corinthians 10:5
[916] Philippians 4:8-9

A Dramatic Victory

---⚓---

Isaiah 40:29 He gives power to the weak. He
increases the strength of him who has no might.

Have you ever seen a dramatic victory? I'm not talking about a quick knockout or a mismatch where someone is in over their head. No, I'm talking about the blood, sweat, and tears kind of victory. You see the pain and anguish in their face as they struggle. How they have endured injury, fight to stand up, and shed tears when they are victorious. That's what it's like for a believer to maintain strong faith during a hard knockdown battle. They get weary, but God increases their strength to overcome.[917]

When you are about to give up, the Lord will give you a dramatic victory. He will strengthen you to push on when you think you are about to pass out.[918] He will give strength when you have none, so that the dramatic victory that you won will be His. There are no quitters on this team, only victors. God gives us the strength to get through it. He gives us the means to endure every struggle, hardship, and trial and come out strengthened.[919] Whether it is a minor skirmish or an all-out brawl, we can win it all.

Have you felt like giving up or dropping out of the race? Have you quit because you felt you couldn't go any farther? If you said yes, get back up;

---

[917] Isaiah 40:30-31
[918] Jeremiah 31:25
[919] 1 Corinthians 10:13

you are in line to gain new strength.[920] Here is your wake-up call. While you're fainting, here comes the power to stand. When you're weak, His power perfects you.[921] Uninvited and unusual trials lead to unconquered strength. Get ready for a dramatic and decisive win. Triumph is ours in Jesus' name. If your weary claim, you promise to conquer in the name of the Lord, and let us all see your dramatic victory.

> **Prayer:** Lord, I ask you for your help in times of trouble. When things look too big, and I start getting anxious, calm me. When problems surround me, be my backup. I will stand in faith, knowing that I do not fight alone. Lend me your strength to overcome. When I am weak, you are strong, so I praise you. I declare I will not give up or give in, but will stand firm in faith through the good and evil. Watch over me and my loved ones, keeping us under your protection. In Jesus' name. Amen.

---

[920] Isaiah 41:10-12
[921] 2 Corinthians 12:9-10

Grace Instruction

---⁂---

Titus 2:11-12 For the grace of God has appeared,
bringing salvation to all men, instructing
us to the intent that, denying ungodliness
and worldly lusts, we would live soberly,
righteously, and godly in this present age.

God's grace revealed in Christ's work brings salvation and righteous instruction. The power of choice is the difference between those who live godly or ungodly.[922] You don't learn a lesson until it's lived. Grace teaches us that we must say no to and repudiate sin before we can live godly. What we learn must become action, or it will only exist as theory. Why? Because it hasn't been proven or made real to us. We can choose to accept what the grace of God teaches us and deny ungodliness and worldly lust, or we can live within them.[923]

To deny ungodliness and worldly lust, we have first to be convinced by God's grace. The Greek word "Paideuo" refers to instructing a child through discipline and training until they achieve their potential.[924] As children, we fail and learn by changing our actions. We all have the potential, but unless we follow Christ wholeheartedly, we won't deny our flesh.[925]

---

[922] Malachi 3:16-18
[923] Titus 3:3-5
[924] Proverbs 22:6
[925] 2 Corinthians 5:14-15

His grace persuades us to surrender our ways to attain His righteousness. We do this by showing restraint when lured to sin, faithfulness when tempted, and character when tried.

You can only go as far in righteousness as you can follow Christ.[926] How we behave towards others reveals what we believe. Some believe that they can't live right before God. They think it's too complicated, and only a handful of believers have what it takes. They're wrong. It is a simple two-step process of denying and living. The Lord will teach you how. Anything you want to achieve is accomplished by denying yourself and doing what's needed. Deny worldly lust and live sober and right. If you release self-pity and desire, you will receive His grace, leading you to righteousness.[927] How do you want to live?

> **Prayer:** Father, thank you for the grace you revealed in your son Jesus Christ. I ask that the same grace that made me your child instruct me to lead a life pleasing to you. Please give me the strength to deny carnal pleasures, pride, and things that distract me from your will. I can do all things through Christ. Bless my home, family, and life according to your incredible grace, in Jesus' name. Amen.

---

[926] Matthew 16:24-25
[927] Ephesians 4:21-24

For the Sake of His Name

Psalms 31:3 For you are my rock and my fortress,
therefore for your name's sake lead me and guide me.

God is a God of many names. The word "God" in Hebrew, Elohim, meaning strong one, is a title rather than a name. We call Him by what we know or need from Him. God revealed His covenant name, telling Moses, I am that I am; tell them YHWH sent you.[928] Some names, such as Adonai or Lord, recognize His position. Other names combined with El or YHWH are redemptive and describe His character and work, such as Shaddai, Shalom, or Jireh, stating that He is the God of strength, peace, and provision. Names are so important that Satan knows your name but calls you by your sin.[929] However, God knows your sin but calls you by your name.

When we ask God to lead and guide us for His name's sake, we declare that all He is in position, power, and goodness are with us when he leads.[930] The psalmist first declares that God is his rock and fortress, trusting the Lord to lead him to safety. If you know Him as your provider, He will lead you to contentment and prosperity. If the Lord is your comforter, He will lead you to healing and encouragement. As Emmanuel (God with

---

[928] Exodus 3:13-15
[929] Revelation 12:10
[930] Psalm 23:3

us), He leads you into his presence.[931] For the sake of His name, He will be what you need.

What happens when we make God our everything and call Him our all?[932] When we give Him all our hearts and His name becomes all things to us, He will lead and guide us in everything for His name's sake. Start serving in God's name, operate with God's help, and finish your task by giving thanks to God. He will perfect us and complete us. He will bestow on us grace, mercy, and peace. He will teach us how to walk righteously and be good stewards of our bodies, time, and wealth. All for His name.

> **Prayer:** Lord, as my Father, savior, and lover of my soul, I ask you to lead me. Please guide me along the right paths and help me discern your will so that I may make the correct decisions. Dispel confusion, conflicts, and competing thoughts. Your name is great and greatly to be praised. Take hold of my family through your provision and protection. Bring us unity in the perfect bond of love. I pray for your hand of peace in our lives and that we have favor in the name of Jesus Christ. Amen.

---

[931] Isaiah 7:13-14
[932] Psalm 73:25-26

Cleaned Up

---⚓---

2 Peter 2:22 But it has happened to them according to the true proverb, "The dog turns to his own vomit again," and "the sow that has washed to wallowing in the mire."

You can't fix a person who isn't ready for change.[933] Why? Because they will turn right back to what they were doing. To encourage actual change in an individual, we must first address their reluctance and desire for the past. Comfort kills motivation. To be righteous, you must be uncomfortable with sin. To reach the next level, we must get comfortable with being uncomfortable. Reluctance means we lack the conviction, confidence, and self-control to change. We will never know what lies ahead without a willingness to leave things behind.[934]

Change can be both powerful and painful. We know how much we need to change, but we are usually only willing to make a change when the change becomes less painful than staying in our current predicament. Many encouraging scriptures encourage us to leave our comfort zones.[935] We can become too focused on the past, like the dog returning to its vomit. Maybe we cleaned up, but our heart pulls us back to our former

---

[933] Proverb 23:7
[934] Philippians 3:12-14
[935] Deuteronomy 31:6

ways.[936] That attachment weighs us down and anchors us to bad habits and behaviors. We become reluctant to leave old things behind and move in a new direction.

As the proverb says, if we don't change, these things will have us in our own vomit and wallowing in the mud.[937] The pig returns to the mire because it cools them down. Things that seem cool are often the things holding you back. Change happens when we value change over complacency. How many families deal with a mess because someone keeps returning to the mud? Without a change of heart and thinking, there will never be a consistent change in us.[938] It's time to get out of the mud, get clean, and stay clean.

> **Prayer:** Lord, make things heavy until your plan for my life outweighs what draws me to the past. I will not look back in fear but will face front in faith. I release the pain of my past for the future glory of your presence and the plan you have for me. Make me uncomfortable with sin and help me to walk by faith and not by sight, knowing the abundant hope you lay before me. Thank you for your mighty work in my life, in the name of Jesus Christ, Amen.

---

[936] Galatians 2:18
[937] Proverbs 26:11
[938] Joel 2:12-13

Strangers not Welcome

Matthew 7:21 Not everyone who says to me, 'Lord, Lord,' will enter into the Kingdom of Heaven, but he who does the will of my Father who is in heaven.

It may shock some who have read this verse about what Jesus was saying. Simply asking to enter the kingdom does not automatically grant us entrance.[939] He is not saying that we shouldn't ask, but simply pointing out that some who ask to come in won't make it in because they are not genuine about the will of God. We often see this verse as applying to others who are either hypocrites or misguided believers. This is true, but the context reveals another group of people.

Matthew 5 mentions three groups of people. The first is the hypocrites.[940] They won't make it in because they are only faking their faith. Another group is the false prophets, who mislead people from walking in truth.[941] Speaking from their flesh, they pretend to teach and speak from God. They are locked out because they move people from God's path. However, the third group is believers who live their lives inconsiderately.[942] Those who profess to be believers yet only consider those who are near and dear to their hearts, rather than imitating God, being there to help all.

---

[939] Matthew 25:10-12

[940] Matthew 7:5

[941] Matthew 7:15

[942] Matthew 7:11-12

He compares the three to bad trees that bring forth only harmful fruit.[943] The will of the Father that Christ speaks of is that we bear good fruit. The fruit of the inconsiderate dies on the vine before it can benefit others. They feel good about giving to those they love, but hold back from giving to others. They are slow to help and can easily ignore God's work right before them.[944] Good fruit means involvement with kingdom growth. It's not sitting on the sidelines. It's overcoming all hurt and obstacles for the sake of Christ. He stands at the door, asking us to bear good fruit. If we don't let Him in now, He won't let us in later.

Prayer: Lord, help me to abide in Christ while you prune me with your word so I can bear fruit. Remove selfish thoughts and motives so my life will be centered and focused on your will. Repair the wounds of my heart so that I reflect spiritual fruit in my daily walk. I ask that you cover my home and family with your loving grace in the name of Jesus Christ. Amen.

---

[943] Matthew 7:16-20
[944] Romans 2:13

From Manna to Maturity

---✦---

Joshua 5:12 The manna ceased on the next day, after they had eaten off the produce of the land. The children of Israel didn't have manna any more, but they ate off the fruit of the land of Canaan that year.

By the hand of God, Joshua brought the Israelites across the Jordan the same way they once crossed the Red Sea.[945] After entering the promised land, the Lord commanded the circumcision of each man at Gilgal. It takes at least a week for grown men to heal from circumcision, but when they stopped, God didn't.[946] Many wrongly assume that manna stopped falling when they entered the promised land, but scripture reveals that it followed them into the promise and did not stop until they ate of the land's fruit.

Manna doesn't just stop falling when we leave our wilderness experience. Until healing happens, manna continues to fall. Circumcision was a wound of worship. Manna falls until the wound closes, and we can worship and feed ourselves without wounds.[947] Some of us are too close to our destiny for the manna to fall. God doesn't leave you alone; He gets

---

[945] Joshua 3:14-17

[946] Joshua 5:2-8

[947] Joshua 5:10-12

you ready.[948] His hand and blessing from above will move to the hand that leads and pushes you forward to destiny.[949]

Manna stopped so the mission could start. God let them become so tired of eating the manna that the Israelites acquired a taste for victory. That's where he wants us. The Lord wants us to handle our business so He can handle our victory. We are to ask for daily bread as fully functioning, committed believers ready to fight for a better future.[950] Don't give up. The Lord takes you from manna to manifestation. Let's feed ourselves and get ready to fight, for the promise is near.

> **Prayer:** Lord, we thank you for the seasons when the manna fell from heaven, but you have called each of us to responsible action. Move your hand to push me beyond provision to promise. Please give me a mind for victory. Cause me to eat from the fruit of your promise and move forward in life. Help me overcome in all things and know your power, in Jesus' name, Amen.

---

[948] Deuteronomy 31:6
[949] 1 Corinthians 16:13
[950] Matthew 6:10-13

Starting Over

---⊼---

Genesis 8:1 God remembered Noah, all the animals, and all the livestock that were with him in the ship; and God made a wind to pass over the earth. The waters subsided.

The world was formless and void. Clouds kept darkness over the waters so no one could see day or night. Yet at the command of God, light appeared, the waters above stopped pouring on the waters below, and then withdrew, forming land. The dark clouds disappeared, the sun shone in the day, and the stars at night. Life originated in the seas and eventually came onto land. The land was ready for plant life to grow. It sounds like the days of creation, but we just described the end of the flood.[951]

God is not afraid to start over, and neither should we be. God began anew in the same way He created.[952] The Lord made a covenant of life with Noah, much like He did with Adam. He brought every animal on the earth to Adam to name them and to Noah to protect them.[953] He gave both all foods to eat with one restriction, and disobeying that law, they shall surely die. Like Adam, He told Noah that he is in God's image and to

---

[951] Genesis 7:17-20

[952] Genesis 1:2-6

[953] Genesis 6:18-20

be fruitful, multiply, and fill the earth.[954] It's incredible that even after all Adam had done, God remembered and had a promise and plan for Noah.

When it seems we must start over again, God provides a promise. After sin, God promised a redeemer, which He fulfilled in Christ.[955] When God starts you over again, He brings a covenant promise. He promised Noah that no one would go through what he went through.[956] Ask yourself what promise you have. We must release what is past, hold on to the present, and hope for the future. God will not forget you. Hold to your faith. He will redeem and bring you through.

Prayer: Lord, I ask you to remember me and blow away my troubles. Be my ark of safety until the time of the promise comes. Take me through every trouble and make my name rise. Help me to deal with the ridicule of those who don't understand my purpose. I ask that you show favor and protect my family. Help me through every change to enter into the promise in the name of Jesus Christ. Amen.

---

[954] Genesis 9:3-7

[955] Genesis 3:15

[956] Genesis 9:13-16

www.ingramcontent.com/pod-product-compliance
Lightning Source LLC
Chambersburg PA
CBHW070902120626
46546CB00001B/97

* 9 7 8 1 9 6 5 4 4 1 0 2 2 *